ALL
IN THIS
TOGETHER

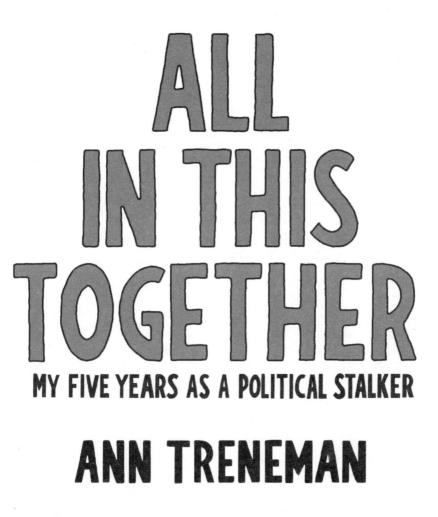

ALL IN THIS TOGETHER

MY FIVE YEARS AS A POLITICAL STALKER

ANN TRENEMAN

\RP\

The Robson Press

First published in Great Britain in 2015 by

The Robson Press (an imprint of Biteback Publishing Ltd)

Westminster Tower

3 Albert Embankment

London SE1 7SP

Copyright © Ann Treneman 2015

ISBN 978-1-84954-916-5

10 9 8 7 6 5 4 3 2 1

A CIP catalogue record for this book is available from the British Library.

Set in Fournier MT Std

Contents

Introduction

'We are all in this together'

George Osborne, Manchester, 6 October 2009

I T WAS GEORGE Osborne's big moment, the speech at the 2009 pre-election Tory Party conference in which the shadow Chancellor, still podgy, voice too high, hair painfully untrendy, set out a package of carefully calculated spending cuts. 'I want a prosperous Britain where my children can be everything they can be,' he told us, on stage in Manchester in front of a giant photo of a suburb. He wanted an optimistic Britain, a Britain with fewer debts, a tolerant Britain. 'And because I want it for my children, I want it for your children too. I want it for everyone's children. Because we are all in this together. We changed the Conservative Party to be ready for this moment. So that when the moment came, people would see us as fit to govern.'

Of course it didn't turn out like that. When George Osborne told the nation that we were all in this together, most people just laughed. And, come May 2010, the people decided the only people who were really all in this together would be, actually, the politicians. It was the first hung parliament since 1974 and the result, after a feverish week, the first coalition government since the Second World War.

It is impossible to be a sketch-writer and not, at times, feel like a stalker.

I can remember in May 2010 running behind the Lib Dem coalition negotiating team as they walked down Whitehall and wondering who that tall
guy with the red hair was. He was, of course, Danny Alexander, soon to be
shortened to Danny A and dubbed the Ginger Rodent, previously the publi-
cist for red squirrels in the Cairngorms, now destined to become part of the
fabled Quad, the foursome (Dave and George, Nick and Danny) who ruled
in coalition land. Quad was one of those words – like Brokeback Coalition,
pleb, Leveson, sluts, dwarf-gate, 'Ed Stone, Eton Mess – that have come to
define the coalition years. No one says Quad now. No one talks about the
Ginger Rodent. The Brokeback Coalition is, actually, broke.

As I stalk past the gargoyles (the stone ones) which adorn the mock gothic
fun palace that is the Palace of Westminster, I often find myself recognising
MPs from their backs. If necessary, I will slow down so I don't have to pass
them. But sometimes I do run into them, face to face. Some recoil. Others
rush forward to take issue with whatever adjective I have used about them.
'Eccentric?' said one MP, looking puzzled. 'What does that mean?' In general,
I find 'eccentric' is a nice way to say 'bonkers' although when asked directly
I proffer the term 'unique' as a substitute synonym.

So what word would I use now for the coalition years? Well, unique is
certainly true, as is eccentric, as is bonkers. But at first, there was no doubt
that the word was 'refreshing'. It's important to remember just how different
it felt then, after the thirteen years of Labour ended with the incredible hulking premiership of Gordon Brown, a man who often felt like a growl, angry
that everyone else, the press, the voters, the country, was not living up to his
expectations. The first sketch in this collection records the Downing Street
rose garden press conference where David Cameron and Nick Clegg were
full of sweetness and light, happy and wholesome, positively fragrant with
possibilities. And that picture, afterwards, which would become famous, of
Dave and Nick, each patting each other on the back, as they headed through
the heavy black door at No. 10, made us all smile.

We know how the story ended – more Grimm than fairy tale. But as I
write, just weeks into the 2015 Tory government, I find myself already nostalgic for those years of coalition. It seems another age, with everyone talking

about 'in the national interest' and, at first at least, Dave and Nick treating each other with the care and attention of honeymooners. I had forgotten, for instance, that Dave came to listen to Nick as he told the Commons about his precious AV ballot. But what struck me, forcefully, as I looked back over the nearly 900 sketches during this time, whittling them down to a fifth of that to be included here, is how the seeds of destruction were sown from the very start. This wasn't a relationship that went wrong. It was lop-sided from the start and it is because this was not acknowledged, especially by the Lib Dems, that it all became as sad as Nick Clegg's face.

So here, then, is what I miss (and a bit of what I don't) about the coalition years:

1. Marriage metaphors. Dave and Nick denied it was a wedding even as they threw confetti all over themselves. We, the press, were wedded to it. The coalition agreement was the pre-nup, the grooms of honour were the old versions of George Osborne and Danny Alexander, the marriage counsellor Nick Robinson of the BBC. They were the Brokeback cowboys, our two gay dads who just happened not, actually, to be gay. You can chart the demise of the coalition by the anniversaries: the first was in the handball arena of the then Olympic dirt pile, the second at a tractor factory. Halfway through, Dave likened their relationship to Rônseal. You know the magic is gone when you talk about DIY.

2. The Lib Dems. There, I've said it. I miss the Lib Dems, with their earnest crusades for doomed causes and their incredible ability to absorb abuse and still burble on about how they are carrying on the traditions of John Stuart Mill. I do think the coalition years would have been significantly different if the Lib Dems had decided not to campaign for the likes of the Alternative Vote or House of Lords reform, the latter an obvious red rag to the Tory bull. What if they had just stuck with their core issue of fairness and concentrated on favoured topics such as free school meals, taking the poorest out of tax, removing the stigma out of mental health? What if, I wondered, as I read through the sketches during that first turbulent coalition year, when students laid siege to Westminster and Nick was burnt in effigy, if they had argued *against* the tuition fee rise and taken the option, provided in the Coalition

Agreement, to abstain as one from the vote? What if, indeed. They chose these battles, but it could have been different.

3. Nick Clegg. There, I've said it again! I miss Nick Clegg singing that he is sorry (I'm so so sorry) and looking sad for the last four years of government and his monthly press conferences that seemed entirely pointless except for the fact that he was the Deputy Prime Minister. I even miss the coalition version of Tory MP Peter Bone, for whom the word eccentric does not suffice, and his obsession with who would rule the country if David Cameron were to fall under a bus. I miss Call Clegg, the LBC programme from which we learnt way too much, including that he had worn a onesie.

4. Ed Miliband relaunches. The Labour leader was the rocket who never had enough boosters, the troublesome politician whom ground control could never fathom. 'Houston, we have a problem' could have been his catchphrase. Twice, three times, sometimes more, a year, we would gather for what became an almost ritualised event. The Tories never tired of mocking him even as they stole many of his moral capitalist ideas (electricity charges, scrapping non-doms). Even One Nation, now the Tory slogan, was once Ed's, launched during one of his trademark memorised speeches. What was the real problem? Was it that he couldn't eat a bacon sandwich? That his name wasn't David? That his teeth were too big? That he forgot to mention the deficit in his last conference speech? But surely the truth is that he is an intellectual and just not much of a political street-fighter. The fact that it ended with him standing next to the 8 ft 6 in 'Ed Stone provided the perfect, weird and, indeed, perfectly weird end to it all…

5. I miss the man formerly known as George Osborne. When the coalition began, George was a slightly overweight wallpaper heir who was politically accident prone. Remember when President Obama called him Jeffrey? Or when he was booed by an entire stadium of people at the Olympics? The man who coined 'all in this together' and gave us the Omnishambles Budget was not, the country thought, together at all. Those were dark days for George, who became known as the Submarine Chancellor, as he dived deep, not surfacing for months. But then he had the best political make-over ever seen: becoming a champion of the unfashionable north, wearing hi-vis at every

opportunity, losing weight and acquiring a new haircut that made him look like Caesar. I miss the old George, a bit pudgy, white-faced, weak-voiced and thin-skinned. The new one is much shinier and not nearly as much fun.

6. Ed Balls and his hand-signals. PMQs is not the same without the shadow Chancellor, who was thrilled to be christened the most annoying man in politics by the Prime Minister. There he sat, his hands constantly in motion. For years, every time Dave and George talked about the economy, Ed would make his 'flat-line' gesture. Any hint of excitement and he would pat the air in a 'Calm down, dear' hand signal. Then there was the shovel ('quit digging!') and, my personal favourite, the wine glass, in honour of the Prime Minister's chillaxing ways. As much as I miss his hand gestures, though, I miss the way he riled the Tories more. They hated him the most. Surely there can be no greater accolade for a Labour politician.

7. The Leveson Inquiry. There will always be inquiries, but there will never be another one like Leveson, where Lord Leveson, or Brian as I like to call him, listened patiently to a stream of celebrities invade their own privacy, washing their own dirty linen themselves so that we, the press, didn't have to. I learnt way too much about the private lives of Max Mosley and Hugh Grant. Surely there will never be a final press conference like Brian's last great theatrical moment when he read out his conclusions, answered no questions and left for Australia. Could you make it up?

8. Britain before the Scottish revolution. It is an amazing fact that, for almost four years, the Scottish question never really bothered anyone very much. There was the occasional pesky midge moment but it wasn't until the referendum was virtually upon us that Westminster realised that, oops, they may have a little problem with the clans up north. You can see how, by sheer neglect, the Westminster elite, as the SNP love to call them, created the situation that exists today. The SNP may have lost the referendum but they are winning the war. Politically, we are all still adjusting to it.

9. UKIP as the fruitcake party. The death of fruitcakery can be timed from the moment in September 2013 that Nigel Farage withdrew the party whip from Godfrey Bloom after his infamous 'sluts' comment. That is when I knew that Nigel was serious about winning the 2014 European elections

(tick), encouraging Tory defectors (tick) and winning seats in the general election (er, only one tick). I'm still not sure that UKIP getting serious really worked for them as a party. Certainly they have not been nearly as successful as the Tory Euro-phobes who began the coalition years as irritants and ended them as triumphant with a firm commitment to a Euro-referendum.

10. Foreign policy, what foreign policy? In the beginning, there was Libya. Actually, maybe that's enough about that (certainly the coalition thought so). Afghanistan was all about getting out. Then there was the Syria vote where the Prime Minister, reacting as if stung by a bee, never went again. So, instead of an actual foreign policy, we had William Hague and Angelina Jolie, or Wangalina as we liked to think of them, fighting the good fight for women victims of war. But I, for one, will miss William Vague, as I thought of him.

The coalition morphed seamlessly into the election which, looking back, was like taking part in a fantasy game, built as it was on the absolute conviction held by almost everybody that we were going to have another hung parliament. All those marginal polls! All those kitchens! All those MPs who never returned. And, yes, I will miss some, and none more than the magnificent stately home that is Sir Peter Tapsell, the perfectly cast Father of the House.

We may not be 'All In This Together' but at least here they are certainly 'All In This Book Together'. RIP coalition years, we won't see the likes of you again – thank goodness.

Ann Treneman
Westminster
July 2015

So Who Exactly Was All in This Together?

DAVID CAMERON: 'Dave', aka, the Prime Minister, leader of the Conservatives, the largest party in the Parliament with 306 seats out of 650, Old Etonian and alternatively known as 'Mr Sunshine', 'Flashman' and 'Mr Angry'.

NICK CLEGG: 'Cleggers' or 'Calamity Clegg', the Deputy Prime Minister, leader of the Liberal Democrats, with fifty-seven seats, Europhile and speaker of five languages. Specialises in apologies and looking sad.

ED MILIBAND: 'Red Ed' or, sometimes, 'Dead Ed', leader of the Labour Party, the opposition with 258 seats. To become leader, in 2010, he beat his brother David, seen as fratricide. Best known for relaunches, moral capitalism, the 'Ed Stone and bacon sandwich difficulties.

GEORGE OSBORNE: The 'Submarine Chancellor' and Tory political strategist, wallpaper heir who found his political mojo by championing the Northern Powerhouse and getting a new hair-cut.

DANNY ALEXANDER: Also known as the 'Ginger Rodent', Lib Dem Chief Secretary to the Treasury and member of the Quad that ruled the coalition.

THERESA MAY: Home Secretary, surprise appointment who turned out to be rather good, becoming the longest-serving occupant since Rab Butler. Ice Queen and shoe fanatic.

ED BALLS: Shadow Chancellor, economist, Gordon Brown sidekick and all-round showman. Brilliant at hand signals and irritating the Tories. Also piano player, lasagne maker and football fan.

MR SPEAKER: John Bercow, famously pint-sized, hated by some Tories for being not as Tory as they are. Controversial, verbally flamboyant, crusader in the battle to update Parliament.

EUROSCEPTICS: Tory backbenchers, previously believed to be swivel eyed, who never tired in their quest to hold a referendum over leaving the EU. Star specimens are Bill Cash and Jacob Rees-Mogg, who I believe should wear a monocle.

ALEX SALMOND: SNP leader and First Minister of Scotland throughout most of the coalition years. Seen as a tartan Mickey Mouse and selfie-king of Scotland. Famously abrasive – and successful – politician.

The First Year

Confetti and Chaos

MAY 2010 — APRIL 2011

THE FIRST FULL coalition government in Britain since 1945 came into being after five long days of negotiations in May with a document immediately dubbed 'the pre-nup'. They were calling it the 'New Politics'. David Cameron, clearly enjoying the trappings of No. 10, displayed a talent for rising above it all. Deputy Prime Minister Nick Clegg embarked on an ambitious programme of constitutional reform (the Alternative Vote and the House of Lords), not to mention keeping busy U-turning over tuition fees. What MPs were calling the Brokeback Coalition was already looking ropey. Meanwhile, for Labour, there was the small matter of fratricide. The Age of Austerity was all around us, but you have to throw some confetti for a year that began with a political wedding and ended with a royal one.

•   •   •

13 MAY 2010

Da dum dum dum … Dave and Nick get married

After a week of talks between the Lib Dems and the Tories,
the press received a missive to go to Downing Street, but we
had no idea why. If I had known, I'd have worn a hat.

FROM THE VERY first sight of the happy couple I knew that this was, actually, a wedding. Nick and Dave emerged from the back door at No. 10 onto a garden terrace dotted with bright green spirals of topiary. Deep in conversation, they processed by the cascading lavender wisteria (wisteria! Dave's fave). Stride mirrored stride, smile begot smile. We could see how well they chuckled together as they came down the garden path towards us. Yes, down the garden path. You could not make it up.

We were gathered, dearly beloved, in the garden of No. 10. The hundred or so velvet chairs were arranged on the lawn – one side for the groom, the other for the other, slightly more boyish, groomette. The garden was a little bit of heaven with its beehive and wormery, dominated by a graceful majestic magnolia. Many of the flowers were yellow and blue, of course, perfectly co-ordinated for the politics. They even had matching his 'n' his lecterns.

The grass really IS greener on this side, I can report. It almost glowed it was so lusciously alien green. The only thing missing was a small orchestra and a tremulous song by Andrew Lloyd Webber.

'Today we are not just announcing a new government,' beamed Dave as Nick beamed back, eyes steady, body turned towards him. 'We are announcing a new politics.'

OMG, as they say, not just a wedding, but a birth too. 'I came into politics to change it, to change Britain,' beamed Nick as Dave beamed back. 'Together – that job starts today.'

Together forever! I have to say they suit each other. Indeed, both looked more relaxed together (forever!) than they do with their own parties. They are both forty-three but Nick makes Dave look a bit older, which, as he is now Prime Minister, is good. I had never noticed his crow's feet until yesterday, but then he laughed more than usual, occasionally throwing his head back. Everyone was talking about their hair (sorry, I wish I could say their policy on nuclear power but it wouldn't be true). Dave's mini-quiff was more coiffed; Nick's more natural.

We guests had brought only questions but, as it was a wedding, they were a bit soft. 'If the phone rings at 3 a.m., do you both have to answer it?' was one. Everyone giggled, especially Dave (or 'David', as Nick calls him). It seems not.

Where was Nick's office? 'He has the Deputy Prime Minister's office in the Cabinet Office,' explained Dave. 'It is pretty close together. This is not going to be a partnership where we have to book meetings.' Nick said that the Cabinet Office was like a warren. 'I have no idea where I am!' he cried giddily.

Birds were singing as they told us about their relationship. They'd set a fixed term of five years (and Parliament will follow suit), so will be renewing their vows at the election in 2015. Yes, Nick would be standing in for him at Prime Minister's Questions. 'I look forward to lots of for-eign travel!' gushed Dave.

It was all ridiculously chummy. Who knew that coalitions were this much of a love-in? If they keep this up, they'll need a joint name (Clameron? Camelegg?). But they both did look transformed. At one point, Dave chortled: 'This is what the new politics looks like!'

Happy days — at least for now.

20 MAY 2010

Nick picks up where 1832 left off...

*In those heady first few days, anything seemed possible,
especially for the Lib Dems, who hadn't been in power since
the 1920s. Nick couldn't wait to change the world.*

T O ISLINGTON, THEN, for the most important speech on political reform since 1832. Don't take my word for it: this is what Nick Clegg, our new Deputy Prime Minister, says.

The location was the atrium of a sixth-form college just off Holloway Road in north London, which may be home to the most kebab shops in Britain. (What did they do in 1832 to get a kebab? Maybe Nick would tell us.) When we arrived, we were given yellow lanyards, a word beloved by Lib Dems for the bit of string that holds your ID card. But the college had run out of ID cards and so we were told to wear the lanyards with nothing in them. As we sat, waiting for Nick, our empty lanyards round our necks, I felt that I was living the Lib Dem dream.

Nick was late. Actually, Nick is always late. Apparently 'Clegg Time' runs about fifteen minutes behind BST. Sure enough, right on Clegg Time, he arrived, preceded by an entourage that already numbered twelve. Then he ducked into another room. How frustrating. It was only when I saw a Lib Dem press officer carry out the sacred (plastic) glass of water for him that I knew the Great Political Reform Speech of 2010 was nigh.

It was very 'Power to the People'. I had hoped that Nick would just sing the John Lennon song, but instead he talked about a 'programme of empowerment'. This is harder to sing. He told us this was 'the biggest shake-up of our democracy since 1832'. He's just lucky that the suffragettes aren't around to chain themselves to the railings over that.

It is a bit of a tradition for Nick that, wherever he gives a speech, there is noise. The moment Nick announced 'The Power Revolution', behind me a dishwasher churned into life. I don't think Nick meant that kind of power. Nick's power revolution will 'put you in charge'. Presumably of the switch.

'Britain was once the cradle of modern democracy,' said Nick. 'We are now, on some measures, the most centralised country in Europe, bar Malta.' Bar Malta? Only a former MEP who is also a Lib Dem would care. I can hear the Libs now: 'My God, we can't be as centralised as Malta – let's have a power revolution.'

Nick told us that he was a liberal (lower case 'l', another example of coalition creep). 'My starting point has always been optimism about people.' Oh dear, this is pure Dave.

There are three steps to Nick's power revolution. First, he's ending the culture of spying. I glanced up at the sign that said we were all on CCTV. Second, he's reforming politics. We've been talking about Lords reform for 150 years. 'The time for talk is over!' he said (talking).

He's set up a committee that is not a 'talking shop'. This seemed a tad unrealistic: is it even possible to mime Lords reform? Only Nick and Dave, being optimists, would know. The third step is about decentralising so we avoid the Malta nightmare.

Nick ended his Great Reform Speech by enthusing: 'Power will be yours!' It seems unlikely, but what do I know? I wasn't there in 1832.

21 MAY 2010

I'd like to report a birth…

The first thing I noticed about the newborn coalition
is that it was a very strange colour.

THERE WAS A gaping hole in the birth announcements in *The Times* yesterday, and this is what should have been in it: LIB-CON. On 20 May, in Whitehall, to Nick and Dave, a child, named Coalition Freedom Fairness Responsibility, thirty-six pages long. No brothers or sisters.

The first thing I noticed about the new infant was its colour. It would be at home on Mars. 'Is it mushy pea or guacamole?' asked a colleague. Actually,

it's lime green with a hint of asparagus. Apparently one colour chart calls it
Tranquil. Basically, it's a muddy version of what you get when you mix a lot
of yellow with a bit of blue: page two is just a Rothko-esque block of this green
that paint makers might think about calling Coalition.

The birth was at the Treasury. The NHS may be concerned by this. It took
place in front of 100 civil servants and fifty press, plus innumerable politicos.
Midwives (mid-husbands?) Oliver Letwin and Danny Alexander looked on
proudly. It had been a nine-day labour (also called negotiations) and no drugs
(only drugs policy) were involved.

'In the end, in politics the right thing to do is the right thing to do is the right
thing to do,' said Dave as he welcomed baby Coalition. Nick looked on ador-
ingly. They got married only last week. On that occasion, Dave said: 'This will
succeed through its success.' I think these will be known as Dave-isms.

The birth was a drawn-out affair, with more speeches than a quadruple wedding. Nick spoke first: 'Even if you've read 100 party manifestos,' he said, revealing
what Lib Dems do in their spare time, 'you've never read a document like this.'

I looked through the thirty-six pages with thirty-one chapters (they went
from B for Banking to U for Universities, so it's not exactly A to Z). It was
partly in Tranquil type and partly in black. To be honest, it DID look exactly
like every other manifesto I've read. But Nick is not the first parent to think
his child ultra-special. I'm beginning to forget that Nick and Dave are from
separate parties. Yesterday they seemed one as they doted on Little Coalition
Freedom Fairness Responsibility Lib-Con (how that child is going to hate the
name; maybe they'll use Co or Free for short).

Now it was Theresa May's turn to speak. She was wearing her *Star Trek*
top, perhaps in sympathy with the little greenie. It's all so male-dominated that
if Theresa didn't exist they would have to invent her. She warbled on about freedom: 'Liberty builds bigger people.'

Then it was Vince's turn, but he was entangled with his mike, so she offered
to fill in: 'I was going to suggest ballroom dancing!'

Vince eventually got to the lectern. 'As the new head of the department for
technological innovation,' he said, 'we make it up as we go along.'

He speaks, of course, the truth.

22 JUNE 2010

Bulldog Dave has a 'Oeuf, oeuf!' moment

The parliament began, as it would carry on, obsessing about Europe.
The Prime Minister was eager to explain his ingenious plan.

I T'S AMAZING WHAT the great British breakfast can do. As you may remember, the EU served one up to David Cameron last week in the hopes of getting off to a good start with him. Yesterday, Dave told the Commons that the jambon-et-oeufs strategy had been a total success in that, now, incredibly, he is leading Europe when it comes to thinking on deficits.

'The summit was rightly focused on securing the economic recovery. It was unanimous that this required early action on budget deficits!' cried Dave. I got the impression that his new best friends, Nicolas Sarkozy and Angela Merkel, would, if their diaries allowed, be over here beside him for the Budget, scythes over shoulders.

Tory backbenchers, most of whom have been unremittingly negative about every Europe statement for the past thirteen years, came in droves to sing Dave's praises. He was their hero. Europe was now following Dave. Wasn't it marvellous? 'We now have a British bulldog representing the interests of Britain rather than a former Prime Minister who was like a French poodle!' cried Peter Bone, a right-winger who looks like Sven-Göran Eriksson, which makes him seem very dated. (Gordon Brown as a poodle? I don't think so but, then, we are in a brave new world.)

Dave said that it was the crisis in Greece (not to mention the oeufs) that had convinced Europe that he was right on budget deficits. 'The one group of people who seem to be completely outside this consensus is the British Labour Party! It's very short-sighted. It's very wrong. They'll come to regret it.'

Acting Labour leader Harriet Harman, spluttering, was a lone voice in the face of Dave-mania. Her line, badly delivered, was that it was the Tories who were isolated in Europe. Britain mustn't let cuts hurt growth. We mustn't fall behind South Korea. At this, Dave pounced: 'If we followed her advice,

I think we would be falling behind North Korea!' The chamber hooted, for North Korea, as Sven would know, had just lost 7–0 in the World Cup.

Harriet blinked. Now Dave chortled again about how all of Europe was backing him: 'The Labour Party are completely isolated!' His message was relentless, his argument crude, his attack total. It was exactly the sort of dog's breakfast argument, though in reverse, that Gordon Brown used to deploy. Woof, woof (or perhaps 'oeuf, oeuf'), as bulldogs say.

23 JUNE 2010

George arrives, axe at the ready

It was hard to see what George Osborne was hiding behind that giant implement, but then we saw it was a VAT rise.

THE GOOD NEWS is that, with his first Budget, Boy George has become a man. The bad news is that it's the axeman. It's hardly an aspirational job. No one says: 'When I grow up, I want to be an axeman!' And yet, that is exactly what Boy George is and, perhaps more worrying, I think he is loving it.

So cometh the hour, cometh the axeman. George certainly looks like a natural villain. It's that pasty skin and black hair. It's perfect for Hammer Horror. Or, *The Addams Family* (a male Morticia). Surely the way he popped up at the dispatch box to chortle, 'Here's Georgie! It's worse than we thought!' owed something to Jack Nicholson in *The Shining*. Has he been watching *The Texas Chainsaw Massacre* for tips? But his horror movie had a twist: George's character was the hero. So it's not The Axeman Goes on a Rampage, it's The Axeman Rescues the Nation. George has his chainsaw and he's going around SAVING people with it. He's scaring us to death FOR OUR OWN GOOD.

George never named the true villain. He just kept referring to his 'predecessor'. It was nicely icy. His predecessor had left a nightmare. He referred, with sadness, to poor Prudence. Like a Victorian maiden, her reputation has been ruined by you know who. 'Past Prudence was the excuse for future irre-sponsibility,' tsked-tsked the axeman. George mentioned the Civil List. Oh my God, I thought, he's going to chainsaw the Queen. But then he told us the Queen had agreed to chainsaw herself. He mentioned child benefit, praising it so much that I just knew, like lions hunting wildebeest, it would end in tears.

I had the same feeling when, on page thirty-two of a 41-page speech, he began to tell us, yet again, how awful it all is. It was like that music from *Jaws*. It tells you disaster looms. Then he struck, raising VAT in a single sen-tence. This brought screams from Labour. 'The years of debt and spending make this UNAVOIDABLE!' shouted the axeman, for that is his catchphrase.

He sat down to Tory adoration and Labour horror. The Lib Dems looked like they'd just been chainsawed. And the axeman? He was satisfied, for it had been almost an hour of pain. It's what he does.

30 JUNE 2010

Health Minister has a (very) small moment of madness

No one could believe it when the swivel-headed
Simon Burns lost it with Mr Speaker.

I FEAR FOR THE health, not to say career, of the new Health Minister Simon Burns. Yesterday Mr Burns went berserk – a technical term, but it was Health Questions so everyone understood – in the Commons, not against the opposition, but the Speaker. Why? Well, like all rage attacks, it was something that would seem tiny to you and me.

It had all begun when Mr Burns had turned round to answer a question from a Tory backbencher. 'Patients are going to be at the heart of the NHS,' said Mr Burns, his head rotating like an owl. At this, Mr Speaker interrupted: 'Can I very gently say to the minister, can you face the House?' Labour MPs cheered. But Mr Burns, who is fifty-seven with a florid beefy look and urbane manner, seemed perfectly normal (always a relative term in the chamber). But then, at the end of the session, Mr Burns was answering another question and this time with his whole body turned backwards.

Labour MPs complained that they couldn't hear. 'You must face the House,' insisted Mr Speaker. 'It's a very simple point. I have made it to others and they have understood it.'

This brought a raucous laugh. Mr Burns plonked down and then, suddenly, exploded, his body contorting, rocking from buttock to buttock, his head bobbing like a cork. 'Stupid,' he said. 'Stupid.'

It was a verbal Mr Creosote moment. Everyone was transfixed. Mr Burns was babbling, incandescent, apoplectic, splenetic. Among the words he fumed was 'sanctimonious'. Mr Bercow ignored him, calling another MP who asked a question on something (though absolutely no one was listening). Then, Mr Burns made a diminutive gesture with his hands and said, clearly: 'Dwarf'.

Mr Bercow, who admits to being vertically challenged, pretended not to hear. It was left to the excitable Tory MP Michael Fabricant, splendid in his buttercup-yellow summer wig, to lay a soothing hand on Mr Burns's shoulder. You know things are out of control when Micky Fab, as my late sketch-writing colleague Simon Hoggart christened him, is a calming influence.

If a panic button had existed, they would have hit it. Many Tories believe Mr Bercow, a former right-wing Tory who drifted to the left and was now a reforming Speaker, if a bumptious and self-regarding one with a habit of making Tory enemies, betrayed their party, but it has never spilled so rawly into the open. Mr Burns left, still in a state.

Everyone was agog. During points of order, Ian Paisley arose, like the ghost of his father. 'Is it in order,' he asked, 'for a member of the front bench to berate, scoff, scold and hiss at the chair whilst a member is trying to ask a question?' Mr Bercow listened, head cocked, as if this was news to him. He then said the incident had not been 'recorded' as he had been focusing on the whole chamber. This seemed unlikely, as if he had somehow missed Vesuvius. But now Mr Speaker came over all, well, sanctimonious. 'I hope that it will not be necessary in the course of the new parliament and the new politics, for that point to have to be made from the chair again,' he said primly.

But no one in Westminster could talk of anything else and Mr Burns certainly did not deny that he'd called the Speaker a 'stupid, sanctimonious dwarf'. Mr Bercow's Labour wife, Sally, tweeted: 'So much for the new politics, eh, Mr Burns.' She referred to 'nasty Tories' and 'low-grade abuse'. Her final response (she packs a lot into one tweet): 'Mr B is Speaker so get over it!' To which I can add only: 'Stretcher!'

6 JULY 2010

Lesson in how to influence no one

Nick makes the wrong friends – and enemies – as he announces the referendum on the Alternative Vote, a system in which voters rank candidates by numerical preference.

IT WAS NICK Clegg's moment in the limelight. Dave slipped in early, next to him. The two men – still on honeymoon, incredibly, after seven weeks – smiled at each other in their special way. At first it went fine. Dave glowed with pride and, at one point, even poured a glass of water for him.

Nick wants to 'empower' (ghastly word) the people by giving them a vote on the Alternative Vote and new constituency boundaries. It may sound laudable but, in the chamber, there was only carping. His reaction was a masterclass in how to lose friends and influence no one.

Labour began by having a bit of fun. Jack Straw, who is having a whale of a time in opposition, said that before the election Nick had called AV 'a miserable little compromise'. What, Jack wondered, had changed his mind? 'POWER!' cried MPs. Nick pretended not to hear, but it must hurt. Over the next hour, he attacked Labour MPs with a viciousness that made me wonder if the Dangerous Dogs Act should be extended. Among his kinder descriptions were 'paranoid', 'churlish', 'patronising' and 'stagnating'.

It was all very entertaining, except for one tiny detail. Nick needs these people.

It is the paranoid, churlish Labour MPs who are going to back him on AV – not Dave, who, no matter how many glasses of water he pours for Nick, is against it.

Austin Mitchell said it was a shame that Nick didn't have the 'guts' to fight for proportional representation. The new constituencies would only hurt Labour. It was, he said, 'the biggest gerrymander in British history'.

Nick stung back, saying that only in the 'weird and wonderful' introverted world of Labour would this be seen as gerrymandering. Gerrymander was the word of the day. By the way, it comes from Elbridge Gerry, an American who presided over bizarre changes to legislative districts (one looked like a salamander). So what does Nick have in common with that lizard? Labour thinks it knows.

9 JULY 2010

John Prescott embraces too much flunkery

I never thought I'd see the Labour heavyweight
wearing ermine. How wrong I was.

H E IS ALREADY being called The Erminator. Others had less kind words to describe the newly ennobled Lord Prescott of Kingston upon Hull. 'Isn't he calling everyone else in Labour a hypocrite these days?' huffed an MP. A peer, rushing in to see the great event, said: 'It's a laugh, isn't it?' Actually, it's more than that. I bet the little ermines of the world never thought that they would be troubled by the likes of Prezza. Yes, he likes croquet. Yes, he likes a Jag (or two). Yes, he thinks he's middle class, but only two years ago, when asked about the Lords, he reportedly said: 'I'm against too much flunkery and titles. But Pauline would like me to. I tell her, "What do you want to be Lady Prescott for? You're a lady already."'

The first person I saw, teetering on black peep-toes in the peers' lobby, was Our Pauline. She looked as if she had stepped out of *Dynasty*. Spotless white suit. Black hat like an awning. So big, in fact, that I could just see only the tips of her spidery eyelashes. Given the views of his lordship (as he now must be called), the hat was particularly impressive. 'I can't stand her big hats,' he has said. 'She has a bloody Berlin Wall of them. I used to get a member of my staff to walk beside her at the State Opening because I was embarrassed by her hats, which you can shelter under if it's raining.'

The only thing it was raining yesterday was flunkeys. The party faithful were being paid back for years of slavish loyalty. Prezza was the third peer to be introduced. Blairites and Brownites filled the benches. I saw Dennis Turner, now Lord Bilston,[1] who as an MP was in charge of the catering committee. New Labour, new toffocracy.

Forget the flunkery, feel the flummery and the frou-frou. The Yeoman Usher led the procession, patent leather slippers gleaming. He was followed by a man dressed as a playing card. Then came the heavy uneven walk of Prezza, his robe just about hiding that chip on his shoulder. The reading clerk, who often flips the tiny pigtails attached to his periwig, looked as if he was struggling to keep a straight face.

Mr Pigtail read out the scroll from the Queen. 'Greeting!' His voice, so mellifluous, seemed to be speaking a different language, though, for Prezza, that is normal. The clerk welcomed 'our right trusty and well-beloved John Leslie Prescott'. I couldn't help but think that, in different times, Prezza might have punched a man in pigtails who called him beloved. Prezza must 'sit among the barons'. He must 'enjoy and use all the rights, privileges, pre-eminences, immunities and advantages' of being among the barons. Somehow I don't think that is going to be a problem for the king of Dorneywood.

The moment was approaching when he had to open his mouth. A nation tensed. 'I, John, Lord Prescott,' he said, lisp banished. He'd been practising in front of the mirror. It worked. He swore allegiance to the Queen and kept God out of it. He was word-perfect. When it was done, peers gave him

---

1   Lord Bilston passed away in 2014.

a hearty cheer and two claps. Prezza, toff-hater, is one of them now. Up in the gallery, Lady Prescott looked thrilled.

27 JULY 2010

Antisocial behaviour in the House? Time to call 101

The new Home Secretary, whose appointment was a surprise, not least because she was entirely the wrong sex for some, begins to show us what she's made of.

THERESA MAY WANTS us to have a new national crime-fighting number – 101. It's for antisocial behaviour and non-emergency crime. In other words, exactly what went on in the House of Commons yesterday. I fear it will be inundated, not least by me.

Mrs May, dressed in her high-collared *Star Trek* outfit, is bringing power to the people. Police commissioners are going to be elected. She's empowering (the language alone is worth a 101 call) frontline staff. 'They will no longer be form-writers but crime fighters.' Oh no, it rhymed. I don't think I can make another call to 101 so soon.

Labour's Alan Johnson began to foam. 'The statement should be entitled Policing in the Twenty-First Century – How to Make The Job Harder,' he sneered. 'You as usual, trot out the infantile drivel about the last Labour government, probably written by some pimply nerd foisted upon your office by No. 10.'

What's happened to Alan Johnson? Everyone used to say that the former Home Secretary was far too nice to be leader of the Labour Party. The apple cheeks glowed, the banter flowed, he was the ex-postie with the mostie. Now it's no more Mr Nice Guy. Does 101 know? He explained that Mrs May had inherited a land of peace and harmony from him; crime had been slashed. She should be grateful, but instead she had unleashed a triple whammy. First came the cuts, then the restrictions on CCTV. And now she had the audacity to try to impose democracy on the police. Wham, wham, wham! Mrs May was a serial offender, a whamaholic.

AJ, spluttering, cheeks on fire, said that Mrs May was driven by dogma and that she was going to drive a coach and horses through police accountability. Is it even possible to do both of those things at the same time? If so, I fear it's another 101 call.

Mrs May hit back – hard. She was rather good. She even clubbed Caroline Lucas, the Green MP who is generally treated as some sort of cuddly mascot. Ms Lucas criticised the idea of elected commissioners, saying that they would be picked for their party. Mrs May snapped that police were not allowed to join any party. WHAM. She accused Ms Lucas of having a 'jaundiced view' of the British people. WHAM. It was like watching a baby-seal-clubbing.

Hello, is that 101?

28 JULY 2010

Showdown for Calamity Clegg

Everyone was thrilled to discover that Tory backbenchers were calling Dave and Nick's government the Brokeback Coalition, after the film about two gay cowboys.

THE COMMONS WAS in a 'yee-haw!' mood. Rowdy doesn't even begin to cover it. The last day of the parliamentary term began with Deputy Prime Minister's Questions starring Nick Clegg, and there was no escaping the *Brokeback Mountain* theme, the movie metaphor obsessing Westminster. 'On the assumption that the Prime Minister and you aren't holidaying together in Montana,' began Jack Straw, with one of his irritating little smirks.

Wyoming, I thought, not Montana. The two gay cowboys were in Wyoming (well, they were fictional, but you know what I mean). But MPs were too busy yee-hawing to care about geography. Ever since it got out that senior Tories refer to the government as the Brokeback Coalition, no one has stopped giggling. I find the comparison odd. *Brokeback Mountain* is a sad film with a tragic ending. Surely Nick and Dave's happy, smiling coalition is more a rom-com, pol-com, sitcom-type thing (provisionally entitled Our Two Gay Dads). But there is no getting away from the fact that MPs love the idea of Nick and Dave as gay cowboys. And Nick, accident prone in every way, has been Calamity Clegg for some time.

Mr Straw did get around to asking if and when Calamity would be in charge of the country. 'The Prime Minister will be taking his vacation in the second half of August,' said Nick. 'He remains Prime Minister. He remains overall in charge of this government. But I will be available to hold the fort.'

Hold the fort! MPs whooped even more. I felt we were, almost, home on the range. Or, as the song goes, 'Yippy-yi-o, yippy-yi-a!' Still, Calamity made a pretty strange cowboy in his beautifully cut Paul Smith suit, the only metrosexual in the O. K. Corral who could, if he had to, take his question time in Dutch, French, Spanish or German. It just wasn't very John Wayne.

And I don't think Big John cared all that much about the Alternative Vote either. Calamity does little else. Yesterday he came under fire from all sides, notably from Edward Leigh, the perpetually outraged Tory back-bencher. He began by calling Calamity his 'new and best Right Honourable Friend'. More giggles at that. Mr Leigh noted that, under the AV system, the Tories in 1997 would have been reduced to a 'pathetic rump' of sixty-five MPs. Mr Leigh is against AV. He wants a separate referendum date and a 'proper debate'.

The Western theme continued. Calamity used the word 'bonanza'. *Bonanza!* This was the second-longest American Western television series next to *Gunsmoke*. I began to see that Calamity was not afraid of a fight. As he talked of voter registration pitfalls, the Labour stalwart Fiona Mactaggart shrieked: 'What are you doing about it?' Calamity looked miffed. 'You scream from a sedentary position,' he said, before screaming right back, 'but what did you do about it for thirteen years?'

The noise level kept going up, as they shouted about the Iraq War, cuts, the size of constituencies etc.

Calamity strode through it all, as bow-legged as Big John, pistols at his side, his faithful horse (Chris Huhne?) tethered nearby. Well, I guess, in the immortal words of Big John: a man's gotta do what a man's gotta do. And this man's fighting.

14 SEPTEMBER 2010

Dinosaurs say we are not all in this together

For more than a decade, during the Labour governments, the trade union leaders had some sort of power and influence. But now all that had changed.

WE ARE WATCHING prehistory being made in Manchester. The dinosaurs are back, roaming if not yet the Earth then certainly the salmon-pink carpet at the TUC conference centre. We watched yesterday as they emerged from the primordial gloop, very much alive and bellowing their hatred of the bankers and the coalition. The scariest dino of them all, Bob Crow (aka B-Rex), watched, eyes flashing, right at home.

What a difference an election makes. For years it has seemed as if the TUC was meeting for its own purposes, not so much a conference as a historical re-enactment society. But now, back in opposition, that has changed – and how.

Political palaeontologists will be fascinated. Take Brendan Barbersaurus, their leader, previously thought to be mild-mannered, a vegetarian who lost his teeth many ages ago. Now, amazingly, he has gone carnivorous. 'What we've got is not a coalition government, but a demolition government!' he roared to applause. The coalition's catchphrase 'We are all in this together' was 'insulting claptrap' (more applause).

He wants to tax the super-rich, mobilise every community, co-ordinate strikes. Then there is Dave Prentisraptur, of UNISON, main-stream, not known for being aggressive. Until now. 'Today we face the greatest test for a generation,' he cried, letting rip at the government, the bankers, the speculators, the profiteers. The new enemy was Barclays's Bob Diamond, on £11 million a year, a man who says he wakes up with a smile on his face.

It is, brothers and sisters, class war. One beast after another castigated our government of millionaires, our Cabinet of the super-rich who wanted to spare the bankers (Bob Diamond smiles! It's an outrage!) and lay the blame on public-sector workers.

'That is a complete lie, a distortion, and we reject it right away!' bellowed Matt Wrack (T-Rex-Rack?) of the Fire Brigades Union. 'The idea of 25 per cent or 40 per cent cuts is complete and utter lunacy. We will stop them in their tracks. IT WILL NOT HAPPEN!'

All this made B-Rex, in the past the most frightening of all, seem rather tame. He warned that all trade union members would, at some point, have to decide if they were going to lie down or fight. 'If the top bankers don't get up in the morning, with the smile that Bob Diamond has on his face, the economy will run as normal,' he shouted. 'But if workers don't get out of bed in the morning, the economy will shut down. We've got to recognise the strengths that we've got!'

Then, finally, into this macho jungle, came Labour's Harriet Harman, Harperson to some, sister dino, the first feminist of the gloop, in one of her last appearances as acting leader. The beasts gave her a warm welcome and she fluttered her support. She received polite applause, nothing more, for she is part of the past now. They believe that they are the future; no longer fossils, reborn to roam anew.

20 SEPTEMBER 2010

Liberal Democrats have a collective identity crisis

The party faithful, meeting at their convention in Liverpool,
couldn't decide if they loved or hated power and so they
decided to do both at the same time. It was so Lib Dem.

THERE IS A Liberal Democrat sign tacked to the door of the ludicrously large auditorium in Liverpool: 'Please be aware that special effects will be in use during this session – including loud noises, explosions and flashing lights.'

That is no way to talk about Danny Alexander, I thought, as I watched the Giant Carrot try to explain to his party faithful why he's cutting us, them, everyone to the bone. 'We are all in this together,' he said. (Oh George, have you actually brainwashed him?) He told them to be proud of the cuts because they are guided by Lib Dem values. Oh dear.

When it was over, I saw one person stand and, seconds later, another. It was a crouching, hesitant ovation of a political party that is, quite clearly, having a massive identity crisis. I can see why. For years, they have been having their days at the seaside (last year the big story was a beached whale). It was all rather gentle and likeable. Now, suddenly, as if they had been kidnapped by Alice in Wonderland, they have become very large and very important.

Loud noises and flashing lights are the least of it. Before, security consisted of a hairy man looking in my handbag: now the entrance looks like departures at Heathrow. There are men with squiggly earpieces, 60 per cent more media and 30 per cent more delegates. At one point, I was caught in a mini-stampede. It's so very un-Lib Dem (it's hard to stampede in sandals).

It's power that's done it, of course. The party faithful are both thrilled and appalled with it. You see it in the way they say the 'p' word – rolling it round as if it were a foreign body in their mouths. And you could see, during the big event of the day, the Nick Clegg question-and-answer session, that they both hate and love it – at exactly the same time.

Nick sauntered onto the stage, Euro chic in open-necked shirt and metrosexual suit. He looked about twelve, as usual, and even more Tory than usual. The tone was set by the first question from a party activist named Linda Jack. She had been a fervent supporter of Nick for the leadership.

'I said then that I would trust you with my life so I could trust you with my party. I still think I can trust you with my life. Can I trust you with my party?' This brought a ripple of laughter and applause. Nick took a deep breath.

'Of course you can, Linda,' he said, sounding forced.

No one agreed with Nick. 'Why are we being blamed for the cuts,' asked one woman plaintively, 'while the Conservatives are being praised for policies we brought to the coalition?' Nick blamed growing pains, the press, political language, machismo and the Labour Party (in that order).

Then came this plea: 'It would be really great to hear occasionally from you and some of the other ministers that you actually don't like a policy that you are announcing.' This received sustained applause.

Nick said that was nuts (I paraphrase). 'My view – and it's my view generally in life – is that if you are going to do something, either do it properly or not at all. If you are part of a coalition government, you OWN that coalition government!' The delegates clapped at that too.

As I said, identity crisis.

26 SEPTEMBER 2010

The shock, the hug and the 'I love you, bro'

*Everyone thought they knew which Miliband brother was
going to win the Labour leadership election. But then, after
an evening of endless bar charts, came the surprise.*

THE MOMENT THAT his victory was announced, Ed Miliband had eyes for only one person – his brother. They locked each other into a hug of hugs, the older brother pounding his brother's back a little too hard, at least eight times.

The rictus grin on David's usually mobile face said it all. At one point, he ruffled his younger brother's bog-brush hair, something he must have done hundreds of times before in their lives.

From that moment, their lives would never be the same again – a genuinely dramatic ending to a contest that has gone on for four long months. Even the last hour had been particularly painful, a political version of water torture as we had to endure self-congratulatory videos and a snail's trail of speeches, including one by Gordon Brown (he lives!). The soundtrack was excruciating – Gordo came out to 'I'm a Soul Man' (I rest my case) – and, when we finally got down to the business of counting the votes, so were the bar charts.

Bar charts. Oh yes, Labour really does know how to throw a party. It was really a very strange event – thousands of people gathered in a dark hall watching a screen with giant bar charts. Surely David Attenborough should be there, whispering, trying to explain to real people about this strange mating ritual.

The numbers were announced by a woman named Ann Black, NEC chairwoman, charisma count of zero. The five candidates had just been clapped into the hall from the pen where they had been held, human rights infringed and, more importantly, mobile phones removed, not allowed to phone a friend or, even more important in politics, an enemy.

From the start, I had been seeking signs of who won, which is a bit like trying to see a black cat on a moonless night. No one even knew who knew. When Harriet Harman came out and greeted Neil Kinnock, a Mili-E man, with double kisses, I thought – ah, there's a sign! But then, did Harriet even know? No one even knew that.

Except, of course, Ann Black, who has, I can tell you, no future as a bingo caller. She recited the numbers, endless lists of percentiles. After the first round (David with 37.78 and Ed with 34.33), she said: 'There are quite a few more rounds to go!' The room was on the edge of its seat. As one bar chart gave way to another, there were 'oooohhhs' and 'ahhhhs'. Then, finally, on the last number, whoops erupted.

After The Hug, The Speech, which was, sadly (because I don't like to spoil the party), just a little bit terrible. Ed stood looking like a thin and tall panda, dark-circled eyes staring out at the hall. His first word as Labour leader was 'conference'. Not a great start.

He praised each of the candidates as if he were an *X Factor* judge. But when he spoke of his brother, it was as if they were in the room alone. 'David, I love you so much as a brother,' he said. 'I have such extraordinary respect for the campaign that you ran, the strength and eloquence that you showed.'

Everyone in the hall was aware of David sitting there, smiling through the pain. Up there on the blood-red podium set, Ed kept saying, 'I get it.' Well, he has got it now. He seemed to be in shock. Afterwards, he stood there gangly, awkward, not knowing what to do, his brother watching.

5 OCTOBER 2010

Toto, we're not in Kansas anymore. We're in power

The Tories met for their conference in Birmingham, the first time they'd held one in power since 1996. George Osborne seized the chance to release his inner Judy.

THE CHANCELLOR STRODE out on stage to an instant pre-ovation and told us how bad things were: Labour had left us on the brink; had crashed the car. It was terrible (and that was just the clichés). But he said that he had stopped the madness. 'Vigilant at all times we remain,' he cried. He praised himself (a trumpet being close to hand) about how he'd already stopped the rot. There was no panic, no danger of a 'deathly spiral' of higher interest rates. 'Our victory is the very absence of war,' he intoned. 'Now, together, we must win the peace.'

What did it mean? Was it a haiku? The audience applauded it all: the war, the peace, the deathly spiral. I suspected that he could say anything – for instance, 'sausages' – and get a clap. He proved this by saying 'Nick Clegg' and, bolder still, 'Danny Alexander'.

He told us hard truths, home truths, straight truths. He brought out the axe, chopping this and that, all for the greater good. 'We are all in this together,' he chanted, for that is his catchphrase.

The audience kept on clapping (were they hypnotised?) Then George, abruptly, left behind his land of pain and ushered us into the Utopia – let's call it the Land of Oz-borne – just beyond reach. I could hear the swell of an entire orchestra. 'Just over the horizon', he cried, 'lies the Britain we are trying to build.'

He was releasing his inner Judy now. Just over the rainbow was a hopeful country, a united country, a prosperous country. Just over the horizon was a land governed by Munchkins (he may not have said that) with imagination, fairness, courage. Somewhere over the horizon was a Britain that is a beacon for liberty. We were all with him now, holding our beacon, over the rainbow, way up high.

George, deficit diva, finished to tumultuous applause, his axe briefly idle.

19 OCTOBER 2010

Tiny biscuit offensive crumbles into the void

The debut speech by Labour's new shadow
Chancellor leaves us with an empty feeling.

I EMERGED FROM ALAN Johnson's first speech as shadow Chancellor feeling short-changed and not a little annoyed. Almost exactly four years ago I went to the same location – the glass box that is the KPMG headquarters near Fleet Street in London – to hear another relatively new shadow Chancellor named George Osborne. I emerged annoyed from that also (well, it's my job), but I can tell you that Mr Johnson was poorer by far.

This is why: Mr Osborne made a speech, took questions and then tried to wriggle out of answering them. He took some risks, put himself out there, had a go. But Mr Johnson hardly felt present as he read out what seemed to be someone else's speech. He took no questions and so, obviously, had no answers. It was like touching a void.

The event had all the awkwardness of a first date. Do you remember Labour's prawn cocktail offensive under Tony Blair to woo the world of business to their cause? I can report that, under Red Ed's regime, it has become a tiny biscuit offensive. We had to negotiate a spiral staircase to get to the biscuits. Except that hardly anyone did. What if you gave a major policy speech and no one came? Exactly this.

We were ushered into a smallish room with sixty chairs and a bright blue backdrop. No Labour signs, no Labour rose. Just deep Tory blue. About half the chairs were full, but it was all media. I could not find one City person who was not from KPMG – and even they were few in number.

The shadow Chancellor was introduced by someone from KPMG who seemed to be, more or less, Head of Stuff. Two shadow Treasury ministers slipped in at the last moment, presumably so that they did not actually have to talk to anyone.

AJ, his red cheeks the only Labour thing in the blue room, looked as if he wanted to be anywhere but there. He read the speech, which had some good lines, with the unbridled enthusiasm of an actuary. He said that the government's deficit plan was built on myths. 'Since the election we have seen another myth emerge: having been in semi-retirement since the 1980s, Tina has reappeared.' The coalition was using Tina (There Is No Alternative) as an excuse for its draconian cuts but, actually, TIAA (There Is An Alternative).

The only reason I can tell you about TIAA is because we were given written texts. Thus I can report that it is a mix of Tory cuts lite, more bank taxes and growth. Otherwise, I doubt anyone in the room could have remembered. Gordon Brown as Chancellor boomed, Alistair Darling tended to drone, but Alan Johnson just recites words.

It ended without applause. Thus a void met a void. Mr Johnson began to walk towards us before remembering that he was too grand (or scared) to take questions. 'Farewell,' he said, exiting stage right, a man frightened by his own shadow job.

20 OCTOBER 2010

Dave says we must never surrender – our time zone

David Cameron's statement on defence spending was so magnificent that he commanded his epaulettes to rise up to salute him.

COMMANDER-IN-CHIEF DAVE LAUNCHED a remarkable military operation – codenamed Operation Flannel – in the Commons yesterday. First he attacked his own forces from land and sea and air, cutting and trimming, slashing and burning. He blamed it all on the official opposition, who, more or less, voluntarily surrendered. Far more deadly was the unofficial opposition (i.e., the Tory Party) who were subjected to a sustained Dave charm offensive.

The result? A truly impressive smokescreen of bamboozlement that swirled around the chamber, almost hiding what had just happened. Through the murk I was hardly able to see Trident, now postponed, or the two aircraft carriers that, after Dave's strike, had no aircraft on them. Through my spyglass, I could only just discern that their vast decks were now being used by what appeared to be piratical skateboarders.

Operation Flannel began with Dave telling us why Britain was great. We have the sixth-largest economy and the fourth-largest military budget. 'We have', crowed Dave, 'a time zone that allows us to trade with Asia in the morning and the Americas in the evening and a language that is spoken across the globe.' Wait a minute, as they say in Greenwich. Our time zone makes us great? Well, at least Dave hasn't cut that yet. Nor has he trimmed a syllable from the English language.

Ed Miliband came over as a rather tiresome polytechnic lecturer, but he did have one rather good question: 'Is it really the case that the best strategic decision for the next decade is for Britain to have aircraft carriers without aircraft?'

Siren alert! Dave, acting quickly, got out the dry ice. 'Let me address very directly this issue of the capability gap,' he said, smoke pumping out of his nostrils. 'There is not a gap in our flexible posture. With our air-to-air refuelling and our fast jet capability we have the ability to deploy force around the world.' Wow, I thought, we've even left our time zone.

'But', said Dave, 'I accept there is going to be a gap in carrier strike.' A gap in carrier strike. So that is what they call an aircraft carrier without aircraft. Mind the gap, as they say. But he wasn't going to, as Labour had, 'push these things off to the future'. 'You've got to make the tough decisions now!' cried Dave, his epaulettes rising up to salute him.

In his very next sentence, he said: 'On Trident...' Forget the capability gap, this was a credibility gap. Sir Peter Tapsell, a majestic galleon of a man, accused Dave of postponing Trident as a sop to the Lib Dems. Dave charged, smoke billowing until I could see nothing, only hear his voice bellowing: 'We are on track to replace Trident. It's the right decision!' Or, as the armchair generals would say, the right indecision.

2 NOVEMBER 2010

Night flight of the Lesser Spotted Gordo

*I got my binoculars out to watch the strange spectacle that was
the former Prime Minister's first speech since leaving office.*

WE HAVE BEEN waiting for Gordo for so long that it was a shock to see him. But there he was, entering the chamber at 10.14 p.m., carrying his moral compass. It was the second time he'd been there since leaving Downing Street, but the first time was a mere flit through. This time he'd alerted everyone he'd ever met that he was going to speak. Often during an adjournment debate there are three people there: last night there were about 200.

Gordo had left nothing to chance. He'd even arranged for ten or so Scottish MPs to serve as his 'doughnut', a parliamentary oddity where MPs clump around another MP to show that he is not alone. There was a mini-panic when part of Gordo's doughnut, arriving before him, sat in the wrong place. So when Gordo scooted along the third bench back and sat down, they had to scuttle along behind him, like hermit crabs in search of a resting place.

The whole event was, as the Tory minister Peter Luff put it, a 'footnote in parliamentary history'. Gordo will have hated that. He has seen himself as many things, saviour of the free world among them, but never as a footnote. His face was impassive as he sat, nervous, hands constantly moving, to his hair, his leg, and finally wrapping around his body.

This was his 'relaunch'. I say this because it could not have been a coincidence that it happened on the same day that he announced he is to campaign for democracy in Burma. Indeed, in what may be the strangest announcement ever made by a former prime minister, he told us that he would be 'guest-editing' his wife's Twitter feed to highlight the injustices of the Burmese junta.

But back to the Commons. It was his first speech from the back benches since 1985. The Lesser Spotted Gordo has been a very rare sight since April. The man who wrote a book on courage has seemed strangely lacking it in a sufficient quantity to appear in public. Apparently he's been busy writing a book about how he saved the world. Since the new government arrived in May, he has missed the Budget, the Comprehensive Spending Review, PMQs, the Strategic Defence Review and many sessions of Scottish questions. And now here he was, practically in the middle of the night, relaunching. The topic, appropriately, was aircraft carriers. It lasted all of four minutes and was, essentially, an intervention in an adjournment debate secured by a neighbouring MP to insist that the maintenance on Britain's two new aircraft carriers (which won't have aircraft for some time) should be carried out at Rosyth shipyard, rather than in France. The fact that it had been heavily briefed that Rosyth would get the contract made the whole thing even stranger.

He began, as if it was PMQs, with tributes to the Armed Forces. He quoted Winston Churchill. He mispronounced Portsmouth as Ports-mouth. It was almost nostalgic to listen to that great booming voice filling the chamber. He spoke eloquently about the dockyard and its place in history and its need for the contract. He sat down, poppy proud on his lapel, his voice still reverberating. Our wait was over. It all seemed most surreal.

9 NOVEMBER 2010

Dave shifts their horizons as only he can

We were invited to what seemed like a giant fridge to be told that the government was scrapping targets – and replacing them with milestones.

IT WAS A completely bonkers event even by this government's standards. Everything about it – the setting, the temperature, the language – was off the chart. At 9 a.m. yesterday, Dave and Nick invited 100 top civil servants, plus the Cabinet, to the giant fridge that is Dunbar Court atrium in the Foreign Office for a pep talk on their departmental business plans. It was so full of nonsense that it makes Jabberwocky look sane.

'Welcome to this wonderfully chilled room,' boomed Dave. Chilled? Actually, I think even bottles of Chardonnay would have found it nippy. The only thing missing was the huskies and the polar bears. The civil servants, who had queued for ages to check their coats, shivered. Rule Number One in the Age of Austerity: Keep your coats on, it's cold in here.

Dave was extremely beamish, as Lewis Carroll might say. His plans are a revolution. It's all about a power shift and a horizon shift. Also, in Dave World, there are no more targets. Instead there are 'milestones'. (I am not making this up).

Dave says that it's about using 'plain English'. I am sure you will agree that 'power shift' is plainly nothing to do with voltage. Instead, Dave is running an extension cable from Whitehall (this may explain the lack of heating) to all of us. So get ready to plug in.

Also, and you can't get plainer than this, Dave's shifting the horizon. That one with the sunsets is the wrong one. Ditto the one with the sunrises. Now, earth meets sky. In future, who knows? Dave insists that Mother Nature (don't forget that she's also lost her child benefit) has got it wrong and he wants her to come up with a new horizon – and it has to be cheaper, too. Also, more plain English, Dave says centralisation is wrong. 'The idea that it's only the people at the top who have the answers is an incredibly negative view of the world,' said the man who had just ordered a new horizon.

Dave wants all departments to report to him every two weeks on progress on their decentralisation milestones. One civil servant (probably ex by now) referred to this as 'tight, central control'.

So what's the word for that in plain English? Well, there are a few, but perhaps 'brillig!' is the best.

11 NOVEMBER 2010

Nick starts to feel the heat on tuition fees

*Outside of Parliament, the students were on the march
protesting against the Liberal Democrats' U-turn on tuition
fees. Inside, Nick Clegg was trying to explain himself.*

NICK CLEGG, BAD heir day. This was the day that Cleggers, as Dave calls him, came into his own as an official hate figure. Outside Parliament, thousands of students marched: one poster said 'Nick Clegg, Tory Boy', another showed flying yellow Liberal Democrat 'hypocrite' pigs. Someone had scrawled on a bed sheet: '"I pledge to vote against any increase in tuition fees" – Mega LOL.'

In the Commons, Harriet Harman, who knows a thing or two about being a hate figure, kept it simple. 'In April,' she deadpanned, 'you said it was your aim to end university tuition fees. Can you update the House on how your plan is progressing?' Mega LOL from Labour. The Tories tried to hide secret smiles. The Lib Dems were as grim as a convention of undertakers.

'Uh,' said Mr Clegg.

'Uh! Uh!' mocked Labour MPs.

Mr Clegg, who should know that hesitation is fatal, scrambled: 'This is an extraordinarily difficult issue.' Labour MPs mocked again. Mr Clegg said that he had been 'entirely open' about the fact that he has not been able to deliver his policy. But the new plan, which actually triples tuition fees to £9,000, was 'progressive'.

'I'm glad you think it's so fair,' said Harriet. 'In April you said increasing tuition fees to £7,000 a year would be a disaster. What word would you use to describe fees of £9,000?'

Mr Clegg gave us all a little lecture on being progressive. Harriet asked why he had gone along with a Tory plan and launched into a tortuously laboured (ha) joke: 'We all know what it's like,' she said. 'You're at Freshers' Week, you meet up with a dodgy bloke and you do things that you regret.'

This brought uproarious LOL-ing. 'Isn't it true that you've been led astray by the Tories?'

Mr Clegg now suffered a complete sense of humour failure. His answers were defensive and delivered with a moral tone so high that it was doing the pole vault. Everything he'd done was for the greater good. He was like a born-again preacher who, when caught in a brothel, claims he's there for spiritual purposes.

Harriet attacked again. I couldn't believe she was doing so well. Now she pointed at the Lib Dems and, like a bad conscience, cried: 'You must honour your promise to students.'

Nick tried to go on the attack – again – but it was like shouting into the wind. Mega-LOL, as the students would say.

24 NOVEMBER 2010

Sacré bleu! Theresa finds the path of most resistance

There is general shock all round as Theresa May briefly embraces a character from the sit-com 'Allo 'Allo! *and shows us that she does have a human side (and it's French).*

'ALLO, 'ALLO. YESTERDAY, the Home Secretary, for a brief but entirely too long moment, slipped into the character of the French resistance fighter, Michelle Dubois, during the immigration statement.

'It is the position…' said Theresa May in her normal voice, before suddenly leaning forward, neck encircled by giant pearls, feet clad in leopard-skin kitten heels. She lowered her voice in what was perhaps meant to be sexy but ended up sounding a bit like a frog-horn.

'I listen very carefully,' she said. 'I will say this oonlee wonze…'

Mais oui! This brought squeals of delighted laughter, even though she had not listened that carefully or she would have known the quote is just: 'Listen very carefully...' And sorry to be a pedant, but this was a statement on the non-EU immigration cap, which therefore excluded Michelle and all the cast of *'Allo 'Allo!* on the grounds that they are French and, of less importance perhaps, not real in any way.

In the Commons, everyone was thrilled, not least Ed Balls, her chief tormentor. For almost an hour, Ed had been orchestrating a campaign to hector her on whether she had dropped the Tory election pledge to lower immigration to tens of thousands a year by 2015.

But Michelle had been coy, saying only that it remained her aim to reduce immigration. She would not, despite repeated goadings, repeat the date. Ed, eyes popping, jumping round like a restless child, thought it was a U-turn.

'You are in a state of quite extraordinary excitement,' said Mr Squeaker, who is, of course, a character himself in every way.

Ed's eyes strobed. But then, Michelle, listening very carefully and saying this oonlee wonze, confirmed that her aim was to do this by 2015. This brought Tory cheers.

Mr Balls, now resembling a jumping bean, popped up after the statement. 'I, of course, commend your chairing,' he said, greasily, to the Speaker. (At times the dialogue in the chamber is beyond parody.) Mr Balls said he had just witnessed 'a U-turn on a U-turn'. Inexplicably, Michelle was flirting with Ed: 'I think that the Home Secretary...' This brought whoops. Ed looked thrilled. 'After thirteen years in opposition,' said Michelle, 'as you'll discover, you make these mistakes.'

I think we all know what René would say to that – and it isn't 'You smart woman!' And then, with only an *au revoir*, it was over.

1 DECEMBER 2010

Itsy-bitsy, teeny-weeny, it's Nicky's tuition fee mankini

It's a mock-a-thon as Nick Clegg is told that voters will judge him for years to come on his tiny new policy on tuition fees.

AFTER HIS APPEARANCE in the Commons, Nick Clegg was heading out to what is, apparently, a top-level meeting in Kazakhstan, which Borat of course believed was the greatest country in the world ('All other countries are run by little girls,' as the anthem goes). I do hope that Nick has packed his yellow Lib Dem mankini but, yesterday, he might as well have been wearing one, for his tuition fees policy left him just as exposed.

Outside, it was a typical Siege Tuesday in Westminster with students protesting in the snow and choppers whirring above the thin blue line. Inside, Nick had got some top Lib Dems (no longer an oxymoron) to come to his Question Time as a sort of thin yellow line. The Ginger Rodent (aka Danny Alexander) was there, but, sadly, no Vince Cable, as he was too busy explaining to TV cameras why he may abstain on the vote over his policy to allow £9,000-a-year fees.

Harriet 'Boadicea' Harman demanded to know how Nick would vote: 'Are you going to vote for, abstain or vote against, as we are?'

Nick 'answered' by asking about Labour's policy: 'Is it a blank piece of paper? Is it a graduate tax? We have a plan. You have a blank sheet of paper!' he crowed.

People would judge him by this, warned Harriet. The only principled stand was to vote against. If he abstained, it was a 'cop-out'; if he voted for, it was a 'sell-out'.

Nick taunted right back: 'Since you don't want to discuss your policy...' Technically, of course, it was his question time, but when your policy is a mankini, you've got to be tough.

Next up was Labour's Chris Bryant, who, as a man who appeared on the internet in his underpants, needed to be there to see this. 'Surely you are man enough to stand up and sign up for what you voted for in the general election?' Nick patronised him (it's one of the many things Dave has taught him), calling Chris 'terrifically excitable'.

The session began to degenerate into something between a blockade and a brawl. The Labour MP John Mann, self-appointed global moral authority, demanded: 'A man tours the country telling people if they vote for him he'll abolish tuition fees. When he has the power he increases tuition fees. What's the best description of the integrity of such a man?' The Man punched right back: 'This must be the same integrity which led the Labour Party to introduce fees, having said they wouldn't in 1997, and to introduce top-up fees, having said they wouldn't in the 2001 manifesto!'

David Winnick, the veteran maverick Labour MP and one of Nick's main tormentors, asked the big question: 'If you are so confident on tuition fees,' he demanded, 'why don't you go and speak to the students who are demonstrating outside?'

Nick, who believes that the best defence is an offence, mocked Ed Miliband. 'Your own leader, I heard on the radio, said he was tempted to speak to the students and then, when asked why not, he said that he had something in his diary. He must have been staring at a blank sheet!' Brave words, though we all knew that the real reason Nick couldn't go outside was his itsy-bitsy policy mankini.

3 DECEMBER 2010

MPs try to fight creature from the black lagoon

MPs were in full cry over the new independent system of monitoring their expenses. Democracy was under threat. But then, they would say that, wouldn't they?

OH THE HORROR, the horror. The expenses debate was like one of those schlock B-movies, The Revenge of the Wronged MPs. While the rest of Britain shivered and shovelled, MPs gathered to emit a collective scream of pain about their expenses. They told terrible tales. There was a claim for a £338 shredder that had not been allowed. One MP had to send a photo of a photocopier (why not, I wondered, a photocopy?) to prove that it existed. Some have had to borrow cars from friends. Can it be more ghastly? 'I am not moaning!' cried one MP.

But they were. They were moaning for Britain, but most of all for themselves. For the past six months, they have had their expenses regulated by the Independent Parliamentary Standards Authority, which they call 'the Ipsa', as if it were the creature from the black lagoon. They hate it and yesterday they tried to do with words what Hitchcock did in his shower scene.

The charge was led by the urbane Adam Afriyie, the Tory MP for Windsor. He accused the Ipsa of being judge and jury, regulator and regulated. Its systems were so time-consuming that it was nothing less than a threat to democracy. Yes, he actually said that. Don't laugh. Almost everyone in the chamber agreed.

The Ipsa was creating a system where only the rich could be MPs. For the rich did not have to put in receipts – they already owned shredders. 'If a member does not have sufficient resources to subsidise themselves,' claimed Mr Afriyie, 'they are then ensnared in a vice-like grip designed to bring them into disrepute with every single receipt that's produced.'

Don't you like 'vice-like grip'? The Ipsa was a giant creature, its huge hairy hands gripping and squeezing the life out of MPs, intent on wrecking democracy and disallowing shredders.

Ann Clwyd, the senior Labour backbencher, spoke softly but urgently. All MPs had been smeared by the actions of a few. 'During my election campaign, someone came up to me and shouted, "Thief!"' she told a rapt House. 'If I had been a man, I would have run after him and punched him in the face.' But since she was not a thief, but an MP, she then used parliamentary privilege to name and shame an Ipsa employee, whom she accused of leaking 'juicy bits' to the press.

More revenge from the Tory Party's Roger Gale. He accused the Ipsa of living in the lap of luxury. The Ipsa rent alone was £348,000 a year. The men at the top of the Ipsa had 'inculcated' a 'climate of mistrust'. 'Let's now call a spade a spade,' said Mr Gale, though, actually, he was calling them something much dirtier.

Mr Gale knew MPs in Kent who didn't live near stations and, because of that, they couldn't claim money back (don't try to understand, you have to be an MP). MPs would not be told where to live by luxurious spades! He issued a warning of what would happen if the Ipsa did not change: 'This House, this democracy, will either be the province of the very rich or juvenile anoraks!'

The almost insufferably sanctimonious Labour MP John Mann got up. 'I am just wondering which I am!' he asked. 'I'm not rich! I've got no inherited wealth!' MPs glared at him. He was letting the side down. Mr Mann told them that if the Ipsa was independent, that meant it was, actually, independent. This brought more fulminating: MPs will not rest until the horrible alien creature is slain or, even better, shredded.

9 DECEMBER 2010

Not-yet-dead Ed hits Dave where it hurts

Ed Miliband's performances at PMQs had Labour in despair. But then he found a bread roll...

I HAVE BEEN QUITE anxious about Red Ed. Last week at PMQs he corpsed so badly that he was immediately dubbed Dead Ed. Worryingly, we haven't seen him since. But, then, Ed is not so much low-profile as no-profile. So, it was with genuine interest that I watched him arrive in the chamber, bog-brush hair newly mown, clutching his typed script.

Dave, who had just flown in from the front line in Afghanistan, was in a manic mood. Next to him, Nick Clegg, the butt of all jokes, seemed like a man in a hostage video. On Dave's other side sat a grim Vince Cable. Dave looked like Action Man.

Ed stood up, feet planted apart. He blinked his ridiculously long blink and asked if it was true that England would have the highest tuition fees in the Western world. As Dave blathered away, I could almost hear Labour's sigh of relief. Reports of Ed's death had been (slightly) exaggerated.

Dave blamed Ed and Labour for the fact that the coalition was tripling tuition fees. I quite liked the sheer temerity of that but then the PM, whose tendency towards arrogance is a weakness, chortled about how only the Tories had been honest. 'One party had the courage of its convictions to see this through!'

Ed pounced: 'You have given it away! One party!'

The coalition brothers didn't look at each other. The Tories may have the courage of their convictions, but the Lib Dems had thrown theirs out the window. Nick looked utterly miserable. Ed noted that, incredibly, the Lib Dems were split four ways on the tuition fee vote. Indeed, one Lib Dem had said that, if he ran fast, he could vote both yes and no.

'A week really is a long time in politics,' commented Ed, with a nod towards Dave: 'Not so much waving but drowning.' It wasn't perfectly delivered. It wasn't even well delivered. But Ed had made his point. Last week, Dave had dismissed him with this one line. Ed had flicked it back.

Ed introduced the subject of 'social mobility', political jargon for what you and I would call class. I knew what was coming. Red Ed isn't crimson for nothing. Dave warbled on about how his great new progressive tuition loan system will help the poor. Ed attacked: 'Only the Prime Minister could treble tuition fees and then claim that it is a better deal for students.'

Dave shouted at Ed: 'You are behaving like a student politician!'

The Labour leader blinked (not waving, but blinking). 'I WAS a student politician,' said Ed, pausing. 'But I was not hanging around with people who were throwing bread rolls and wrecking restaurants.'

Labour erupted in joy. Class war! Eton! Bullingdon Club! Nothing makes them happier. Dave should have seen it coming. Ed was now throwing the entire loaf. 'You do not understand the lives of ordinary people up and down this country!' he lectured. If PMQs was a food fight, then Ed probably won it by a bap.

IO DECEMBER 2010

Inside like a siege, outside a peasants' revolt

The vote on tuition fees came after a day of
prolonged agony for the Liberal Democrats.

THE BODY LANGUAGE of the Lib Dems said it all. The votes were being counted and the chamber was heaving, the wells crammed with MPs, jostling and craning. Simon Hughes, the deputy Lib Dem leader, was sitting on the bench, which makes a change from the fence he'd been on all day (maybe he had splinters). He'd just rejected an overture from Red Ed Miliband to vote 'No' with him. The fence may be uncomfortable, but it was his home.

Nick Clegg, hate figure or future guru, depending on your view, stood in front of the Lib Dem benches, locked in fawning conversation with one of his loyalist MPs. It was the first time I had seen Nick smile all day. He'd been there at the very beginning of the debate to hear Vince Cable give a Nutty Professor-type speech, hands shaking, argument rambling. Nick had fled afterwards, returning five hours later to vote.

Tim Farron, Lib Dem president, young, blond and ambitious, had voted 'No'. Now he meandered round, looking for a chum. Nick turned his back to him as Tim circled, until he'd done an entire shun pirouette.

The top three in the Lib Dems – Nick, Simon, Tim – had voted three different ways, and none was talking to each other. For a party that loves to bond, it had been a terrible day as they had wrestled with their consciences, which grew until they were like boa constrictors coiling round.

Labour MPs shouted when the result was announced, for they'd cut the government majority of eighty-three to twenty-one. They pointed at the sparsely populated Lib Dem benches. For a brief moment, a pensive look occupied the Prime Minister's usually mobile face. It was his coalition government's first big test, and he'd won, though it didn't feel like a celebration.

Outside, students had enlisted the statue of Winston Churchill in their struggle as they occupied Parliament Square. The cold, crisp air smelt of cordite and vibrated with sound – whistles, chants, shouts, tubas. As I came out of the vote, I could hear them chanting: 'Shame on you! Shame on you!' From the inside, it felt like a siege; from the outside, a peasants' revolt.

The best speech of the day, by far, belonged to John Denham, the shadow Business Secretary. When he was in government, John bored for Britain. But yesterday he was tough and eloquent. Where Vince had been fumbling, overcome by Labour MPs giving him the full blowtorch treatment, John was listened to with something, at times, quite close to silence.

'I was a minister once who resigned on a point of principle,' he said (the Iraq War vote), speaking directly to the Lib Dems.

> After you've done it, you realise it wasn't half as bad as you thought it would be. The self-respect you gain far outweighs any temporary loss of position, power or income. This decision matters so much to so many people, I say to the House, if you don't believe in it, vote against it.

They listened in silence. In the end, the Lib Dem ministers stayed firm, but, make no mistake, it was the hardest day for them.

21 DECEMBER 2010

There is snow crisis here, really

The snowstorm hit the country with a vengeance, throwing air, road and rail into complete chaos. The Transport Secretary was up to his knees – and still digging.

I AM GOING TO issue an extreme weather warning to Philip Hammond, the Transport Secretary, or, as he was dubbed in the House, the No-Transport Secretary. The country was snowed under, very little was moving but, in Phil's world, it was all going rather well.

The road and rail network had performed 'broadly satisfactorily', he said. There had been 'some disruption' on the trains but the roads had been OK since Saturday. I began to wonder if the No-Transport Secretary had been anywhere over the weekend. He did admit that, when it came to Heathrow, there were lessons to be learnt. It was 'a very real challenge'.

So there you have it: a very real challenge. I wonder when, in Snowman Phil's world, a challenge becomes a crisis. When hell freezes over perhaps? Phil is tackling this with a kind of elegant languor that you almost have to admire. He has, he told us, not breathlessly, been talking to colleagues from other departments 'on a daily basis' since Friday. But he had – and this is real hold-the-front-page stuff – issued a 'Snow Code' to tell people how to clear their pathways without fear of legal problems. I am not making this up, though at times even I can't believe it's true.

Maria Eagle, his small but explosive Labour shadow, laid into him. If things were going so well, why were people stuck at railway stations? Why were people in their cars for thirteen hours? She accused him of being in charge of the Department for Chaos.

Phil hated that. 'I think after a heavy dump of snow, we've had a heavy dump of political opportunism! You talk of chaos. Do you remember the chaos last year when you ran out of salt?'

Snowballs came thick and fast from the Labour back benches. After one particular vituperative outburst from John Spellar, Phil said: 'People will see you've got nothing to offer except a meaningless rant!' Phil said that Labour seemed to want him to institute 'some kind of Moscow central-control'. Tories laughed but, actually, Russia does know more than most about snow.

Tom Watson, the Billy Bunter look-a-like, started to shout. 'What we are asking for is leadership! People are sleeping on airport floors! They've been turfed off trains! They have been frozen in their cars! They are cold in their homes because they are not getting deliveries of domestic fuel. Where is the Prime Minister? He's the Invisible Cam!'

The Snowman hated that. 'I can tell you that people sleeping on airport floors are not helped by this kind of ridiculous rant. What they need is a calm, measured, considered response. That is what we are doing. This is an extreme weather event. We will do better than his government did last year.'

Actually, Snowman Phil, I think people sleeping on airport floors probably enjoyed that ridiculous rant.

20 JANUARY 2011

MPs play to gallery as Devil wears Thatcher

No one could believe it when a Hollywood legend dropped in to watch the weekly madness that is PMQs.

I WAS WONDERING WHY Ed Miliband and David Cameron seemed more nervous than usual at Prime Minister's Questions when I spotted, in the VIP seats, the pale and luminescent face of someone who looked exactly like Meryl Streep. I peered closer. The trademark tortoiseshell specs could not hide the fact that it was, actually, her – a Hollywood A-lister watching our weekly political panto.

I willed PMQs to live up to Meryl.

She is our most famous observer since Brucie of *Strictly Come Dancing* fame. Later, I learnt that Dave had 'facilitated' her visit as she is to play Mrs Thatcher in a movie called *The Iron Lady* (I had rather hoped it was to be a musical called Maggie Mia, but this is not the case).

So, how to explain yesterday's PMQs to Meryl? Well, to coin a film title, it's complicated. First, an apology for some shameful overacting in the chamber. Yes, Mr Speaker, I mean you.

For the past few weeks, PMQs has been a flippant affair. This week it was far more serious. Ed began with a short, sharp question about hospital waiting times. Dave, lamely, said: 'We want waiting times to come down.' The jeers were overwhelming and, as he struggled on, Mr Speaker pounced. After all, Meryl was here, and he wanted to shine.

'Order!' he cried, for it is his catchphrase. 'Last week, a ten-year-old constituent of mine came to observe PMQs and asked me, "Why do so many people shout their heads off?"!' He paused before shouting: 'It is rude and should not happen!' Was it my imagination or did Mr Speaker, having delivered this little cameo, glance over to Meryl?

Dave and Ed resumed tearing chunks out of each other. 'You are taking the "national" out of the National Health Service,' shouted Ed. 'Why are you so arrogant as to think you are right and all the people who say you are wrong are wrong?' At which, Dave, neatly, shouted: 'First of all, you are wrong!' There was a great deal of smoke and fire but in the chamber the Devil does not wear Prada (sorry, I had to get that in) but is, instead, in the detail, and yesterday Dave failed to explain exactly why he is reorganising the NHS.

It all ended, for this is certainly not Hollywood, badly. Ed tore into Dave for breaking promises, at which point Dave threw down his briefing notes (I'm sure he hoped that Meryl noticed the measured yet powerful way he did this). 'The same old feeble pre-scripted lines,' Dave said with a perfectly pitched chuckle. 'I am sure they sound fantastic in the bathroom mirror!' So who won? Only Meryl, I'm afraid, who didn't leave the chamber until Norman Baker began to drone on about sustainable transport. I think it was the words 'community bus' that, finally, made her flee.

22 JANUARY 2011

A reckoning of sorts as Blair voices his regret

The appearance by the former Prime Minister before the Chilcot Inquiry was a traumatic event for everyone in the room.

TONY BLAIR WAS nearing the end of his marathon session at the Iraq inquiry when, behind him, a woman dressed in black began to cry, openly and silently. Her face, etched in grief, crumpled. Mr

Blair could not see her, but I swear he must have felt her. Suddenly the entire room seemed to swoon with emotion.

'I wanted to say something,' said Mr Blair, and his voice, previously so confident, agile, powerful, began to crack. His almost preternaturally blue eyes blinked too quickly.

The audience was full of those who had lost family members in Iraq. They had waited years for an apology, dreamt of it, prayed for it, raged for it. Now it was nigh, it seemed a surprise. 'At the conclusion of the last hearing, you asked whether I had any regrets,' Mr Blair said, staring ahead at the committee, though surely his words were for the sixty people behind him. 'I took it as a question about the decision to go to war and I answered that I took responsibility.'

The woman – later I was told it was Sarah Chapman, who lost a brother in Iraq – was still crying.

If this was Hollywood, Mr Blair would have turned around and faced them. But it isn't (even his acting talents appear to have their limits) and so, instead, the audience in this strange claustrophobic basement room could only watch his back, clad in an immaculate blue suit, with red and wary eyes. The disembodied voice continued: 'That was taken that I had no regrets about the loss of life, and that was never my meaning or my intention.'

The whole place was a flotation tank of emotion. 'Of course, I regret deeply and profoundly the loss of life, whether from our own Armed Forces, those of other nations…' No one heard the end. 'Too late!' cried someone. 'Too late!' echoed another.

Mr Blair's back did not move, there was not even a wrinkle of acknowledgement.

'Quiet please!' shushed Sir John Chilcot, who hates outbursts and has worked hard to avert them for the past fifteen months. Mr Blair, gathering himself, began to expand on lessons learnt. Two women in the audience stood up and turned, until they had their backs to him. They stayed there, silent witnesses, silent protesters, for a minute, before leaving early.

The last time Mr Blair had faced the committee was a year ago – the occasion of the famous non-apology. Then he had begun nervously and ended on a rampaging high, warning the world about Iran. This time he oozed confidence and righteousness throughout. We could see the word IRAN in big letters in one of his binders and, sure enough, there was a dramatic plea on that.

But it will be the regret that we remember. Other than the 'Too late!' outburst, there had been only one intervention from the audience when, after Mr Blair praised the military for its willingness to follow orders, the room had rumbled with anger.

Now, as he walked from the room, his eyes never flicking from the side exit, a voice crackled through the air. 'Your lies killed my son,' said Rose Gentle. 'Hope you can live with it.' Then the audience left quietly, almost dazed. 'He'll never look us in the eye,' muttered Sarah Chapman.

This may indeed be the case, but the scene in that room yesterday seemed to me like some sort of reckoning. Imperfect and messy, yes. Dysfunctional, certainly. But a reckoning, nonetheless.

26 JANUARY 2011

There's no excuse like a snow excuse

The Chancellor displays a talent for making bad news even worse.

MEMO TO DAVE and Co.: the next time there is bad news, don't make it worse. As the appalling growth figures were announced yesterday, George Osborne loomed onto our screens, coatless, in front of some dead twigs in the No. 10 garden.

We haven't seen much of George lately. Indeed, I think my last sighting was that photograph of him skiing in Klosters in that lovely skull-and-crossbones-patterned snood. This time he had ditched the snood but he was just as scary.

'The weather had a huge effect,' announced George. 'It was the coldest December in 100 years. People couldn't get to work.' (Though, of course, some could get to Klosters.)

The man from the BBC noted that, if you stripped out the snow (which sounded painful), growth would still be flat. 'The weather clearly had a bad effect,' insisted George. 'Look, we've had bad weather. It's the worst December for 100 years.'

Surely, though, this was the worst case of blaming the weather in 100 years. As a commuter, I am an expert on excuses. I have heard it all: the wrong kind of snow, leaves, ice, hail. But now George had gone one further: the wrong kind of news was on the line, it must be the weather's fault. (Snow in December: who knew?) In three minutes, George blamed the weather eleven times. The other thing he kept saying was: 'We are not going to be blown off course by the bad weather.' Even though, actually, it was obvious to everyone that they just had been.

Vince Cable, allegedly in charge of growth, was due to hold a celebratory press conference yesterday morning. It was abruptly cancelled and blamed on the traffic (the worst traffic in 100 years). The press conference was rescheduled for 12.30 p.m. I got there on time, one of ten journalists in a room that could accommodate 100. Vince was fifteen minutes late (the wrong kind of news means delays all day).

My, but it was a grim affair. I have seen mortuaries that were merrier. Vince has the air of a man who is walking the plank but still looking around to see if anybody has noticed that he is. One hack noted that, in Lord Mandelson's day, these events were held to announce various cash injections. 'We are not able to throw money at problems,' noted Vince bleakly. The deficit had to be the priority. 'It has been very painful. This department has had to take a 25 per cent cut in spending. It's tough.'

Vince was alarmingly off-message on the weather: 'We had a bad quarter, lots of it weather-dependent, not all of it.' Not all of it? I do fear for Vince's future. Sometimes you don't need a weatherman, as Dylan once almost sang, to know which way the snow blows.

I FEBRUARY 2011

Bottoms up! Here's to the Lansley health revolution

The Health Secretary struggles to explain his
bottom-up, top-down NHS reorganisation.

BLOOD AND GUTS, threats and screams of pain. In so many ways the health debate was like a scene from A&E on a Saturday night. It was like *Casualty* but with much more talk about bottoms.

I thought that Andrew Lansley, the Health Secretary, the technocrat's technocrat, might blow a gasket (a technical term understood by all A&E doctors). He didn't help himself, because he never does. 'The purpose of this Bill can be expressed in one sentence…' he began. Labour MPs interrupted, shouting: 'It's a scandal.' Mr Lansley grimaced.

The thing about plotting a revolution is that it helps to be a revolutionary. Mr Lansley, phlegmatic and laborious, is anything but. He is about as inspiring as a toothbrush. He loves detail. The whole speech felt like small print. The language is all about pathways, empowerment – and bottoms.

'An NHS organised from the bottom up, not the top down,' said Mr Lansley. What does it mean? Can someone at the top order a bottom-up revolution? There is a rumour that all it means is that Mr Lansley is putting himself forward for Rear of the Year. He attacked Labour for their endless reorganisations (he is an irony-free zone).

Mr Lansley has been doing health, in opposition and now in power, for seven years and believes that no one understands it as he does. I thought he might hit a Labour MP who dared to ask about hospital closure. 'Time does not permit me to explore the extraordinary ignorance of that,' he said in a bottom-up, pain in the rear sort of way.

John Healey, for Labour, treated the policy like a piece of gum on his shoe and pleaded with the Lib Dems, looking pathologically glum, to see it for what it was: partial privatisation: 'This is not your policy but it is being done in your name.'

Behind Mr Healey sat a tremendously excitable David Miliband. What a joy to see him in the chamber. Some people's emotions show on their sleeves, Mr Miliband's are on his face. Cheeks out, lips popping, forehead scrunching. In a short, sharp, eloquent speech, he dismissed the Bill as a 'poison pill'. I do hope that the Miliband returns to the front bench soon. He is much missed.

No debate on the NHS would be complete without a loud sneer from the Beast of Bolsover. 'Why on earth should the Health Service be changed?' cried Dennis Skinner, feet apart, ancient sports jacket flapping. 'All those miners in my constituency who were wanting those knees replaced, those hips replaced, they've all been done! That's what the people in Bolsover know.'

He sat down to cheers. Mr Lansley looked disgusted. Clearly bottom-up does not include Bolsover.

2 FEBRUARY 2011

Weary Lordships suffer weird brand of democracy

Labour peers delve deep into the Hegel–Heidegger post-modernist argument as they try to derail the AV referendum Bill.

T O THE LORDS, to see Day 16 of the epic battle being waged by Labour peers to thwart the AV referendum and the Parliamentary Voting System and Constituencies Bill. I'm afraid that I must report that the filibustering had now reached a philosophical point of madness.

It was Day 16, Hour 85, amendment 110ZZA and 110ZZB, and the debate was whether the Electoral Commission should be required to tell us what we are voting for on 5 May, i.e., explain the AV voting system. The proposition was that they should do this in an 'unbiased' and 'impartial' way and in plain English.

The view of Labour's Lord Davies of Stamford, formerly known as Quentin, was that this was impossible. Lord Davies, who, as an MP switched from the Tories but is best known perhaps for having the worst comb-over in Britain, explained why both he and Hegel were sure that the Electoral Commission could never attempt this. 'The anti-positivists, the traditional Hegel–Heidegger post-modernists, would say there is no thing as objective reality anyway,' he announced. As it happens, he proclaimed, the positivists would also advise the Electoral Commission such a thing was not possible.

'It is asking human beings to do what no human being can do,' announced Lord Davies. 'I don't think any of us can produce an opinion which is genuinely unbiased. I think it is philosophically impossible and practically impossible.'

At this Lord Anderson of Swansea popped up, confusing his nineteenth-century German philosophers. Had Lord Davies just been talking about Nietzsche's view of 110ZZA?

'Hegel!' cried Lord Davies.

'Then I wonder if one might follow the Marxist dialectical and have a thesis, an anti-thesis and a synthesis,' offered Lord Anderson, immediately coming up with a problem for this. 'No one actually favours the alternative vote,' he proclaimed.

A fellow Labour peer disagreed: 'Mr Clegg!'

Lord Anderson considered this. 'In God-like isolation he may well be but I suspect that even Mr Clegg does in fact prefer other systems!' he said. 'What is clear is that the AV is a total orphan system.'

A Lib Dem got up wearily. 'Are you aware that the leader of your own party supports AV?' he asked. Lord Anderson admitted he had never spoken to Red Ed (unlike Marx, with whom he obviously has regular contact). But he still knew that, given a choice, Mr Clegg, Mr Cameron and Mr Miliband would prefer another voting system.

As this nonsense raged, Lord Strathclyde, the Tory Leader of the Lords, sat, like a mountain, impregnable. How can he stand it? I glanced over to see if the new Black Rod, Lieutenant General David Leakey, introduced only an hour earlier, his lace cuffs and jabot a wonder to behold, was in his place. He was not. Good man.

I knew that I also could not take much more. Now Lord Foulkes explained that, whatever Hegel and Marx put together on AV for the voters, it would have to be made available in Punjabi, Polish and, most importantly, Welsh. And it all needed checking. Hadn't someone once said that, when translated, the Welsh were asked: 'Do you believe in God or would you prefer a daffodil?'

Oh dear. It seems incredible that there are not only more hours of this but more days. Democracy has never been this weird.

9 FEBRUARY 2011

George wins bare-knuckle bout on points

*Ed Balls, the new shadow Chancellor, and the replacement for
Alan Johnson, gets extremely over-excited by his own debut.*

ED BALLS RUSHED into the chamber at the very last moment, late for a very important date. He looked completely thrilled to be there. This was the moment: he had dreamt about it, plotted for it, wished for it. Now it was real and he was face to face with Boy George, the Chancellor.

It's only Treasury Questions, but not to these two. For them it is gladiators. It is bare-knuckle boxing. It is a duel. Such is the animosity that, if we lived in another age, they would have been standing in a field with pistols at dawn. The press gallery was mobbed. The chamber was almost full. It was a good match: brain v. guile, economic geek v. political cad. Or, as I see them, bulldog versus scorpion.

For Ed, it was all going so well before anything actually happened. I am sure, in his mind, there was even incidental music, maybe something from *Rocky*, as he arose to ask his first question. 'It is an honour,' he boomed, 'and a great responsibility to shadow the Chancellor at this critical time.' I could almost see his heart beating faster. George sat across, sneers flickering across his face like scudding clouds.

Ed's first question was all about snow and it was so long – 172 words – I felt that I needed a husky to keep up. The gist of it was that it snowed in Britain and the economy dived, it snowed in America and its economy grew. 'Can you tell the House, is there something different about snow in Britain?'

The scorpion rattled his tail. 'You are a man with a past,' said George, letting rip about how Ed, singlehandedly, had caused global financial chaos.

Ed growled that George should spend less time on the ski slopes of Switzerland and more listening to Americans in Davos. His next 'question' was, again 172 words long, about how bad things were, especially with growth.

'You clearly had a lot of time to prepare that, but I'm not sure it all came out as expected,' George sneered. I read, via the blogs, that some thought this a reference to Ed's old stammer. But, to be honest, I just think that Ed's question was too long and complex, not nearly as good as when he practised in the mirror.

George claimed that Ed had knighted Fred 'The Shred' Goodwin and had brought fiscal disaster to this country. These were, frankly, ludicrous claims. 'We have got a plan to clear up his mess,' he trumpeted. 'You have no plan at all!' You know who George reminded me of? Gordon Brown when he was Chancellor. Dominant. Confident. Brash. Both men would hate that. But it's true.

15 FEBRUARY 2011

The Big Relaunch takes place in a very small room

Dave strips down to his shirtsleeves as he tries to get closer to the people.

I F YOU DON'T know what the Big Society is, then you are reading the right piece. Only yesterday morning, I too had no idea what the Big Society was. I was plagued by questions. Not, sadly, how do you make the world a better place, but questions such as why isn't it called the Large Society? But then I went to the Big Relaunch and discovered all the answers.

The first thing I learnt: Big Society, small room.

So small, indeed, that it was standing room only and so cosy that it bordered on nauseous. Dave was in the middle, stripped down to his white shirt (which, as all Dave-watchers know, means he is trying to get closer to the people). He roamed around a little circular bar table, wired for sound with his microphone pack on his belt.

Big Society, huge personality.

The Prime Minister's warm-up act was John Bird, the founder of the *Big Issue*. He arrived and suddenly shouted: 'Knock, knock!' He then shouted back at himself: 'Mayonnaise!' This brought stunned silence, followed by John, singing: 'Mayn-eyes have seen the glory of the coming of the Lord...!'

Oh dear. That's the thing about a crammed room – it's hard to leave. Mr Bird told a joke about a man who goes into a shop and asks where the camouflage jackets are. The shopkeeper answers: 'They're good, aren't they?' At this point, Mr Bird shouted (at himself, again): 'That's Ken Dodd!'

We were all rather grateful when the Prime Minister arrived. Dave gave us his definition of the Big Society. It's vague but it's not. It's not one thing but lots of things. It's about us having power. It's not a cover for cuts. It's not going to make him popular. Whatever it is, he's passionate about it. The one word that summed up the Big Society was 'responsibility'.

Big Society, lots of sharing.

Dave took questions. He was told that the Scouts have a 50,000 waiting list because there are too few Brown Owls because of all the criminal bureau checks. Dave agreed that was terrible and revealed that he had run a Sunday School crèche 'very badly' and 'very occasionally'. The Big Society is all about transparency. Dave's forcing councils to reveal all so we can be empowered to run our local failing pub. (Yes, I know it sounds strange. I am only the messenger.) Dave can't tell councils what to do: 'This is a democracy. It is not a dictatorship.' He sounded wistful.

One of the Big Society people there told us that there is a 'global marketplace for sharing'. She wants to 'harness the power of sharing'. After all, many people didn't even know their neighbours. 'Obviously I know mine,' chortled Dave. 'It's George Osborne!' This got a laugh, I know not why.

Someone told Dave that she was 'confused dot com' about the Big Society. I do hope that you, dear reader, are no longer confused dot com. We now know that the Big Society is: small rooms, knock-knock jokes, big ideas and harnessing the power of sharing. Well, it's a start. Remember, you read it here first.

16 FEBRUARY 2011

AV is bathed in starlight and rivals fail to twinkle

The 'No' campaign got off to an interesting start
with an anti-politician political launch.

WE HAD BEEN enticed to the No to AV launch with the promise of a 'special guest'. I immediately thought of the Prime Minister. The pro-AV camp had already scored the double coup of Colin Firth (who has played a king) and Helena Bonham Carter (ditto a queen). The 'No' campaign needed some glamour. In lieu of an actual prince, surely Dave would have to step in.

The event was held in the London Film Museum with, yes, a red carpet. My hopes raised. In the room I looked around for someone 'special' but saw a random collection of people, famous only to their own families. Then I saw that the cameras were trained on a moustache, as large and fuzzy as a giant inky caterpillar. It was Lord Winston of baby fame.

Was he the celeb? I felt let down, though, actually, that moustache could win an award for best supporting facial hair. But where were the other heavy hitters? Even Lord Prescott, who is political royalty, was absent. As the event began, I looked around the room. The BBC's John Pienaar was the most famous person there.

The idea, as became clear, was to hold an anti-politician political launch. It's a novel plan, like the Oscars without actors or the Brits without musicians. And, as the event unfolded, it became clear why no one has ever done it before.

The panel was made up of an ex-MP, Jane Kennedy, Lord Winston and A. Nother (he never told us his name). Carole Walker, of the BBC, the second-most famous person there, asked Lord Winston how he felt about being an anti-politician politician. 'I am a member of the House of Lords,' he said. 'I am not a politician.'

Argh. The whole event seemed to be submerged, as opaque as the grey and grim waters of the Thames that flowed outside the window. No one answered any questions directly. Finally one journalist exploded about the anti-politics politics: 'If it quacks it's a duck, and you quack.'

The quacking got louder. Someone noted that the Yes to AV campaign had glitz and glamour but that the 'No' campaign had, well, Lord Winston. What did he have to say to that?

'I can't really answer that. I think they are lovely people. Not that I know them,' he burbled. 'I would love to talk to Colin Firth. I don't know if I would be able to persuade him.'

Jane trilled: 'They may have the beauty but we have the brains!'

Lord Winston didn't like that. 'I think you'll find that Colin and Helena are both very intelligent people.'

At which point Jane murmured: 'I'm digging myself a hole.'

And how. Let's just all forget the whole thing ever happened.

18 FEBRUARY 2011

Tree-a-culpa as forest plan is cut down to size

The Environment Secretary feels humble as she fells her forest sell-off policy.

SO THE LADY was for turning after all. As Maggie T almost said: Yew turn if you want to. Yesterday Caroline Spelman did just that on forests. The Twittersphere is calling it a tree-a-culpa, a word that demands a definition of 'epic grovel'.

'I would first like to say that I take full responsibility for this situation,' said Ms Spelman, her voice flute-like and small. Everyone had got the 'wrong impression' about her policy on forests so she was axing it and setting up a new board (sorry but she is). She ended simply: 'I am sorry. We got this one wrong.'

She wilted onto the front bench. There, with her in her hour of need, was George Osborne. Yes, that bad. If I were Caroline, I would know it was over. When the Dark Lord – the man who gave you the chainsaw and urged you to use it – comes to show his support, the clock is ticking.

Mary Creagh, for Labour, was more than a little bit chippy. Her response included the execrable line: 'Today the air is filled with the sound of chickens coming home to roost.' Ghastly. A Tory cackled: 'Bwack bwack bwack bwack.'

Ms Spelman wittered away, as she does in her lady-who-lunches way. But then, struck by her own magnanimity, she noted: 'As regards humility, perhaps ultimately that is the difference between you and me.' The Tories cheered. Was she really bragging about her own humility?

Labour MPs sympathised with her, saying that the PM was just as much to blame for this 'humiliating climb-down'. 'Is it not deplorable', declared Sir Gerald Kaufman, 'that you have been made to stand in the corner with the dunce's cap?'

Ms Spelman, humility expert, bristled: 'It is only humiliating if you are afraid to say sorry. One of the things that we teach our children is to be honest. It is not a question of humiliation, it is my choice.'

Sir Peter Bottomley popped up to announce that he'd once said he was sorry in the House. Ms Spelman twittered back that he was a living example of how you can apologise and continue to do valuable service. 'I think it is a very good example why humility is a good quality in a politician,' she fluttered.

At which point, a voice boomed out: 'If I say so myself.'

This brought laughter, though not from Ms Spelman, who is missing a sense of humour as well as of irony.

Ms Spelman, controversially, now came out in favour of honesty. 'I can assure you that honesty is always the best policy. That is indeed what I always try to teach my children.'

I looked at her. Was that a halo I saw? We should have known that a yew-turn is just too sappy for words.

8 MARCH 2011

A Vague attempt to set up a no-flies-on-us zone

The Foreign Secretary reminds me of someone
as he explains his policy on Libya.

I KNEW THAT THE Foreign Secretary was about to arrive when I heard the deafening whirr of a helicopter over Parliament. His mission, as I discovered from top secret sources (Twitter), was to penetrate the Commons and establish a credible position on Libya. Or, as the spies would call it, 'finding a hotel'.

For this, the Foreign Secretary had taken on a new identity. 'The name's Vague, William Vague,' he whispered to himself as he rushed to take up his position to begin the task of covering himself in verbal camouflage. He wished, just for a moment, for a bit of glamour. James Bond, 007, dazzled at the craps table while he, Vague, 000, had to endure having the same kicked out of him by politicians who didn't even have numbers.

His arch-enemy, Labour's Wee Dougie Alexander, didn't look even remotely menacing. He called Vague a 'serial' bungler and then, emboldened by this rare show of boldness, Wee Dougie moved on to mockery: 'The British public are entitled to wonder whether, if some new neighbours moved into the Foreign Secretary's street, he would introduce himself by ringing the doorbell or instead choose to climb over the fence in the middle of the night.'

William Vague smiled the smile of a man who had to grin and bear it for his country. Wee Dougie was being silly. William Vague 000 would do neither. He would arrive, instead, by chopper with night-vision goggles and a map in invisible ink.

The attacks came thick and fast. Everyone was cautioning him about a no-fly zone. Vague was vague. On this day it was his job to establish a 'no-flies-on-us' zone. It was a struggle. Sir Ming Campbell, the Lib Dem who may not know that his codename was Vase, said he regretted what he was about to say. 'Isn't it clear this mission was ill-conceived, poorly planned and embarrassingly executed? What are you doing to restore the reputation of the UK?' Vague threw more camouflage into the air. The UK was leading the world in diplomacy. As for Libya, the opposition there said they would 'welcome' more contact.

Ben Bradshaw, hair standing up like a cockatoo, asked: 'If the object of this mission was to make contact with the leaders of Free Libya, why didn't they just go straight into Benghazi as scores of international journalists have?' Vague, replied, teeth gritted: 'Whenever we deploy diplomats into a dangerous situation, we provide a level of protection based on the professional and military advice.'

He was being as bland as blancmange. But some attacks were beyond ridiculous. There was even one Tory MP who accused him of sending a ship (HMS *Cumberland*) named after a pork sausage to a Muslim country. Honestly. The final insult came when a Labour MP accused him of 'overdosing' on James Bond. At this, Vague thought of what Bond would be doing at that moment, a blonde at his side, playing craps. Surely Vague's was the harder mission.

9 MARCH 2011

A happy ending to cheer Snow White

Dwarf-gate ends well, much to our surprise.

BREAKING NEWS. I COME straight from Health Questions, where, much to everyone's shock, Simon Burns, the minister in constant need of anger management, has ended his feud with the Speaker. Snow White will be pleased. She is known, unlike one of her famous seven little men, to have been Unhappy about the entire saga.

It all began, once upon a time as they say, when Mr Burns was ticked off by the Speaker for not facing forward when addressing the chamber last June. At this, Mr Burns, more firecracker than slow fuse, began to live up to his name. His face got redder and redder until, twitching with anger, jumping round the bench as if he had been hijacked by Mexican jumping beans, he began to mutter loudly, calling Mr Bercow a 'stupid, sanctimonious dwarf'.

Mr Bercow ignored the outburst.

Others did not. The Walking with Giants Foundation objected and Mr Burns apologised, but not to Mr Bercow. The Speaker, who admits to being vertically challenged, is believed to be 5 ft 6 in. But I do not think that even makes him the shortest man in the Commons. (By the way, the man with the shortest name is Tim Yeo and no one abuses him.) The feud simmered on. Mr Speaker is a man whom many Tories love to hate. They resent that he used to be right wing but became left wing, though now, of course, as Speaker he is supposed to be no wing (do keep up at the back!). Plus there is the issue of his (very tall) wife Sally, last seen featured in a newspaper, wearing a bed sheet and talking about sex. Snow White would not approve of that either.

But I digress. The plot took an unexpected twist a few months ago when the Prime Minister, of all people, repeated a joke in which a mythical minister backs into Mr Bercow's car. 'I'm not Happy,' says the Speaker to the Minister. 'Well which one are you then?' came back the reply. Cue uproarious laughter.

Yesterday, at Health Questions, Mr Burns was being his usual pugnacious self. Labour MPs, on the warpath over the unpopular NHS reforms, were needling him very badly and some of their 'questions' were completely off the subject.

'Mr Speaker!' objected Mr Burns.

Mr Bercow did not rule the question out of order and, instead, advised Mr Burns that the Labour MP wanted to meet him.

I feared an explosion. 'Mr Speaker!' exclaimed Mr Burns. 'You are a wise owl to be able to interpret what honourable members opposite are thinking but may not be saying!'

At this, an owl sound – which I can only translate as 'twoooot' – could be heard. And Mr Bercow was, unmistakably, happy. 'Wise owl is the kindest description you have ever offered of me. I'm going to take it that you mean it!' he said to much laughter. 'It's the best I'll get!' At which point, a Labour MP shouted: 'It's a hoot.' It's also a happy ending but then, don't forget, in fairy tales, as opposed to politics, everything ends happily ever after.

11 MARCH 2011

Pooh-Bah Patten suffers interference on telly habits

*MPs were amazed as Lord Patten of Barnes, a
candidate for BBC chairman, explained why he loves
programmes on tractors and wheat production.*

T O SEE LORD Patten of Barnes in action was to see a man who was, emphatically, not of the people. He was wonderfully grand, a talking Taj Mahal. When he ran Hong Kong, he was called Fat Pang, but now, surely, we must upgrade him to Grand Pooh-Bah Pang.

My only question, after he appeared for two hours before MPs, was not whether he was big enough for the BBC but whether the BBC was too small for him. Surely what he needs is not a corporation but a small but immensely erudite country to run.

He was gloriously out of touch. The Tory MP John Whittingdale began by asking what TV he watched. Well, he said, the night before he'd watched an 'extremely good' programme on BBC Four on wheat production and tractors. He'd then switched to *MasterChef*. He said this with a flourish, as if it were wildly hip and groovy. 'I went from BBC Four to BBC One with no stopping point.'

He doesn't watch breakfast television. 'I listen to the *Today* programme, as most people in this room do.'

Mr Whittingdale interrupted: 'But not most people in the country.'

By way of an answer Lord Patten said that he had watched *Strictly Come Dancing*. His voice was tinged with pride.

He loved Radio 4. He mentioned Melvyn Bragg on string theory as a particular joy. He woke up to Radio 4 and went to bed with it. 'Interesting life,' he noted (he is saved from total Pooh-Bahness by a sense of humour as dry as the Sahara).

He said he was also guilty – now raising his hands in an arrest pose – of listening to Radio 3. But what about 6 Music? Pause. 'Honest injun,' he said (something I haven't heard for decades), 'no.' I suspect he had no idea what it was.

How about Radio 1? 'Only when trying to get to Radio 3 or 4!'

When was the last time he'd watched *EastEnders*? Pause. 'Um. I should think longer ago than I last had a McDonald's.'

I think that means never. The Labour MP David Cairns noted that what little TV Lord Pooh-Bah did watch was hardly seen by anyone else (by the way, just in case you want to catch it, that wheat programme was called *Mud, Sweat and Tractors: The Story of Agriculture*).

'The fact is that I watch the sort of television programme which you would expect somebody with my background to watch. I'm sixty-six, I'm white, I'm relatively well educated,' he noted. (Fact: he is the Chancellor of the University of Oxford.) But most people are watching something else, persisted Mr Cairns.

'I'm not going to pretend that I'm suddenly going to morph into a sort of sub-Reithian enthusiast for programmes which it would be perhaps difficult to place in the Temple of Arts and Muses which is over the door of Broadcasting House,' he said.

Mr Cairns was remorseless: 'I get the sense that your idea of going down-market is to watch BBC Two!' This got a laugh.

'Last night I watched in fascination *MasterChef*, which is on BBC One!'

It was wonderful. I really think he needs his own TV programme, Master Class with Pooh-Bah. Go on, BBC, you know it makes sense.

22 MARCH 2011

PM explains why Libya is not Iraq

*The political generals explain why we should go
to war, but the poor infantry have doubts.*

D ENNIS SKINNER, THE Beast of Bolsover, his voice rasping, cut to the chase as he stood to question the Prime Minister. 'It's easy to get into a war, it's much harder to end it.' How, he wanted to know, would we all know when the Libyan war was over?

The Prime Minister grabbed the moment. 'This is different to Iraq,' he said. 'This is not going into a country, knocking over its government and then owning and being responsible for everything that happens subsequently. This is about protecting people and giving Libyans a chance to shape their own destiny.'

That this was not Iraq was the über-theme of yesterday. For the spectre of that war, sanctioned eight years ago to the week, did not hover so much as haunt this, the most important debate of the first year of the parliament. It was a riveting occasion.

The politicians did not let themselves down. This is one Hansard that I will keep. For once, the leaders, eloquent and passionate, really were all in this together. Ed nodded while Dave spoke. Dave nodded with Ed. And Nick Clegg, whose party was the only one to oppose Iraq, nodded with everyone.

Mr Miliband gave, easily, his best speech. He noted that the debate was conducted in the shadow of the history of past conflicts but also, for him, his family's past. 'Two Jewish parents whose lives were changed forever by the darkness of the Holocaust yet who found security in Britain.'

His brother David watched from the farthest back bench as Ed continued:

> In my maiden speech I said I would reflect the humanity and solidarity shown to my family more than sixty years ago. These are the kinds of things we say in maiden speeches, but if they are to be meaningful we need to follow them through in deeds, not just words. That is why I will be voting for this.

If the leaders were united, the poor bloody infantry had more doubts. 'There is nothing glorious in war, nothing romantic,' warned Kris Hopkins, a former soldier who is now a Tory MP.

Bob Ainsworth, the former Defence Secretary, spoke in a voice laden with the experience of wars gone wrong. 'I am a late and very reluctant supporter of this operation,' he said heavily. 'It is relatively easy to support things on day one and relatively difficult to support them on month three.'

Perhaps the best speech came from the Tories' Rory Stewart, the former soldier and diplomat, who noted how easy it was to become captivated by fear.

'This is very, very dangerous. It is very dangerous because we must again and again get out of that kind of language and get into a language which is humble, which accepts our limitations.'

The chamber was rapt. They are going to war, but not with their eyes wide shut.

31 MARCH 2011

The most annoying man in politics is annoying

Ed Balls is thrilled when the Prime Minister
gives him a special accolade.

WHO IS THE most annoying person in British politics? Forget the issues of Libya, tuition fees and police cuts. At PMQs, the only question that mattered was that rather annoying one. But this being Britain today, the event began with breaking wedding news.

Dave noted that Red Ed was to wed (Wed Ed?). Ed said he may ask Dave's advice on his stag do and Dave beamed back: 'When I was Leader of the Opposition, I would have done anything for a honeymoon! You probably feel the same.'

I'm afraid that, for Dave & Co., the honeymoon is over. The Prime Minister will be pleased that this is the last PMQs until after Easter. Yesterday, Ed beat him on the issues (tuition fees and police cuts) until finally Dave, clearly annoyed, fell back on his old standby, the personal attack. 'Has anyone seen a more ridiculous spectacle than you marching against the cuts that your government caused?' he chortled. 'I know Martin Luther King said he had a dream – I think it is time you woke up!'

Dave began to have a grand old time, insults flying like pigs. This was Flashman at his finest (which is also, of course, at his worst). His answers got more and more, shall we say, blithe, not to say glib. Labour was barracking, with Ed Balls on particularly irritating form. Ed sat almost across from the Prime Minister, heckling him about how he hadn't been briefed, which must have been all the more annoying for being, manifestly, true.

Suddenly the PM stopped, in mid-answer about enterprise zones in Stoke, and snapped. 'I wish that the shadow Chancellor would occasionally shut up and listen!'

'YEAAAHHHHH!' cried Tory MPs.

Ed Balls was thrilled. His mouth, always open, like a frog catching flies, snapping shut with satisfaction. Did I hear a ribbet? The PM shouted: 'Am I alone in finding the shadow Chancellor the most annoying person in modern politics?'

Ed Balls, who loves a bit of am-dram, poured a glass of water and offered it to the PM. 'No!' barked Dave, looking over at Ed Miliband: 'I have a feeling that the Leader of the Opposition will one day agree with me!' Perhaps, but not yet. So, who is the most annoying person in British politics? Ed Balls so wants it to be him but, I have to say, it's a very crowded field.

27 APRIL 2011

Sir Peter brings MPs a Punic Wars dispatch

*The Father of the House reminds us why we must
never forget Tripolitania and Cyrenaica.*

O F ALL THE armchair generals in the Commons – and there is a small battalion – the grandest armchair of all is occupied by the majestical form of Sir Peter Tapsell. At eighty-one, he is our version of Father Time or, in this case, General Time Gone By.

I swear that I could hear a faint trumpet fanfare as he arose, as round and grand as Humpty Dumpty, pre-fall, in a three-piece suit, his mahogany tan set off by a white pocket handkerchief. 'May I suggest that it may be over-optimistic to assume that the civil war in Libya will cease when Colonel Gaddafi departs the scene because, as you know, Tripolitania and Cyrenaica have been estranged dating back to the Punic Wars...' I quite liked that 'as you know'. So did William Hague, for he did, of course, know. It felt like a quiz question gone out of control (how I wished for a 'fingers on buzzers' moment so that all MPs could tell us those infamous Punic War dates).

Sir Peter paused, possibly for a reverie on his service in those wars, '...which is why Ernest Bevin in 1946 wanted to restore Mussolini's single Libya to their two historic entities.'

The chamber was rapt, eyes agog, lips twitching upward. 'Moreover,' continued Sir Peter, for that is how he talks, his words marching slowly, a lexicon on parade, as he explained to the Foreign Secretary that the only possible lesson of the Punic Wars was that partition was the way ahead.

Mr Hague inclined his head in tribute.

'I absolutely take your point about the Punic Wars and the historical division between Tripolitania and Cyrenaica,' he said, just to show off a bit. But what was right in previous centuries, or indeed millennia, was not right for now. There would be no partition.

Sir Peter rocked back, medals clanking, looking pleased to have raised the issue, oblivious to the titterers in the House who probably think that BC means Before Cameron.

His fellow armchair generals spoke in code but, basically, seemed to want to get rid of Libyan leader Muammar Gaddafi any way we can, and pronto. We should, they said, arm the rebels. Sir Malcolm Rifkind said that he welcomed the military instructors that we have sent but more was needed. 'These are not instructors,' said Mr Hague primly. 'It is a military liaison team.'

I looked over at Sir Peter. Is this what they said in the Punic Wars? No boots (or, perhaps, sandals) on the ground? Don't send instructors, only a liaison team? In the name of Tripolitania, we should be told.

28 APRIL 2011

Dave decides he is a Winner

*No one quite knows why the Prime Minister decided to unleash
his inner Michael Winner on the Labour front bench.*

D AVE, DEAR, CALM down. It's only PMQs. But, actually, if you
want to blame someone for your outburst, I've got a list for you.
There's been the distraction of the royal wedding (calm down,
dear, it's only a morning suit). You could blame Ed Miliband because you
always do. Or Ed Balls for shouting at you. Or how about Andrew Lansley,
for having to answer questions about his top-down bottom-up NHS hash-
up? Or you could blame yourself. Sorry about that last one.

It's my belief that Ed Miliband is the culprit. He planted the seed a few
minutes earlier. He'd asked Dave why 98.7 per cent of nurses disagreed with
the NHS shake-up. (Don't you feel sorry for that 1.3 per cent of a nurse who
doesn't agree?) 'Inevitably,' said the PM, sounding weary, 'when you make
changes in public services, it is a challenge taking people with you.'

Ed shook his head, mock sadness in his Labrador eyes: 'Dearie me, that
wasn't a very good answer, was it?' Dearie me? When is the last time you
heard anyone who didn't own an antimacassar say 'dearie me'? I am not sure
that anyone ever says this who is not in *Midsomer Murders*.

It is my theory – for there always is a theory in Midsomer – that this
'dearie me' was the subliminal trigger for what happened next. Dave had been
boasting that the reforms were supported by the former Labour MP How-
ard Stoate. 'He is no longer an MP because he lost the election,' noted Dave.

Angela Eagle, the feisty shadow Chief Secretary, screeched: 'He stood
down!' Dave looked at her and, for unknown reasons that would require
years of therapy to uncover, decided to channel Michael Winner and his car
insurance commercial. 'Calm down, dear,' he said to Angela. 'Calm down.
Calm down.'

Tory MPs crowed with laughter. 'Listen to the doctor!' cried Dave, which, actually, is rather creepy when you see it written down. Dave read out a Dr Stoate quote to a scene of Hogarthian mayhem.

'I said calm down! Calm down, dear,' he chortled. Yes, Dave, I think we've got it by now: the collective noun for this many dears has to be a herd of insults.

Dave began to mix up his Inner Winner with his other alter ego, Flashman. It was a dangerous derring-do (dearie-do?) territory. Dave glowered at Ed Balls, the shadow Chancellor, who was gesturing towards Angela Eagle and, confusingly, his wife, Yvette, also on the front bench. For one mad moment, a duel loomed.

Dave challenged Ed: 'I will say it to you if you like.'

Ludicrous. Ed Balls was shouting: 'Apologise!'

Flashman dismissed this. 'I am not going to apologise,' he said. 'You do need to calm down.'

But no one was calm. 'I think the Prime Minister has finished!' bellowed the Speaker. I do hope not. After all, it was only a joke.

30 APRIL 2011

Everybody back to Sam and Dave's

*It was just your normal royal wedding street party
with cupcakes by Samantha herself.*

I T FELT MORE like a theatre set than a real event but, on this day, perhaps that was normal. Downing Street, usually the coldest of streets, felt a much warmer place yesterday decked out in homemade bunting and wreathed in smiles. Clues that it wasn't your normal street party included the five-piece brass band, the personal ice-cream cart and a giant screen overlooking all.

Then there were the guests. The Prime Minister and his wife Samantha didn't arrive until 3.59 p.m., straight from Buckingham Palace, he still in morning dress, she still missing that hat. They arrived just after Babs Windsor, who is apparently the official street party czar for London.

I have to say, though, that the stars of the show were the cupcakes, made by Sam Cam, who didn't wear a hat for that either. She made them – chocolate, complete with edible icing pictures of Will and Kate and Union Jacks shaped into hearts – with two of her guests, Alina and Fynn Kiewell, ages nine and six, who had raised £2,020 for Save the Children in a swim-a-thon. This was their reward, and they were having a blast.

Dave is wonderful at these events for he has the gift of making the totally unreal seem quite normal. He sauntered among the ninety guests, all invited by charities and served by Downing Street staff, most dressed up in red, white and blue. He drank lemonade from a Union Jack cup, signed autographs and even accomplished a few high-fives.

Samantha chatted away, completely at home (but then, of course, she was).

Eventually Dave came over to the press pen (also festooned with bunting), eyes sparkling, morning suit a little tight around the middle. 'It has been an amazing day, the whole country has had something to celebrate.'

It was, he said, 'like a fairy tale'. A journalist noted that this was the new generation. Dave nodded. 'It's the day we've seen the new team.' I quite liked that: the new team. What was his lasting memory of the day? 'There is something about singing Jerusalem in Westminster Abbey with the whole orchestra behind you and you feel the roof is going to lift up and that there is no greater country and no greater place to be.' And then he was off, to find a Union Jack cupcake.

The Second Year

Hacking, Riots and Omnishambles

MAY 2011 — APRIL 2012

THE POLITICAL YEAR began with the electoral disaster (for the Lib Dems) of the AV referendum and ended with the re-election of Boris Johnson as London mayor. The economy continued to bump along the bottom of what seemed a very deep ocean. Then there was Libya and the London riots. But the big issue, and overwhelming drama of the year, was the phone-hacking scandal and the resulting Leveson Inquiry. Then, of course, came the Omnishambles Budget. We're all in this together? Really?

•   •   •

7 MAY 2011

Nick misses out on the AV count

*Everyone who was no one was there as the results came
in for the Lib Dems' Great AV Referendum.*

YOU COULD ALMOST see people thinking, as they roamed around
in a cavernous 'nerve centre' of the AV count: Whose idea was this
anyway? And, as if in answer, there stood the quintessential Lib
Dem, Simon Hughes, in his summer beige suit, mouth constantly moving,
emitting a stream of equally beige words.

Who needs Nick when you've got Simon? It says everything that, for at
least an hour, as the count began, Simon Hughes was the most interesting
man in this room at the egregiously misnamed ExCel centre, a giant tin can
in the badlands of east London.

As Simon finished one pre-record, only to be grabbed by a TV guy, I
scrambled behind him. 'Simon!' I cried. 'You are the biggest celeb in the
room.' He smiled, a man totally happy for that moment: 'As opposed to an
elephant!' Actually, there was room for an elephant or two – make it a herd
– in the room. The Great AV Vote Count didn't begin until 4 p.m. for reasons that no one could really understand. Maybe everyone wanted a siesta.
At least it gave Chris Huhne time to announce the result on TV before the
count even began. He loves the attention so much. I asked someone if Nick
was coming and they raised one eyebrow. Say no more.

A stage was set up in the corner for 'announcements'. On the opposite
side were three platforms for the TV broadcasters and their spaghetti soup of
cables. In between was a yawning expanse of carpet which, gradually, began
to fill. Every result, for hours, was No. Broxbourne, early on, was incredible
(4,988 Yes, 19,386 No). Danny Alexander was our new elephant in the room
(don't knock it, it's a step up from being a ginger rodent).

Labour's Lord Reid swept in. 'The people have spoken,' he said, terse
and scornful of a referendum hatched in a 'backroom deal'. He attacked the

insults and whingeing of the Lib Dems. I realised, as I listened to the bile, that I have missed him very much, the wire wool politician of the Labour years.

It soon became clear that the people had not just spoken, they had shouted, catcalled, boomed, screamed, cried, jumped up and down and kicked the door down. As Amy Winehouse once sang in her song 'Rehab': 'No, no, no...' Was it a rout? Not quite. Some boroughs of London, home to the Guardianista rebels, had voted Yes it seems. The dinner party circuit was at odds with the nation. Well someone has to be. I felt like sending Nick a postcard: Wish you were here...

13 MAY 2011

The year of Living the Dream is (almost) over

Dave and Nick hold their first anniversary party
in a dirt pile with inspirational signage.

WHAT A DIFFERENCE a year makes. Last May it was 'The Wedding' in the sun-dappled rose garden at No. 10. This year it was 'The Handball Event' in the giant lunar-like dirt pile that is the Olympic site in east London. It was heaven – for JCBs.

Whose idea was it to come to Diggerland for their first anniversary? As we were bussed there, an Olympic guy pointed at what looked like another pile of dirt. 'That's a sewer!' he noted.

The whole thing felt a bit like North Korea, with flags and billboards exhorting us to do good things. 'Be safe, be healthy, be considerate, be proud,' waved the flags. Outside the Handball Arena, there were six little flags that waved 'Complete' at us. Everyone had that awful logo on their lapel.

The Handball Arena – 'Complete!' – had 7,000 multi-coloured seats. It was like being in the middle of a bowl of Smarties. Apparently they do this because then it won't look so empty on TV if the seats aren't all occupied.

No one seemed to know a thing about handball: it was soccer with hands, someone said, and it was huge in Iceland. Nick and Dave were there to talk about youth unemployment. About 120 business leaders and apprentices had been bussed in (see what I mean about North Korea?). Nick and Dave arrived, various ministers in tow, a bit late, a bit rushed.

'I don't know anything about handball!' trilled Dave. 'Mind you, I'm a politician, so that won't stop me talking about it.'

Nick gazed at him through tired, bloodshot eyes. Both gave short speeches on how to tackle the scourge of unemployment and took questions from the apprentices. It was all very well-meaning but the whole event felt stage-managed and false.

Lucy Manning, from ITV, noted: 'A year ago we were in the warm and fuzzy atmosphere of the Downing Street garden.'

Nick stubbed the toe of his shoe into the floor. 'Fuzzy?' he asked, looking almost bashful. 'What does that mean? Fuzzy?' It was noted that, in the rose garden, there had been much joshing about how, when asked during the election what his favourite joke was, Dave had answered 'Nick Clegg'. But, now, he was asked, wasn't it true that Nick Clegg had become a joke? Nothing fuzzy about that question.

Dave warbled on about how he felt the same about the coalition. He and Nick had 'robust discussion, even arguments, in private'. 'And,' he said, 'we've obviously got used to each other's jokes in the last year!' Nick smiled at him and chuckled: 'They change – not!' Dave smiled at him and chuckled back.

It was a moment of warmth and, well, fuzziness. Despite it all – the AV referendum, tuition fees etc. – they still have at least a bit of the old chemistry, one year on.

18 MAY 2011

Chris Huhne tries not to get his point(s) across

It was a very British scandal: Who needs the likes of New York's Dominic Strauss-Kahn's shocker when you can wallow in the Energy Secretary's speeding points saga?

SMUG. SUPERIOR. LECTURING. Patronising. That was Chris Huhne when he came to the Commons to tell us about his fourth carbon budget triumph. As I looked at this man, infuriating in a hogging-the-centre-lane sort of way, belligerently insistent of his rightness in all things, I could see that his estranged wife Vicky Pryce may have a point.

Ah yes, points. With Mr Huhne embroiled in the Great M11 Speed Zone Scandal, Labour MPs took joy in asking pointed questions with the word 'points' in them. Indeed, they may be giving each other points for such points.

At various points (sorry), Stephen Pound, the court jester of the Labour benches, would bellow at Mr Huhne: 'How many points was that?'

Mr Huhne, face set, colourless lips in a grim line, ignored that and any other references to his wife's claim that he had asked her to accept speeding penalty points incurred on the M11 after he had flown to Stansted in March 2003.

Oh, the mundanity of it all! As I watched Labour MPs delight in all references to transport – even the word 'accelerate' brought joy – I thought how very British it all was. In New York they do scandals right, with Dominique Strauss-Kahn with his Air France first-class cabin and a $3,000 hotel suite where he had sex with a maid. Here we have the Lib Dems, a trip on Ryanair to Stansted and a 30 mph speeding zone on the M11. If this scandal were a car, it would be a Ford Fiesta.

Mr Huhne droned on. Soon Labour MPs were reduced to random shouts of 'What about Stansted?'

Finally, Geraint Davies got to the point (sorry) by asking if Mr Huhne thought lowering the speed limit would help the carbon targets. 'Or do you think the speeding limit for cars should be raised like the Transport Secretary and presumably your wife?'

Mr Huhne, deadpan, said this wasn't his responsibility. 'It is well above my pay grade.'

It was a relief for everyone when Mr Huhne left just as a Labour MP was setting out a Ten-Minute Rule Bill called Dangerous Driving (Maximum Sentence). You couldn't make it up.

15 JUNE 2011

Putting lipstick on a pig of an NHS Bill

The Health Secretary's 'pause' in his NHS reforms had ended and now, as he told the Commons, he was ready to make his-tory.

THE TONE FOR the day was set early in Andrew Lansley's statement when the Health Secretary warbled that, in the NHS: 'I want there to be "No decision about me without me."' At which point a Labour MP shouted: 'What about your job?' Cue hilarity. But Mr Lansley ignored that heckle. He may have just conducted a 'listening exercise' of epic proportions (i.e. The Great Pause) but that doesn't mean he can't be selectively deaf.

'Humiliating!' spat shadow Health Secretary John Healey at Mr Lansley. Mr Healey's voice was deadpan, his eyes in his long, thin Reggie Perrin face fixed on his foe: 'You have spent the last nine months telling anybody who criticised the government's health plans that they were wrong.' (At this, Emily Thornberry, at his side, acting as a backing singer, chirped 'Yes! Yes!') Mr Healey glared at Mr Lansley: 'Today you admitted you were wrong.' Emily chirped even more.

But, of course, Mr Lansley had done nothing of the kind, for he is, simply, whatever the situation, always right. I have always thought he looked and acted a bit like Barney Rubble of Flintstone fame and, true to form, nothing fazed him yesterday. Even the sight of Dennis Skinner (speaking of dinosaurs) was met with a level-headed stare. 'We are witnessing a new Frankenstein monster, all to pacify these tin-pot Liberals,' sneered the Beast, while the Lib Dems looked, well, potty.

Gradually, a theme emerged to the Labour abuse: pigs. Frank Dobson said the reforms had pretended to produce a 'collaborative silk purse out of a competitive pig's ear'. Kevin Brennan opined: 'You've got a bit of a tendency to be pig-headed and cloth-eared when people disagree with you.'

The porcine abuse prize of the day goes to the Labour MP who demanded to know why Dave wasn't there. 'Isn't it true the reason is, as was said across the Atlantic, you can put lipstick on a pig but at the end of the day it is still a pig. Isn't that proved with the NHS Bill?'

'Order!' shouted Mr Speaker, noting that this was of dubious taste, as if MPs cared about such things.

Mr Lansley infuriated Labour by refusing to be riled and, from his own side, there was only love. He was so caring, so wise, so entirely kind. At one point Mr Lansley, almost but not quite embarrassed, mused: 'I don't think it's about me.' Really?

24 JUNE 2011

Lions, tigers and bears! Oh my!

I watched the ultimate example of a political three ring circus as, ludicrously, the coalition whips tried to squash the mouse that roared.

WILD TIMES IN the political jungle. Whips. Chains. Cages. The government tried everything to tame its backbenchers over a motion to ban wild animals in circuses. No. 10 may be able to control lions, tigers and bears, but not Mark Pritchard.

The Tory backbencher wanted a ban. No. 10 did not. Yesterday, Mr Pritchard was the mouse – some would say rat – that roared. 'On Monday I was offered reward and incentive,' he revealed. 'If I didn't call for a ban, I was offered a job.'

But Mr Pritchard would not be bribed. 'It was ratcheted up last night where I was threatened. I had a call from the Prime Minister's office directly and was told that unless I withdraw this motion, that the Prime Minister himself said he would look upon it very dimly indeed.'

Ahhhhhh, cried the Commons, riveted by such a public career suicide. I have to say, it really was just like a movie.

'Well, I have a message for the whips and the Prime Minister of our country,' Mr Pritchard declared (where was the swelling soundtrack?).

> I may just be a little council-house lad from a very poor background, but that background gives me a backbone ['Yeah!' shouted the crowd]. It gives me a thick skin ['YEAH!' again] and I am not going to be kowtowed by the whips or even the Prime Minister on an issue I feel passionately about. We need a generation of politicians with a bit of spine, not jelly. I will not be bullied by any other whips!

The whips were flying round the chamber like bats out of hell. The hapless minister, Jim Paice, whose balding pate and horseshoe of hair is alarmingly clown-like, perused his papers with obsessive interest. Now he was the one in the cage: forced to defend a policy which said that, basically, we would not enact a ban because of a potential legal case in Vienna.

There was a bizarre speech by a Tory named Andrew Rosindell, who insisted wild animals in circuses are not wild at all. 'I am fed up with animals being used as a political football,' he cried (now that would be cruel). He said 'tenth-generation circus tigers' should not be 'wrenched' away from their home.

So, Mr Rosindell was asked, would he say that third-generation slaves in America had felt less enslaved? 'I am sorry that the debate is being dragged to such a level,' despaired Mr Rosindell.

His was a lonely voice (actually the word used by a Labour MP was 'idiotic') as MPs jostled to castigate the government.

Like all animal stories, there were some 'ahhhh' moments, such as when the Tory MP Bob Stewart told us: 'I found a bear in a cage – in no-man's land in Bosnia. He was entirely miserable. Wouldn't even be coaxed out of his cage by honey. We managed to ethnically cleanse that bear out of Bosnia!'

Wow. Bribes, threats, Europe, slavery and now bear ethnic cleansing. Mr Paice hadn't looked up from his papers once. The Commons was revolting, the animals were out of the cages. I don't think anyone was really surprised when Mr Pritchard announced that the government had decided to allow a free vote.

The Labour MP Jim Dowd said, gloomily, 'To paraphrase George Orwell, some votes are more free than others.' But, in the end, the motion was nodded through – cue Born Free music – without a vote. For once, it was the government that was whipped.

29 JUNE 2011

Aggression? It's just not Michael's bag

Thwack! Michael Gove was on feisty form as he fought Labour over the looming teachers' strike.

I THINK I KNOW who bought Margaret Thatcher's iconic killer handbag at that charity auction for £25,000. It was Education Secretary Michael Gove. Yes, I know the black Asprey doesn't accessorise well with his suit, but he was certainly wielding it with force – bash, bash, bash – in the Commons yesterday.

Mr Gove had been dragged to the House to explain what was going on with tomorrow's teachers' strikes. Labour's Andy Burnham – he of the bedroom eyes – accused Mr Gove of being 'high-handed' and wanting to return to the battles of the 1980s.

At this a Tory shouted: 'RUBBISH!'

But Mr Gove kept his voice on an even keel, each word distinct, as if clipped from a newspaper. His manner was über-über-polite and utterly passive aggressive. He critiqued Mr Burnham's speech as 'irresponsible'. Whack (also, for consistency's sake, he pursed his lips). It was 'inappropriate' – the great sin in the world of über-über-polite – to 'ratchet up the rhetoric'.

Whack. Andy took up a defensive position with his arms. Mr Gove did his own ratcheting. Andy had been 'pandering' to the unions. Mr Gove said 'of course' he was keeping the law under review. The 'of course' was ominous.

Why, asked the Labour bruiser Tom Watson, didn't Mr Gove leave the chamber and try to avert the strike? Mr Gove waved the black Asprey. 'The question for Labour MPs is what are you doing to keep our schools open?'

David Winnick, the ancient but respected warhorse, got out his own rather ancient ragtag of a handbag (was it macraméd?). Many teachers felt that the government had declared 'war' on them. 'They are sick and tired of a Cabinet made up of a good number of multimillionaires taking an attitude so hostile.'

Mr Gove's voice grew ever more clipped – we're talking bowling greens. 'I hope you will reflect on your rhetoric and recognise that it is not helpful to your own community.'

Finally the Beast: class war, classroom war, it's all the same to Dennis Skinner. 'This smug, arrogant government has revelled in the part that it's played in this dispute,' the Beast of Bolsover growled. Mr Gove said that he respected Mr Skinner's passion, then bashed him too. Baroness T will be proud.

7 JULY 2011

Ed unleashes his inner volcano

The Labour leader asked for an inquiry into the
hacking scandal and, amazingly, got one.

ED MILIBAND IS a natural geek and when I think of him I often cannot help but hear the words 'science experiment'. Thus it was yesterday when he faced his biggest test to date. For Dave it was also tricky. Indeed, the PM, having just come back from Afghanistan, must have wished that he had stayed in the relative safety of Kabul.

Everything was in Ed's favour but, with a man whose nickname is Milibanana, that means nothing. Ed often tries to construct the political equivalent of a volcano for the science fair but, being made of papier-mâché, it never erupts. This time he had almost too much material at hand: phone hacking, police corruption, Andy Coulson, the BSkyB decision. This was either going to be Vesuvius or just very, very confusing.

He began with a promising rumble, voice low, tone serious. The country was appalled. Would the PM hold a public inquiry? The Prime Minister answered directly that, yes, he would. This is almost a first and so you know how serious it was. Ed was 'encouraged' by his response. His voice, still low, oozed reason: he listed a series of suggestions for the inquiry. Dave nodded.

Could Dave hear that rumble? Maybe not. The PM began to worry out loud that he didn't want to rush an inquiry. Ed, suddenly his consigliere, advised that it was important to do something now. 'Just because we cannot do everything, it does not mean we cannot do anything,' he soothed, Mr Proverbs.

Then, voice so even that it wouldn't have moved a spirit level, Ed switched topics to BSkyB. Surely the PM should delay the decision. The PM, voice rising, did not agree. Then, suddenly, Ed roared: 'I am afraid that that answer was out of touch with millions of people up and down this country!' Magically and, frankly, amazingly, Ed's volcano was sparking into life. As Dave spluttered in return, Ed tsk-tsked: 'This is not the time for technicalities or low blows.'

It all sounded rather, well, prime ministerial. Infuriatingly for Dave, there was more to come: 'With the biggest press scandal in modern times getting worse by the day, I am afraid that you haven't shown the necessary leadership,' sighed Ed. That took chutzpah: a month ago Dead Ed couldn't have led a conga queue. Now, suddenly, he was an expert. 'If the public are to have confidence in you, you've got to do the thing that is most difficult and accept that you made a catastrophic judgement by bringing Andy Coulson...' The name was met by Labour screams. Lava spewed. Heat rose. Ed shouted: '...into the heart of the Downing Street machine!'

Dave hated this. But Ed had built the perfect volcano and, for once, there wasn't much he could do.

13 JULY 2011

The day Clouseau became Keystone

The Home Affairs Select Committee summoned the top cops to ask them about phone hacking. Their answers were alarming.

I T WAS, SIMPLY, incredible to see Britain's top cops try to explain themselves when it came to the phone-hacking debacle. These are the men who are, or were, in charge of counter-terrorism in our country, and they don't even seem to know if their own mobile phones have been hacked.

First up was Yates of the Yard, John to his friends. In 2009 he took an entire day to dismiss the idea that the 11,000 pages of evidence about hacking might hold anything new.

Yesterday he appeared defensive, withdrawn, unhelpful, superior. A tabloid hack might call him 'tight-lipped', but that does not do justice to the tension there (can you be 'tight-faced'?).

'Do you think your phone was hacked?' asked Keith Vaz, the rotund head of the Home Affairs Select Committee, who sees himself as some sort of Watergate-style interrogator (I am sure he is already thinking about who will play him in the film).

Mr Yates said that he had suspected it had been years ago, but he couldn't prove it. He didn't know about anything more recent. Mr Vaz, who adores drama and believes that life is, if not a stage, then there to be stage-managed, provided Mr Yates with a list of known hacking victims from *The Guardian*'s website.

'Is that the first time you have seen the list?' asked Mr Vaz.

Mr Yates nodded, leafing through. Gordon Brown's name was on there. So were other police officers'. 'As is my own,' said Mr Yates in an almost robotic voice.

The Labour MP Steve McCabe noted mildly: 'You just don't sound like the dogged determined sleuth that we would expect.'

The robot hardly reacted. I didn't think that it could get worse – and then the man who used to be his boss, Andy Hayman, arrived before us. Tall, cocky and way too relaxed, he took a job as a columnist with News International (*The Times*, as you ask) two months after retiring.

Was it true that, while in overall charge of the original phone-hacking inquiry in 2006, he had accepted hospitality (as in dinner) from the company? 'Yeah!' he cried, entirely happily.

Was his own phone hacked? 'I haven't a clue!' he cried. Well, his name was on the list. 'If I am, so be it!' he cried. 'I've got nothing to hide at all! The shopping list will be there! And the golf tee-off time!' It was a car crash. Mr Hayman said that, as a boy, he had wanted to be a journalist. He never thought about how it looked. But he had never done anything improper. Of course he couldn't influence anyone! No line had been crossed!

'All of this sounds rather more like Clouseau than Columbo,' noted Mr Vaz drily. Other MPs weren't so nice. Wouldn't the public just see Mr Hayman not as a top cop but as a 'dodgy geezer'? Dodgy geezer? It's perfect casting: I think he will have to play himself in the movie. Forget Clouseau. Think Keystone. If it weren't so scary, it would be funny.

20 JULY 2011

A bit small for a hate figure, but the jowly old guy was the star

There was already too much drama going on as Rupert and James Murdoch came to testify but then, suddenly, Wendi jumped up to defend her man.

I T WAS THE first time that I have seen Rupert Murdoch in the flesh, but can I just start this sketch by saying – Wendi Deng! Slap, bang, wallop! Forget Wonder Woman, this was Wonder Wendi to the rescue the moment that her man came under attack. The historic session was almost over when it happened. I say historic, though what I may mean is hypnotic. James Murdoch, motor-mouth, talking incessantly, his flat American accent seeming to render almost all words meaningless. 'I share your frustration,' he kept saying to MPs, though I doubted it as they struggled to follow even one of his sentences to its end.

Rupert, though, spoke in short, dare I say tabloid, sentences in raw-boned Australian, punctuated with pauses so long and unexpected that you felt that, like a ha-ha, you might fall into them. 'I would just like to say one sentence,' he announced at the start. 'This is the most humble day of my life.' I am told that, in the overspill room, this got a laugh. In the real room, it seemed from the heart, if a bit Hollywood.

My first thought on seeing them walk in was that Rupert was quite small to be such a big hate figure. It was a cramped room, holding only fifteen press and thirty members of the public. Now four people stood up with signs that said 'The people vs. Murdoch'. They left as silently as they had protested.

We then got on with the serious tedium. Very occasionally, like a rare butterfly, a new fact flitted into the room, surprising everyone. Some MPs – Jim Sheridan, Alan Keen, Thérèse Coffey – seemed from another planet. Others, like Tom Watson, are starring in their own movie and have little room for us.

And yet, in this room of egos, there was no doubt who was the star: the old jowly guy, sitting slightly slumped, eyes often closed. When someone noted how often prime ministers kept asking him to No. 10, he shot back, quick-draw: 'I wish they'd leave me alone!' Everyone laughed and, again, it seemed true.

Wendi sat directly behind her husband, long hair hanging down, fussing over him, rubbing his back. When Rupert spoke, he often banged his hands on the table until, at times, I felt a bongo rhythm developing. Wendi reached out to stop him. James, eyes wide behind rimless spectacles, also tried to intervene.

'My son is telling me not to gesticulate,' noted Rupert, suddenly the octogenarian being watched by the protective son.

They seemed, to be honest, to be in their own cocoon. Rupert does a good line in homespun straightforward tycoonery. 'There is no excuse for breaking the law at any time,' he announced, reminiscing about his father, a great campaigning journalist. James is more managerial, setting great store by internal processes and committees. MPs, faced with these two, in sync with each other, seemed stymied.

I was sitting in the front row, just behind the Murdochs, at the far left. At almost 5 p.m., more than two hours in, a man stumbled up from behind, plastic bag swinging. He took a white paper plate with foam on it and, as the whole thing went into slow motion, he smeared the foam on Rupert. Wendi launched herself like an Exocet as the guy said: 'You are a greedy billionaire.'

Wendi, papers in hand, hit the protester in the face. She fell to the ground but scrambled back up. It was chaos but Rupert just sat there, silent, blobs of pine-smelling foam on his nose. 'I got him!' Wendi crowed, rarin' to go.

A policeman, also with foam on his face, watched. Rupert still said nothing. Wendi used bottled water to clean the foam off. James, angry, wanted to know how the guy had got past security. 'This is a circus,' he fumed. 'Honestly, this is a circus.'

We were all being ushered out of the room. James demanded an adjournment. But it was Rupert, jacket off, defoamed, who had the last word. 'It's fine. Let's carry on,' he said, looking quite unfazed by that, or, frankly, anything else that day.

21 JULY 2011

Where's Wendi when you need her?

*Parliament was actually extended a day for Dave to rush
back from Africa to tell us all about, well, Dave.*

I THINK WE NOW know why Dave cut short his Africa trip. He felt that we weren't getting enough Dave with our daily Hackgate. So yesterday was a Dave marathon. He warbled his way through a two-and-a-half-hour Commons statement, answering 136 questions, then opened a Hackgate debate. It was impossible not to conclude, as we staggered out, that there was such a thing as too much Dave.

But not, I suspect, for Dave. It was a performance of pent-up frustration that began, and I do not welcome this innovation, with what may be the first political pre-apology. 'If it turns out I have been lied to,' he cried, with melodramatic flourish, 'that would be a moment for a profound apology. And, in that event, I can tell you I will not fall short!'

Ed Miliband seems to be suffering from Hackgate fatigue and, unusually, failed to call for anyone's resignation (any will do it seems). The PM, when it came to Andy Coulson, had been caught in a 'tragic conflict of loyalty'. Dave was scathing. 'What I would say is stop hunting feeble conspiracy theories and start rising to the level of events.' He attacked Ed for petty party-political point-scoring before embarking on what can only be called an orgy of the same.

Dave lavished praise on Dave for being so transparent and for not, like Gordon Brown's wife, holding a slumber party for News International's red-haired Rebekah Brooks ('I've never seen her in pyjamas!'). 'We now know who was, if you like, the Slumber Party,' shouted Dave, obviously enjoying himself, 'and it was the party opposite!' The smugness was overwhelming.

My favourite moment came as Dave was wallowing in self-praise about how he was the kind of man who never ran away from anything and took responsibility for every decision that he had ever made. Suddenly he stopped and looked over at his tormentor, Ed Balls, the shadow Chancellor who was heckling him for hiring Mr Coulson. 'Look! You hired Damian McBride! You hired Alastair Campbell!' Amid the shouting and the outrage, Dave leant across the dispatch box and cried: 'GOTCHA!' Oh, please. Everyone claims that Hackgate is about the victims, but yesterday it was totally tabloid. How I yearned for Wendi Deng to rise up and administer a smart slap.

9 AUGUST 2011

Calamity Clegg strikes again

London was rioting and the Deputy Prime Minister rushed to be the first on the scene. It was not clear, however, if anyone really wanted him there.

BY THE TIME that Nick Clegg got to the badlands of Tottenham yesterday, that particular bit of London wasn't burning so much as having a barbie. The only aroma that I could detect on this fresh spring-like day was that of barbecuing ribs. Overhead, a helicopter purred. On the ground, it felt a bit like a holiday.

Sorry, shouldn't have mentioned the holiday. As Nick sees it, he wasn't so much on holiday as 'working from Spain'. He was in 'constant contact' with Dave, George, Vince, Chris, William (I just hope he's got them all on Friends and Family). Now he was back, and determined to be our first 'leader' to visit the badlands (not to be confused with riot tourism).

Except that Tottenham, by that time, was more the sadlands. The High Road, where the now famous Carpetright was located, had been cordoned off for more than a day. Nick's team told me that I wasn't allowed to observe him meeting victims and community leaders on police advice. I don't know why.

By then, Nick was in what was probably the safest street in Britain, swarming with police and no one being allowed beyond the cordon.

Earlier, Nick had addressed us on television from what appeared to be a dentist's waiting room. 'We are standing shoulder to shoulder with those who condemn the violence,' he announced. I don't know about 'we', but in Tottenham he was only standing shoulder to shoulder with those allowed in the sterile zone.

My only chance to see our acting leader in the flesh was a question-and-answer with LBC radio in Southwark, south-east London. About seventy people were there, a thin crowd, which meant they were stacking the chairs before it started. Maybe people wouldn't care if Nick were still on holiday (or working from abroad, as we must now call it).

Sirens wailed nearby but the only calamity heading our way was named Clegg. If you were as accident-prone as the Deputy Prime Minister, would you try to enter a room from a balcony? And yet here was Nick, coming in from the outside, like Milk Tray man with a schoolboy haircut.

'Here's the Deputy Prime Minister,' cried the LBC host Iain Dale. But as Nick came, a gust of wind blew over his four nine-foot-high 'Meet Nick Clegg' banners.

Nick laughed: 'It's radio, isn't it?'

He told us about his visit to Tottenham but the audience was more upset about the bankers. Why weren't the banks lending to small businesses? Why wasn't Nick making them do it? Nick just kept saying it was all going to be better.

'You say that we are all in this together,' noted one man. 'Prove it.'

Nick launched into another soliloquy that was cut short by a terrible racket.

'Speaking to businesses...' began Nick, though I couldn't hear the rest for the noise.

'What is that?' asked Nick.

'Ducks,' noted Iain Dale.

'In here?' asked Nick.

No, out there, where all the bad things are.

6 SEPTEMBER 2011

Tinker, tailor, soldier, spies – and Dave

David Cameron came over all le Carré as he told us about the
fall of Tripoli and a secret inquiry about you know what.

AVID CAMERON ARRIVED in the chamber on two separate missions. The first was to take the credit for the fall of Tripoli while not taking credit for it. The second was to say almost nothing on the subject of spies and the inquiry into how much they knew about torture and rendition. He had studied le Carré. Now he must deliver. Tinker, tailor, soldier, shhhh. That was his motto.

It helped, of course, that when it comes to Libya, his enemy was his friend. Thus Labour MP after Labour MP arose to praise Dave. 'Can I commend your leadership?' they asked. Dave bobbed his head ever so slightly, for to do more would look wrong.

The Tory praise was more effusive and Dave knew he had to take action. When Nicholas Soames, whose breadth and depth bring the words 'aircraft carrier' to mind, noted how magnificent it all had been, Dave said that the Libyans deserved all the credit. In terms of his role, he said the word that came to mind was 'humility'. (Historians, take note.) He then told us that he was a 'practical liberal conservative' and that this had been a 'practical liberal conservative intervention'. 'It's a way of thinking!' he chirped.

The spy thing was trickier. Dave hardly mentioned it in his statement. Indeed, he'd wanted to write that bit of the speech in invisible ink, just to show he knew how to do it, but his advisers told him that no one would know and so what was the point? Instead, Dave settled for praising the spies for their 'vital work'. 'And because they cannot speak for themselves,' he said, 'let me put on record once again our enormous gratitude for all they do to keep our country safe.'

Everyone nodded. No one knew what he was on about but it was impossible not to agree. Dave said there would be no 'rush to judgement'. Everything must be looked at 'in context'. I think this is practical liberal conservative code for 'I never want to hear about this again'. Everyone nodded sagely at this too. Sir Ming Campbell, the Lib Dem who has made nodding sagely into a virtual art form, praised Dave for being 'circumspect'. Dave looked back at him circumspectly, for the Lib Dems were an unreliable lot.

Sure enough, now Sir Ming noted: 'When dealing with unsavoury regimes in the shadowy world of intelligence, it is necessary to maintain both fastidiousness and distance so as to avoid accusations of impropriety or illegality.'

Dave said that Ming was entirely right which, in the world of spies and politics, could mean absolutely anything. Dave went into default gush mode: 'It is important to put on record our thanks to the security services and what they do.' But what do they do? Jeremy Corbyn, career peacenik, asked if the inquiry would be in public.

Dave looked pained at the very idea. 'Some of it will be held in public,' he said, 'some of it, by necessity, will be held in private.' To this, everybody nodded. To which I can only add: shhhhh.

Addendum: No one was surprised when the inquiry was later scrapped.

9 SEPTEMBER 2011

Cruella cloaks an absolutely icy chill over her antagonists

Theresa May, Ice Queen, was the unexpected success of this government. Here, in an appearance before the Home Affairs Select Committee, she shows what's she's made of (brrrrr).

I SHIVERED AS I watched Theresa May at the Home Affairs Select Committee yesterday. The Home Secretary's change from human to Ice Queen continues apace. She is already down to the perfect temperature for Chardonnay. Her goal, as I understand it, is to reach frozen pea levels soon.

Keith Vaz, the headline-hungry committee chair, noted that she had delayed her plans to elect police commissioners. Why the U-turn? It will cost an extra £25 million, which was worth 2,000 police officers.

Cruella, as I cannot help thinking of her, flicked an icy stare. To sum up her answer: 'Blah.' Or, to use her favourite word: 'Absolutely blah.' (Everything is 'absolutely clear' and 'absolutely right' though not, obviously, absolutely fabulous.)

'Isn't this a decision that has been taken because Nick Clegg and the Lib Dems have decided to put party issues above the high principles that you and the Prime Minister feel are important in terms of democratic accountability?' asked Mr Vaz oilily, who is not called Vas-oline for nothing. Cruella emitted more (absolutely) frozen words.

'So Mr Clegg had nothing to do with this?' asked The Vaz. Her red lips, the only colour in her outfit that had not been inspired by an X-ray, pressed together. Clearly Mr Clegg had everything to do with it.

She poured herself a glass of water which, amazingly, did not freeze on contact. 'I can assure you that this money is not coming out of the policing settlement,' she said.

From where, then? Cruella would say only that she was in 'discussions' with the Treasury. For once, I felt sorry for the Treasury: it can't be easy negotiating with her. Bring a hot water bottle is all I can say.

Indeed, I'm not sure she does negotiate. Over the next hour and a half she slapped down the Prime Minister over whether an American could ever run the Metropolitan Police and Boris Johnson as to who decides such things.

The Vaz asked if Boris had a veto. The word was too inflammatory, too interesting, too accurate, for Cruella. 'We are not going to be thinking in those sorts of terms,' she said.

Then there were the riots. What had caused them? More lip pursing. It was too early to say. Ken Clarke, the Justice Secretary, had blamed the riots on a 'feral underclass'. Cruella was not having it. 'It's not helpful for politicians to suddenly speculate over what happened,' she noted.

Brrrr. Cryogenicists will want to study her soon. Absolutely.

28 SEPTEMBER 2011

Ed says he's not Tony ... but who is he?

*Labour met in Liverpool for their convention and their
leader explained what moral capitalism was.*

THE BEST BIT of Ed Miliband's end-of-conference speech was when it was over. Justine joined him on stage, eyes wide. The pair looked like two baby birds (he a magpie, she a wren) who had just flown the nest. The crowd was on its feet, clapping like mad, as Florence and the Machine pumped out 'You've Got the Love'. They had the love! Ed and Justine pecked (as lovebirds do). Then they embarked on a journey, as they like to say in politics, wending their way through the crowd. But instead of exiting at the side through the curtain, they climbed the stairs at the back which looked positively Machu Picchu-ish. At the top, someone had opened the double doors and we could see that, outside this dark, subterranean, nether-worldly conference hall there was indeed a place of light and air.

Ed and Justine turned to wave, light flooding round them, infusing them, turning them into strange-looking beings. It looked quite religious, a modern William Blake painting: Ed and Justine Ascend to Heaven. Then they turned and, poof, were gone.

It was the perfect ending for a speech that was more of a sermon anyway, with its moral capitalism in which the good are rewarded because they want something for something and the bad are not because they want something for nothing.

How to tell good from bad? What about those of us who will settle for anything at all? These are all questions we will have to ask Ed when he gets back from heaven.

He looked impossibly young, with his sticky-up hair, his long blink, his unlined face. 'I'm not Tony Blair,' he said to cheers. How strange is that? Somehow I can't quite imagine TB ever having to define himself by saying, 'I'm not Ed Miliband.'

Ed told us that we were in the middle of a 'quiet crisis'. He says that in the twenty-first century we all have to make a choice. 'Are you on the side of the wealth creators or the asset strippers?' he demanded. 'The producers or the predators?'

I immediately felt drawn towards the predators: raptors, lions, wolves. After all, what did producers do other than make films (or, possibly, lay eggs)? But now Ed jumped in: 'Producers train, invest, invent, sell.' Aha. 'Predators are just interested in the fast buck.' So producers good, predators bad. I had not realised that, in addition to reinventing capitalism, Ed was reordering the natural world.

What would Darwin say? But, then, of course, Ed is not Darwin.

4 OCTOBER 2011

By George, he has the answer: it's graphene

I can date the beginning of the Northern Powerhouse from the Chancellor's speech at the Tory Party conference in Manchester.

G EORGE OSBORNE FAMOUSLY says that he has no Plan B. Yesterday we found out why. What he's got is a Plan G. Yes, that's right, G. It doesn't stand for George or growth (don't be silly) but something much more exciting: graphene.

What is it? At first, we only knew it rhymed with Noreen. His speech had been preceded by an adoring presentation by his Treasury team ('Glory to George!' they cried). The Chancellor arrived looking sombre. If we had mood music, it would have been a dirge. It began as a speech about pain, a blueprint for his signature economic policy of sadomonetarism. He told us that we were anxious, worried, losing our jobs, our careers, our hopes. There was a crisis in Europe, our banks, our deficit. Then, hilariously, he chirped: 'But we should be careful not to talk ourselves into something worse.' It was like a horseman of the apocalypse wheeling round in mid-gallop to trill: 'Let's have some fun…'

Every once in a while, with Tourettian bouts of optimism, he would cry: 'Together, we will ride out this storm!' He made fun of Ed Balls, the man he loves to hate. 'Economic adviser to Gordon Brown,' he scoffed. 'I'm not sure I'd put that on my CV if I were Ed Balls. It's like "personal trainer" to Eric Pickles!' Everyone laughed: George loves a fat joke, cruel to be unkind, that's our horseman of the Apocalypse, riding out the storm.

He told us a series of rather smallish things he's trying out, like lowering carbon targets and making it easier to sack people. He's going to do something called 'credit easing' – no one had any idea what it was (printing money, actually) but everyone clapped anyway.

So where was the big idea? Now, suddenly, George told us we were in Manchester. 'The city where the first computer was built, where Rutherford split the atom.' The crowd was looking at each other. Was this University Challenge? George said that only this morning he'd met two 'brilliant' scientists who'd won the Nobel Prize for Physics. 'Their prize was for the discovery of a substance called graphene.' The word 'graphene' was met by silence, the crowd too baffled even to applaud.

To me, and I suspect many, graphene sounded only like the first name of a country singer. George explained that it was the strongest, thinnest, best-conducting material known. More blank stares. Actually, with the help of Wikipedia, I can report that it is an allotrope of carbon, whose structure is one-atom-thick planar sheets of sp2-bonded carbon atoms. So, really, almost exactly like a country singer.

George says that graphene is going to be used in everything from aircraft wings to microchips. It's the Coca-Cola of allotropes. We are inventing a national research programme to take graphene 'from the British laboratory to the British factory floor'. Do you remember Gordon Brown's 'British jobs for British workers'? Well this was British jobs for British allotropes. 'We are going to get Britain making things again!' he cried.

So there you have it. Plan G. Allotropes riding to our rescue, conquering the horsemen, saving us from the storm. The crowd clapped, they knew not why.

20 OCTOBER 2011

Mr Reynard says he's (a bit) sorry in Hollywood style

Things can change in an instant in politics and here they did so for Liam Fox, who resigned as Defence Secretary amid a welter of confusion over the role of his special adviser. So was he sorry? You decide.

D R LIAM FOX'S personal statement was a cinematic event. Forget the idea of an apology. This was a Hollywood moment. It was not so much mea culpa as me-me-me-aculpa. I had to admire it for the sheer chutzpah or, as this is a fox, chutzpaw.

Fox: The Movie kept us waiting.

The build-up felt like forever. The rumours that he was about to appear in the Commons had been circulating for more than twenty-four hours. Yesterday began with PMQs where the most important person was yet again absent. Still, that didn't mean that he wasn't the star. PMQs came and went and then there was a statement. The only sign of a fox in the chamber was the faux fur gilet worn by the Welsh Secretary, Cheryl Gillan. But Fox fans kept streaming in and so I assumed he would be arriving soon. Sure enough, at 1.48 p.m., Mr Reynard swaggered in to loud cheers and headed up to where a gaggle of friends had gathered to form the support doughnut that surrounds all apologising politicians.

He arose to more plaudits. It's a funny Foxhunt that ends with the quarry as hero. Still, he began brilliantly: 'Two weeks ago I visited Misrata in Libya. I met a man who showed me photographs of his dead children. A few days later I resigned from the Cabinet. One was an unbearable tragedy. The other was a deep personal disappointment. I begin with that necessary sense of proportion.'

That was his finest moment. His wife, Jesme, tremulous, watched from the gallery. The rest of the speech can be summed up thus: he's a bit sorry but not very. He's done nothing seriously wrong and many things seriously right. To a swelling soundtrack, he told us he had no bitterness and then proved it by castigating the sensationalist press who had hounded his relatives. 'I believe there was, from some quarters, a personal vindictiveness – even hatred – that should worry all of us.' He switched into Kate Winslet mode, gushing like a broken tap, thanking everyone he had ever met. He praised Jesme (more cheers). It had been hard for her to see him being attacked 'in a very aggressive way'.

When it ended, Tory MPs filed up to clap him on the shoulder and kiss his ring. Desmond Swayne, Dave's parliamentary private secretary, gave him a whacking great bear hug. So that's how it ended: bear hugs fox. As I said, Hollywood.

21 OCTOBER 2011

To the barricades in their pinstripes

There was the smell of cordite in the chamber as the Eurosceptics revelled in securing a debate on whether to hold a Euro referendum.

THERE IS REVOLUTION in the air at Westminster. Think Paris 1789. Berlin 1989. Tripoli 2011. You think I exaggerate but, for Tory Eurosceptics, this is right up there. The people have spoken, they have done the British equivalent of storming the Bastille (i.e. they have signed an e-petition). The result is that there is to be a debate on whether we should hold a Euro referendum.

Forget the Arab Spring. This is the Tory Autumn. 'YEAH!' the besuited revolutionaries shouted yesterday from their 'awkward squad' bench in the Commons when the debate was officially scheduled by Sir George Young, Leader of the House, bicycling baronet and thus the personification of the ancien régime.

It seems a very British revolution.

As I write – and, as with all revolts, things can change in a tweet – the vote on Monday is certain to be lost. Because, although the people have spoken, the MPs have been gagged. They must vote not as the people would have them but as the government demands.

The air yesterday was rippling with rumours of revolt and resignations. 'The government is split from top to bottom!' crowed Angela Eagle for Labour to yet more cheers (and not all of them from her side). Why, asked Angela, had the debate been moved forward from last Thursday to Monday? The rumour was that the government was frit. Sir George insisted that the debate had been moved so that the Foreign Secretary could fit it into his diary: he would 'enhance' the event.

One by one, the rebels stood up, rattling their sabres. These are men with proper revolutionary names like Nuttall and Reckless. And Pritchard, as in Mark. He took on his government – and won – over wild animals in circuses. Now he aims to do for the people what he did for lions and tigers. He decried that all MPs were being whipped to vote 'No'. 'Is it any surprise that the British public are increasingly frustrated that this place is more out of touch than ever on the European question?' he asked.

Sir George's face was like a mask. 'Whipping matters, happily, lie in the capable hands of the Patronage Secretary,' he announced, referring to the Chief Whip. So stay tuned. Whipping matters. Reckless ways. It's democracy, but not as we thought we knew it.

Addendum: The debate was as predicted. The best speech, by a mile, was also the shortest, delivered by Charles Walker, a maverick Tory who is working at becoming an eccentric (and succeeding). 'If not now, when?' he asked and then sat down. It was hard to know who the Euro rebels hated most: the EU, Sarko, the Lib Dems or the whips. Andrew Bridgen, a Tory MP, noted how he'd received a huge number of e-mails in favour of a referendum. 'I've had only one phone call against – from the Whips' Office!' The government won the battle. The war was another thing.

11 NOVEMBER 2011

Big Tom, glamour and the Mob

Labour's Tom Watson can't stop himself from turning the final hearing with James Murdoch into a scene from The Godfather.

THERE HAS BEEN much speculation about who is going to star in the inevitable film about Hackgate. I had always thought Tom Watson, chief interrogator, could be played by Philip Seymour Hoffman. But after yesterday I realise that was naïve. It is obvious that Mr Watson will cut out the middle man. He will just play himself.

At yesterday's second hearing – or sequel, as we Hollywood types would say – James Murdoch was in the hot seat. But the big man in the room, in every way, was Tom 'Tommy' Watson, aged forty-four, the former Brownite bruiser MP now reborn as Hackgate investigator. Just yesterday morning he tweeted: 'Late, late night playing Portal 2. Early, early morning drafting questions and listening to the Clash on full blast. #brandnewcadillac'. Wow. The Clash, Portal 2 and Hackgate. What a combination.

'You are familiar with the word Mafia?' Big Tom demanded, hair slicked back, chin dimple emoting.

Mr Murdoch's thumbs tapped together. 'Yes, Mr Watson.'

'Have you ever heard the term omertà, the Mafia term they use for the code of silence?'

Mr Murdoch poured a glass of water. 'I'm not an aficionado of such things.'

Maybe it was the word 'aficionado', but Mr Watson now went seriously Tony Soprano until, finally, he demanded: 'Mr Murdoch, you must be the first Mafia boss in history who didn't know you were running a criminal enterprise.'

It was an offer that Mr M could refuse. 'I think that is inappropriate.' (I do like that word 'inappropriate', the ultimate British word of revulsion, and it seemed even more so spoken in his flat pan-American accent.)

Other MPs were taken aback by the speed at which Hackgate had become *The Godfather*. The mild-mannered Tory Damian Collins tried to retrieve it by announcing: 'You weren't a Mafia boss but it wasn't exactly *Management Today*.'

Finally, there was Louise Mensch. If Tommy Watson provides the guns, she has the glamour. Yesterday, she had on her new face-lifted face and a Metallica Arènes de Nîmes lanyard from a gig two years ago. This may have been a subtle way of telling us that her husband manages Metallica. I suspect that she thinks that is even cooler than the Clash.

'I apologise in advance,' she announced, saying she would have to leave after her questions. 'We have children the same age, I think, and I have to go back home and pick them up from school.'

To which Mr Murdoch replied: 'Good luck.'

What a film! Awesome, as the Clash would never say.

22 NOVEMBER 2011

The Dowlers keep it real and then Hue Frant arrived

Everyone always says that Hackgate is about the victims and so, finally, we heard from the Dowler family at the Leveson Inquiry before everything went all seriously celeb on us.

'SHE'S ALIVE!' SALLY Dowler cried, both hands flying up with her voice, telling us how she felt when she rang her missing daughter Milly and found some messages had been deleted. For a second, just that one, Mrs Dowler, so neat and composed, showed us the thrill of hope of that heart-stopping moment.

It was the most dramatic, and cruellest, moment in a long and strange day at the Leveson Inquiry. They were watched by others in the 'core victim' section: Max Mosley, Hugh Grant, a man who was Jude Law's lawyer, a writer who had dated an MP. And, then, there were the Dowlers, extraordinarily ordinary, polite, contained, modest. Without them, the inquiry would not work.

They testified first, sitting forward at the witness desk, shoulders slightly hunching forward, tense, hands in their laps. Bob Dowler is tall and large, his voice deep and level. Mrs Dowler small, her eyes deep and vivid. They take British understatement to a new level. Sally had been 'really cross' when a private re-enactment walk was photographed. When they found out about the hacking, she hadn't been able to sleep for three days as she thought back on those unexplained moments when she had thought 'something untoward is going on'.

Something untoward. That's one way of putting it. They were asked about their meeting with Rupert Murdoch. 'He was very sincere,' she said quietly. They talked about their struggle to be fair to all when in the eye of the media storm. 'We tried the best we could,' said Mr Dowler.

At the end, Robert Jay QC, counsel to the inquiry, asked if they had any recommendations on how to curb the press. 'I think we will leave that to you,' they said, smiling at Lord Justice Leveson, compact and balding, steely but also verging on the avuncular. 'How very generous of you,' he smiled back.

Then they were gone and it was all downhill. Joan Smith, novelist and journalist, immediately took us into the heady world where politicians and journalists dine with former presidents in places like Venice. Graham Shear is a solicitor to many slebs, including footballers, a word he adored repeating, almost petting it, as if he still could not quite believe it. He talked endlessly, not in paragraphs but pages, about lawyers and their fees, watched raptly by dozens of lawyers, all getting fees.

The finale was a two-hour bravura performance by Hugh Grant (or, as the giant screen that carried the simultaneous transcript called him, 'hue frant'). Mr Grant has cast himself in a new role – press campaigner, fighter for truth in a movie tentatively called Hacked Off, Actually. But it's all hampered by the fact that he has stardust on his shoulders and a face that won't sit still.

Everything seemed larger than life. Every time he does anything, the press are there. Every time he goes to hospital, the details are leaked. Plus, don't get him started on the girlfriends (the transcriber referred to 'Elizabeth Hurrilly').

My favourite moment came when Hugh revealed he doesn't have publicists as much as 'anti-publicists'. One helped to put out a statement on his new baby (keep up at the back!) while he was filming in Germany. 'It was not ideal,' he noted drily. 'I was dressed as a cannibal at the time.' As you do. If it seems a world apart from the Dowlers, that would be because it is.

25 NOVEMBER 2011

Harry Potter and the great S&M party

J. K. Rowling, Sienna Miller and Max Mosley: it's just another day at the Leveson Inquiry.

'I CAN'T PRETEND I have a magical answer,' Joanne Rowling said to the Leveson Inquiry. 'No *Harry Potter* joke intended. That slipped out.' The entire room smiled back at this intense Hermione-like figure, blinking in her round Harry Potter specs.

Joanne had held us in her thrall, a famous woman who has fought infamously hard to guard her privacy, now telling her secrets, what has hurt her, upset her, made her furious. At one point she was talking about being accused of wearing a fur coat (she was not), and I saw on the large screen that carries the simultaneous transcription it had become a 'fury' coat. I thought that was quite Harry Potteresque.

The day belonged to two pale beauties – Sienna Miller and J. K. They seemed so fragile as they told us of their celebrity prison, the paparazzi stalking, how for them fame has become a prison of paranoia (which appeared on the transcript as 'partner annoyia')

And, then, sandwiched in the middle, was Max Mosley. Oh dear. At seventy-one, he is devoting much of his life – and fortune – to privacy and the press. He has fought to clear his name after the 2008 *News of the World* headline: 'F1 boss has sick Nazi orgy with five hookers'. He admits the S&M but denied the Nazi slur and won in court. 'You have to be quite eccentric or very determined before you bring a privacy action,' he said yesterday. How about both? It was impossible not to have sympathy. Mr Mosley lost a son to drugs, a son unable to deal with the ramifications of the *NoW* story. He says of the press: 'They had no human feeling at all.'

But, like a bad imp, Mr Mosley could not stop slinging a little dirt. He had a go at Paul Dacre, the editor of the *Daily Mail*, who had accused him of being guilty of 'unimaginable depravity'.

'Well, first of all, it reflects badly on his imagination,' noted Mr Mosley. The *Mail* website was preoccupied with 'schoolboy smut'. What did this say about Mr Dacre? 'He may have some sort of strange sex life but it's not up to me to get into his bedroom,' said Max. 'It's his business. And equally if somebody has a slightly unusual sex life, exactly the same thing applies.' (I like the 'slightly' there.)

Mr Mosley said that the women in 'my little party, as I like to call it' were 'totally enthusiastic' and went on: 'They love what they do! The very idea they were exploited is offensive!' He compared Mr Dacre to a hyena. Mr Mosley was on a roll. It wasn't really Harry Potter's world.

20 DECEMBER 2011

George struggles with the Jesus question

*The Chancellor turns a question about Jesus into a film called
Whoops Apocalypse. If you ever want to imagine what a
sneer in action does at Christmas, this is your answer.*

THE CHANCELLOR WAS confronted over his Vickers bank reforms yesterday with a question I suspect he had never even thought of asking himself: what would Jesus do? 'Are you spending too long talking to the money changers?' asked Labour's Malcolm Wicks in a blatant bid to play the Wise Man in the Commons 'Winterval' play.

George Osborne looked irritated. He'd just spent one and a half hours on the phone to Europe! And now he was supposed to ring Jesus too? Labour was SO demanding.

Was that frankincense I saw in Mr Wicks's hands? It certainly wasn't gold, for Gordon Brown had sold it all. 'Would you feel that when Jesus overthrew the money tables, he should have waited six years before acting?' demanded Mr Wicks, a reference to the bank reforms being in an inbox marked 'Long Grass' (snakes also being big in the Bible).

Mr O tried not to sneer but you cannot turn a Scrooge into a saint or even a Santa just like that. 'I wouldn't say that what we are undertaking is of biblical proportions here,' he insisted, though, only moments before he was claiming that these were the biggest banking reforms in our 'modern history'.

Ed Balls, who owns his very own Santa costume, said that he had already apologised for not regulating the banks enough when Labour was in power. Shouldn't the Chancellor, who had wanted less regulation, also show a little humility? Scrooge twitched his lips into what was, even for him, a superlative sneer. I wasn't at all surprised when that turned into a rant aimed at Santa (i.e. EB).

'For you to complain that we aren't doing enough is frankly ridiculous,' he said. 'You are the man who advised that Fred Goodwin should get a knighthood. That is your record!' George's long thin fingers – even his digits are Scrooge-like – pointed at Ed. 'Frankly, your mealy-mouthed apology reminds me of that film Whoops Apocalypse!' he said, mimicking: 'I'm sorry I brought down the entire British economy, can we all please move on now.' He looked at Ed again: 'That is what you have done.'

So there! But who was this? Was it the Ghost of Christmases Long Past? Arise Dennis Skinner, who noted that, if the banks are split up, wouldn't that just mean even more bankers? 'The chances are that the most reviled group of people in the land are going to multiply!' MPs liked that modern slant on the Miracle of the Loaves and Fishes. It's going to be a great Winterval.

11 JANUARY 2012

So, Ed, are you waving or drowning?

New Year, yet another New Ed but the relaunch does not go quite to plan.

I HAD A SINKING feeling at Ed Miliband's relaunch, not least because, behind him, floating in the grey waters of the Thames, was a relic of a ship. HMS *President*, an Anchusa Class corvette of the Royal Navy, was built in 1918. Now she is an 'event space' for parties. That ship has seen her share of relaunches, but possibly nothing quite like Ed's.

They say that Ed had a Zen-like calm about him. He's going to need it. You know things are not going your way when even *The Guardian* crossword has it in for you. The clue for eight down yesterday was: 'Miliband upset in cut vacillation.' The answer was 'indecision'.

Oh cruel cryptic world!

The next indignity came when Ed Indecision was interviewed by John Humphrys on the *Today* programme. This can best be summed up by three initials: SOS. Highlights, or, more accurately, lowlights, including John hinting that Ed was too ugly to win and a born loser (I paraphrase), and Ed countering that he had deep inner belief in his ability to lead the nation.

We were in a 'man the lifeboats' situation and it wasn't even breakfast. The media had been told to arrive at 10.45 a.m. for an 11 a.m. speech. The theme was The New Reality. The Tories insisted that this was Ed's sixth relaunch, but Labour was equally adamant that it wasn't a relaunch at all. Instead, it was a landmark, a new direction, the most important Ed speech since his last most important Ed speech. In other words, a relaunch.

Labour had invited some 'real people'– essential these days for all relaunches – from London Citizens, the community organisers. Elevenses came and went: we all watched the empty podium and, behind it, the party ship, looking as grim and grey as a hangover.

As we waited, we saw that the BBC was flashing up the trailer 'David Miliband speech' as it showed the empty podium. Oh dear. Where was Ed?

I half expected to see him floating by in a rubber ring, a man overboard. Ed ended up being thirty-five minutes late to his own relaunch.

He said The New Reality was that there was no money, which hardly seemed all that new to me. Ed has some new Blair-like gestures involving flapping arms. He remains, at heart, a geeky lecturer, crying out for a whiteboard and a special pen. He is taking on even more crony capitalists than before and accused the PM of stealing his theme. Dave, he said, has accepted this as the 'new battleground'. Ed had a message for him: 'Bring it on!' He flung his arms out like wayward oars. Waving or drowning? You decide.

12 JANUARY 2012

The Scottish referendum brings panda-monium

*The Commons became a zoo as confusion reigned as both the
UK and Scottish governments made announcements about
how to go about holding an independence referendum.*

A S LUCK WOULD have it, Scottish Questions preceded PMQs and so we had a double dose of tartan taunts. The Prime Minister arrived just in time to hear the Scots Nat Pete Wishart, formerly of Runrig and so the closest thing that the Commons has to a rock star.

'There will be an independence referendum in 2014...' shouted Pete.

'YEAH!' cried his fellow SNP rowdy Angus MacNeil.

Pete played on. 'I see that the Prime Minister has walked in!' he cried, voice rising over the war drums as he invited the PM to come to Scotland as soon and as often as possible.

'YEAH!' cried Angus, emitting what can only be called a Dr Evil laugh: 'HA HA HA HA!' Pete added the punchline: 'The PM is the best recruiting sergeant for a "yes" to independence vote that we have!' Pandemonium. My, but the Scots Nats are on a high. All politics is tribal but Scottish Questions was like a football match. In contrast, PMQs seemed positively sedate, an English tea party with Dave and Ed, pinkies extended, nibbling cucumber sandwiches with the crusts cut off, sipping their Earl Grey with a slice of lemon, while agreeing that the English know best when it came to this Scottish vote thing.

'Too many in the SNP have been happy to talk about the process but do not want to talk about the substance,' nibbled Dave. Ed said bravely: 'May I agree with you?'

Dave, rosy English cheeks glowing, said that he feared that the SNP didn't want a referendum but a 'neverendum'. Ed, even more bravely, agreed: 'This is not a fight about process.'

So there you have it, take a memorandum on the neverendum: the English say it's not about process. It took, oh, seconds for the Scots Nats to set them straight.

Angus Robertson, the leader of the tribe and positively cuddly by SNP standards, arose to say that the Scottish government had been elected with a mandate to deliver an independence referendum. The other three main parties (how the Scots love to fight everyone at once!) shouted him down. 'They were! It is a fact! In contrast, the Conservative Party have fewer Members of Parliament in Scotland than there are giant pandas in Edinburgh Zoo! Why is the Prime Minister trying to emulate Margaret Thatcher by dictating to Scotland?' So now you know. This fight isn't about process, it's about pandas. I like the madness of the political equation: Tories equal pandas equal Thatcher. It's all getting, as I'm sure the adorable Tian Tian (aka 'Sweetie') and Yang Guang ('Sunshine') would agree, rather beastly.

The good news for Ed, who has eyes like a panda, is that he could easily be mistaken for one. And, don't forget, Sweetie was the BBC's female face of the year. That takes care of the gender problem: who says politics is all about men? So forget process, think pandas. The Scots Nats are putting the bamboo in bamboozling and the panda in panda-monium. It's going to be wild.

18 JANUARY 2012

Mr Bone's dogged pursuit of the unthinkable facts

*The Tory MP continues in his quest to find out who would
be in charge if the Prime Minister falls under a bus.*

THE TORY PETER Bone does not appear to be particularly morbid. Indeed, he actually looks remarkably like Sven-Göran Eriksson, albeit a taller, more hulking version. His love of stripes means that he is often, as yesterday, wearing a double set – stripy shirt under pinstriped suit – a combination that would make a zebra jealous.

For the past few months, Mr Bone (and his wife Mrs Bone, on behalf of whom he claims to ask most questions in the Commons) have been obsessing about who would be in charge of the UK if the unthinkable happened and Dave fell under a bus. I have to say that, in this age of transparency, it seems a perfectly good question to me.

But not, it seems, to the government. Last month Mr/s Bone asked the Defence Secretary (no answer). Then s/he zeroed in on the Deputy Prime Minister. 'Appropriate arrangements would be made in that very unfortunate event,' said Nick Clegg. 'Your morbid fascination with the premature death of your own party leader is not a subject for me, it is a subject for the Chief Whip.'

But yesterday, Mr Bone, fearless if ultra-polite, returned to the subject, as indefatigable as a dog with, yes, a bone. This time he was asking William Hague, the Foreign Secretary, who was in the Commons en route to Brazil, a trip that must seem all the more essential during these dark, cold January days.

As Mr Bone arose (not a short event), there were cries of 'Where's Nick?' and 'Mrs Bone!' What, asked Mr Bone, would Mr Hague's role be in a 'national emergency'? Mr Hague, pate gleaming like a mirror (I am quite sure that he polishes it with Windolene), said his role would be to support the Prime Minister and the government.

'You might have a problem with that,' warned Mr Bone. 'Is it true that under government plans, if the Prime Minister was killed during a terrorist attack, it would be the Foreign Secretary who took charge of the government until the Queen could choose a new Prime Minister?' Mr Hague shook his head, pate no doubt sending alarming mirror signals into outer space. 'Well, I can assure you that continuity of government plans are in place to deal with any catastrophic destabilising incident,' he said. 'We don't consider it appropriate to talk about these plans in public.'

I would think that, in most countries, the chain of command would be considered an essential fact to know. Mr Hague, no doubt his mind already on Copacabana and the need to pack some factor fifty for pate protection, repeated that 'arrangements' would be in place.

'I cannot assure you that there will be a place in the bunker for Mrs Bone!' he announced.

Mr Bone looked disappointed (and Mrs Bone may be more than that). But I have to ask: if Mrs Bone isn't in the bunker, who is?

25 JANUARY 2012

All inhale at a whiff of Branson wisdom

*MPs breathed in the glamour of it all as the Virgin
boss told them to decriminalise drugs.*

SIR RICHARD BRANSON blew into Westminster, a gust of glamour, his white-blond lion's mane blowing behind him, to tell the Home Affairs Select Committee his views on drugs. His very presence seemed to put Keith Vaz, the celebrity-crazed committee chairman, into orbit. He was on a high, albeit a legal one.

Sir Richard was there because he sits on the Global Commission on Drugs Policy. His answer to our drug crisis is quite simple – decriminalise the lot and treat it as a health issue. It is an interesting policy but MPs could not seem to quite get over the fact that the man, the legend, the hair, was in front of them.

'You yourself have smoked cannabis,' noted Mr Vaz with a tinge of wonder in his voice.

'I would say 50 per cent of my generation had smoked cannabis,' soothed Sir Richard.

Mr Vaz looked at him solicitously. 'And it hasn't been detrimental to your health?' Sir Richard, glowing with his Necker Island perma-tan, bared his two big white teeth, which flashed at us from among his Van Dyke beard combo of moustache and goatee. 'If I had been smoking cigarettes I would have been very worried,' he said, eyes twinkling.

MPs' eyes, already orb-like, got even bigger. They were, very definitely, inhaling now, heady with it all.

David Winnick, septuagenarian Labour, couldn't stop himself from crying: 'I've never taken a drug in my life!' Then he added: 'Other than prescription!' Mr Vaz tut-tutted. 'No need for further confessions. One is enough.'

Sir Richard noted that skunk cannabis was too strong but other types were less harmful than alcohol. Mr Winnick looked askance. 'You're not saying drugs should be sold in supermarkets?' he asked, adding: 'Buy your heroin and get your cannabis free!' (Where do MPs get these crazy ideas?) Are you getting the feeling that the committee has quite a steep learning curve ahead of them when it comes to drug policy? At one point an MP referred to drugs as 'the stuff'. It was hardly *The Wire*.

Mr Vaz began to burble on about how the committee would be going to Colombia as part of its inquiry. (Bogotá, you have been warned.) 'We will be travelling Virgin!' trilled Mr Vaz.

Sir Richard flashed that smile again. 'We use fuel on our planes,' he said, adding something about 'flying high'. Then he stopped himself, quite wisely.

28 FEBRUARY 2012

The battle to stay awake in the Land of Nod

*The fight over the Health Bill in the House of Lords
proved to be the perfect cure for insomnia.*

I HEADED TO THE Lords to view the battle over the Health Bill. It was narcoleptic. The warriors fighting the good fight over amendments 38B, 79A, 82A, G83, 84, G85, 86, 86A, 86B, G88, 89, G90, 91, 92, 93, 102, 110 116 deserve some sort of medal for showing bravery in the face of an intense danger of napping. I myself had to curb my somnambulism to tell the tale.

So, dear reader, welcome to the Land of Nod, where nothing less than the future of the NHS is at stake. And yet, even knowing how wildly vital this all is, it was still so very, very hard to focus when the subject at hand was how to stop conflicts of interest on the Clinical Commissioning Groups, which are new groups made up of GPs who will be giving contracts to, yes, GPs. It seems that, without amendments, there were no safeguards. Wildly important – but those words 'clinical commissioning groups' are just so zzzzzzzzzz.

'Is this sufficient? I don't think so!' barked Labour's Lord Hunt of Kings Heath, who was an absolute terrier all afternoon. (How does he do it? Coffee? Red Bull? We need to know.) 'It's the weakest corporate governance of any public body in this country! This is going to explode in the government's faces.'

Earl Howe, who was, for the afternoon, the government, didn't even look up at that. Silver-haired, sleek, smooth as a pebble. I suspect that, like a seal, he may be waterproof. What would dare explode in his face? And would he even look up if it did? Baroness Barker, a bollard in tweed, arose from the Lib Dem benches. She was worried that if we made too many rules about conflicts of interest – such as forbidding GPs from awarding contracts that they might personally benefit from – then we might make it so no decisions could ever be made.

Or I think that's what she said. It was like taking a dip into a pool of nonsense with her circular sentences and verbal cul-de-sacs. Around the chamber, eyelids were pulled by a force no less than gravity. Oh, it can feel like a dream in the Lords with its fairy-tale golden throne and glowing candelabra. I caught one of the chainmailed statues that hold up the lavish Pugin ceiling closing his eyes.

Stay awake! Thank God for the moment of clarity brought by Lord Winston of the Giant Moustache, who was a vision in mustard corduroy, as he explained how easy it would be for a conflict of interests to arise. But, somehow, as he detailed a new procedure for examining the uterus, I felt it was just all a bit real.

Earl Howe does not speak so much as susurrate. He accepted some of Baroness Bollard's amendments. But he would make no blanket ban on conflicts of interest which were, instead, to be 'managed' with 'integrity'. He assured us that the clinical commissioning groups would be helped by the health and wellbeing boards who would be helped by … oh, I give up.

They called the vote. The government won. The Battle of 38B et al. was over.

Now for 38C…

8 MARCH 2012

Arise Sir Peter Tapsell, this was your finest hour

The Father of the House gave an address fit for a
Queen as MPs debated the Diamond Jubilee.

WHEN SIR PETER Tapsell arises, I always expect a flock of birds to disperse. A statue come to life, he is eighty-two going on 182, imposing in his impeccable three-piece double-breasted suit. The handkerchief, snow-white, curtsied from his top pocket. His words processed slowly, assisted by a lisp: each one gift-wrapped, with some sporting bows as well.

'At the time of the last diamond jubilee, the Father of the House was Charles Villiers,' he said. 'He had started his distinguished political career in the parliament of King William IV, had sat in this House for sixty-three years, and was aged ninety-five.' MPs shouted: 'MORE!' 'By comparison with him, I am a mere parliamentary debutante.'

He said 'debutante' with such a flourish that it was (briefly) calligraphied in the air above him.

Sir Peter insisted that he was not alive in 1897 (surely that cannot be true) for Victoria's diamond year, though he could remember George V's Silver Jubilee in 1935. The 'hit tune' – he said this as if it were dangerously trendy, as if his next word might be 'daddy-o' – of the time was The Daring Young Man on the Flying Trapeze.

Mr Villiers, shortly before his address in 1897, had sent the Queen a personal gift. 'A parasol,' said Sir Peter, though the lisp made it sound more mysterious. 'I have presumed to follow his example,' announced Sir Peter. Mr Villiers's parasol had been 'dressed' in Chantilly lace. Nothing French for Sir Peter. His lace was from Nottingham! I wondered when the last time was that anyone dressed a parasol in the Commons.

The House was rapt. 'For my generation the abiding memory of our Queen is her stunning beauty when she came to the throne,' Sir Peter proclaimed. 'There is nothing more inspiriting in the whole world...' he paused '...than a beautiful woman!' He said 'woman' as if it might be 'goddess'. It was a very grand way of saying 'Phwoar'.

He paid tribute to her stamina in her many travels. 'I once asked a courtier how she did it,' he said. 'He answered, "By not eating salads, shellfish and watermelon while travelling."' A top tip indeed.

He ended by quoting a 'poet and parliamentarian' about another queen of hearts: 'Tell me, if she were not designed / The eclipse and glory of her kind'. Those the words of Sir Henry Wotton, friend of Donne, Jonson, Milton and, or so I imagine, Tapsell.

16 MARCH 2012

Bong! Don't they know what time it is?

*It was a race against time to stop the idea of
charging people to tour Big Ben.*

ONG! THE BIG Ben debate was, actually, a real ding-dong. On one
side were those who believe avidly that tours to the clock tower
should remain free. On the other were those who think charging
taxpayers £15 to walk up 334 stairs that they already own is a price worth
paying in Austerity Britain.

The plan, until Tory Robert Halfon got involved, was to start charging for tours as a way of paying for their cost of £100,000 a year. Mr Halfon
managed to secure a debate on the issue – itself worth a few bing-bongs –
and insisted: 'Those who support the charges argue that Big Ben is not part
of our democracy – it is simply an adornment. This is patently not true. Big
Ben is the most recognisable British icon in the world!'

Labour's Thomas Docherty intervened: 'Surely Her Majesty the Queen
is the most recognised icon in the world!'

'Hear, hear,' murmured MPs. (Did I hear Big Ben chime in too?) Even
if Big Ben isn't the Queen, it is still iconic. Think of James Bond and the
extra chime in *Thunderball*. Think of Richard Hannay hanging off the hand
in *The 39 Steps* (what happened to the other 295?). The musings got rather
out of hand (tick tock) and, fittingly, the Speaker imposed a time limit. MPs
were up against the clock.

Mr Halfon said that if Parliament wanted to save money, it could cut out
the 'obscene' food waste. Tory MP Jake Berry thought that if they rented
out Speaker's House for the Olympics, they could get £20,000 a night. Jacob
Rees-Mogg, man of the people (vox populi, vox dei), insisted sacrifices must
be made even if it meant contributing to the cost of bound Hansards: 'I actually like rereading my own speeches – somebody has to.'

Bong! Time to get back on track. 'We are not a theme park!' barked

Mr Halfon. 'I am reminded of the parable of the money lenders at the temple. Let's not become a place of just money lenders – about money, money, money. Let's be the Parliament of the people, by the people, for the people!'

But, argued others, what did a clock mechanism have to do with democracy? 'The ability to climb the clock tower isn't essential to the enhancement of our democracy,' noted Sir George Young, the Leader of the House. 'There is a difference between access to the clock tower and access to the chamber.'

Bong! Big Ben seemed to be winning the argument (I wasn't surprised for it was a race against time). Labour's Kevin Brennan said the idea of charging for the clock tours would take us all in a dangerous direction:

> My fear is that in a few years we will see the supreme irony in this place of huge corporate events and dinners for the bankers – the very people who put us in the mess that necessitates all this fiscal cutting. They will be the only people in here, having their swanky champagne parties and dinners in Westminster Hall or on the terrace, while our constituents are being charged simply for the privilege of looking around their own Parliament. That is where all this is headed. Whether we accept the amendment or the motion, the [House of Commons] Commission needs to listen to the voices of people in the House and think again.

And, incredibly, that is just what happened. The proposal was dropped. Big Ben's 334 steps will be free to climb for you and me. Bong!

22 MARCH 2012

Upstairs, downstairs riff comes over as a bit rich

This was the Budget that would soon be called a shambles
but, on the day, George thought he got away with it.

I T WASN'T LONG after George Osborne stood up that it became clear that he was trying to recast himself. No more Mr Bad Guy. Now he was a Robin Hood figure, giving to the poor by taking from the rich.

About fifty minutes in, he started referring to them as just The Rich. 'Thanks to the new taxes on The Rich I've announced, we'll be getting five times more money each and every tax year from the wealthiest.' David Cameron, behind him, raised one hand, opening and closing it, fingers spread out in what may be his version of the Vulcan greeting. 'Five times!' he mouthed. 'Five times!'

High five! But, wait a minute, aren't THEY the rich? At times like this, the line-up of those three public schoolboys – Dave, George and Nick Clegg – on that front bench just looks like a huge casting error. They kept 'high fiving' themselves as George chanted that he was using his 'five times more' money to help the poor.

'What planet are they on?' shouted Labour leader Ed Miliband.

I have to admit that I hardly recognised Ed. He was that good. Tories and Lib Dems flashed more jazz hands. Five! Five! Ed ignored them, insisting that all of this was a sleight of hand. The Chancellor wasn't Robin Hood but a character in *Downton Abbey* who, with his top-rate tax cut, had made each of his millionaire friends £40,000-a-year better off. 'While everybody else is being squeezed, what's the Chancellor's priority?' he shouted. 'A tax cut for his Christmas card list!'

Nick, Dave and George looked like guilty schoolboys.

'You talked about tax transparency!' shouted Ed. 'Let's have some! Hands up in the Cabinet if you are going to benefit from the income tax cut.'

Everyone looked self-conscious. Philip Hammond, the Defence Secretary and a self-made millionaire who is destined to play a smoothie in our Fantasy Cabinet Downton, shook his head. 'No!' he mouthed. But no one else moved a facial muscle.

29 MARCH 2012

It's all pie in the sky as Mr Pasty tells a porky

David Cameron, trying to face down the revolt over the Chancellor's new pasty tax, remembers when he last tasted one of those things that Cornish people eat.

SO THIS IS what it has come to. Yesterday David Cameron held a press conference at No. 10 on the Olympics. Behind him stood a furled British flag. In front of him, on the lectern, was the unicorn and the lion crest. Lord Coe was there, as was Jacques Rogge, the International Olympic Committee President.

And Dave was talking about pasties.

'I am a pasty-eater myself!' cried Dave. He then more or less proved that he is not by trilling: 'I go to Cornwall on holiday.'

(Note to Dave: pasties are not a geographically limited food, they are sold throughout the land.)

'I LOVE a hot pasty!' he insisted.

OK, we get the idea. You are not too posh to pasty. You think we should all be in this together, down Greggs, buying pasties with 20 per cent VAT in the national interest.

Surely it was time for Dave to move onto, say, security plans for the Olympics. But it seemed not.

For the Prime Minister was playing catch-up (or should that be ketch-up?). The day before, Chancellor George Osborne had been asked by Labour's John Mann when he'd last been to Greggs to buy a pasty. 'Look, I can't remember,' George had sneered. At which point, Mr Mann had sneered right back: 'That kind of sums it up.'

You've heard of street cred? Welcome to the politics of pasty-cred. For, in a brilliant food-fight manoeuvre yesterday, Labour's Ed Balls and Ed Miliband actually went to a real live Greggs in Redditch to buy man-of-the-people sausage rolls. Eight of them! Dave's people told him it all looked very cinéma vérité. The two Eds were even filmed queuing as if they were real people! Why, Dave wondered, hadn't his press people thought of that: actually going to visit the little people to eat some of their ghastly little pies?

Yes, he would have got indigestion, but it would have been the perfect antidote to all that fiddle-faddle, twiddle-twaddle about *Downton Abbey*, millionaire donors and kitchen suppers. What a missed opportunity! It could have been just like the husky photo, just with baked goods. Instead, he was stuck here with M Rogge and not a pasty in sight. So Dave did the next best thing: he relived his last pasty moment, chew by chew.

'I think the last one I bought was from the West Cornwall Pasty Company. I seem to remember I was in Leeds station at the time.'

His eyes got a dreamy look (or was that shifty?). 'The choice was whether to have one of their small ones or large ones, and I have a feeling I opted for the large one. Very good it was too!'

Too much information, I'm afraid. Sometimes Dave forgets that in the parallel universe that is the real world it is quite easy to check his facts. It didn't take long to ascertain there hadn't been a Cornwall Pasty stand at Leeds station since 2007.

Where is this all going to end? For Dave, I suspect, at Greggs with a hot pasty in his mouth. At least he won't be able to talk.

17 APRIL 2012

The Bradford Spring blows into town

*George Galloway loses no time in explaining his place
in history, fresh from his Bradford West win.*

G ORGEOUS GEORGE GALLOWAY arrived fashionably late to his own mini-press conference in Westminster yesterday, accompanied by a small entourage of beautiful people. 'Who's that?' I asked about one young lady even more gorgeous than George. 'The wife,' said one hack. 'The fourth one.'

Someone produced a crib sheet on her. Her name is Putri Pertiwi, she's twenty-seven to his fifty-seven, and she's a Dutch-Indonesian anthropologist. It turns out that they got married less than forty-eight hours after George's sensational Bradford West by-election win. This, then, was the honeymoon.

George once used the word popinjay to describe Christopher Hitchens, but he's no stranger to the mirror himself. He's quite the dandy: grey three-piece suit, neat stubble, black suede shoes. Putri had on precarious orange shoes with silver heels. George approached the tiny media scrum. Had anyone else, asked the man from the *Morning Star*, ever made such a comeback? 'Churchill,' noted George. 'The only other person to win six elections in two countries in four different constituencies.'

Ah, yes, the modesty. I had forgotten about that. 'It's great to be back but I'm just the advance party. There is an army mustering in the north, in the great industrial and post-industrial cities of this country, an army of discontented, alienated people who feel that this place has let them down.'

The voice is just as beguiling as ever. We haven't heard it from the back benches since he was defeated in 2010 but now, in the chill spring air, the cadences rolled by like waves. 'New Labour is terrified of any other by-elections and I understand why. This concept that I have coined, it's rather rude, three cheeks of the same backside, pretty much sums them up.'

Putri was glued to his side, eyes gazing into the rolling news camera.

George doesn't seem to breathe, the oxygen of publicity being enough for him. 'Still, this is the parliament. This is the sixth time that I have been elected to it, two different countries, Scotland and England, and four different constituencies. Something of a record, at least post-war,' he said, neatly erasing Churchill, as is only right of course.

20 APRIL 2012

May-Day as Theresa has a date crisis

The saga of our attempt to deport Jordanian cleric Abu Qatada took yet another ridiculous turn as the Home Office got the European Court time limit wrong for his appeal.

WHAT A DIFFERENCE a day makes. Earlier in the week Theresa May had been a hero for arresting Abu Qatada. By yesterday she had become a fool who couldn't count. (I paraphrase, but not much.)

'Yesterday the Home Office said the appeal deadline was Monday night but European Court officials said it was Tuesday night,' Labour's Yvette Cooper said. 'So on the Tuesday night deadline, while Abu Qatada was appealing to European Court judges, the Home Secretary, who thought the deadline was Monday night, was partying with the *X Factor* judges.'

'AHHHHHH!' cried Labour MPs. 'SHAME!' Shame indeed. For a moment it was unclear who was the greater threat: Abu Qatada and his battle to thwart British justice or Theresa May attending the same event as singer and judge Tulisa Contostavlos. Then the moment passed and we all knew the answer: Mrs May.

This then was the great debate yesterday. When does a day begin and end? How long is three months? And is the X in *X Factor* really something to do with multiplication? 'We are talking about a simple mathematical question,' insisted Mrs May. 'The European Court's judgment was on 17 January. The period of three months within which we were allowed to refer ended at midnight on 16 April.'

Labour MPs did not agree. It was not simple mathematics. It was complicated. For them, this was not about multiplication but division. Labour timelord Keith Vaz explained that, actually, forget the Moon and the stars, the Sun and the Earth, for it all hinged on Article 43 of the European Convention on Human Rights. 'If you look at the cases of *Praha* v. *the Czech Republic* and *Otto* v. *Germany* you will see the time limit begins the next day.'

This was breaking news. Praha and Otto. What a combo. They sound even dodgier than the *X Factor* judges. Maybe Mrs May should be partying with them. The Tories weren't having it. 'Claiming that 17 April is within three months of 17 January is rather like claiming that New Year's Day is on 2 January!' harrumphed Andrew Bridgen. And Tory Michael Ellis explained that, in Article 43, the crucial words were 'within three months'. As he explained: 'So Monday 16 April was within three months, whereas Tuesday 17 April would have been three months, not within three months.'

So that's clear then. Labour explained that no less an expert than the BBC said that the three months weren't over until 17 April. 'Did your officials ever put before you the decision whether to go forward on 17 April or 18 April?' demanded Clive Efford. 'This is an important question!'

But not as important as this one from Dennis Skinner. 'Does the Prime Minister know what day it is?' This got great guffaws. 'Yes!' insisted Mrs May.

Well, whatever day it is, it sure wasn't Mrs May's day. How Mr Abu Qatada must be laughing.

25 APRIL 2012

MPs call in the jester for advice on drugs

The Home Affairs Select Committee was agog as Russell Brand
arrived in a tangle of tattoos, jewellery and opinions.

RUSSELL BRAND, UNLIKE a lot of famous people, is larger in real
life than you expect. He blew into the Home Affairs Select Committee hearing room like a bad wind: tall, hairy, loud. 'Allo!' he cried,
turning to a packed audience. He turned back to the MPs. 'Allo!' He took off
his black hat, punctuated by pheasant feather, and shrugged off his jacket.
The committee stared as one, jaws dropping. Bare arms! Tattoos! Jewellery!
His sleeveless grey vest was torn in all the right places, his belt was rock star,
his necklace involved hundreds of strands of silver and crosses.

Mr Brand, as the MPs called him, was there to talk about drugs and his
belief in abstinence-based recovery. 'I was sad lonely lonely unhappy detached
and drugs and alcohol to me seemed like a solution to that,' he announced,
needing no warm up.

'Once I dealt with the emotional spiritual mental impetus I no longer felt
the need to take drugs!' Russell flashed a wicked smile. The MPs seemed to be
more or less in shock. Keith Vaz, the celeb-crazed chairman of the committee, noted: 'You were arrested roughly twelve times...' Russell interrupted:
'It was rough! Yes!' Everyone laughed and Brand was thrilled. He is a terrible show-off and manic with it: eyes darting, tattoos dancing as he gestured,
voice like a machine gun. He was with Chip Somers, chief executive of the
detox centre Focus12, who, in comparison, seemed in slow motion. Russell
kept telling us about Chip's evil past. 'He was an armed robber! You don't
mind if I tell 'em?' he said, hitting Chip on the arm.

Russell was on an instant first-name basis with everyone. Keith Vaz was
'Keif'. The Tory Michael Ellis was just 'mate'. Actually, I think I saw all the
MPs flinch when Russell called him that.

Keith asked 'Mr Brand' about legal highs. Was that what young people preferred these days? 'I don't know, because I'm not young enough anymore,' burbled Russell. 'But I do know that young people will always want to get high. As I said before, Keif, it's insignificant the substance they are using. If you are a drug addict, you are getting drugs. That's it.'

Russell is against methadone treatment because it doesn't get to the root of the problem. 'What we need is to give love and compassion to everybody involved. If people commit criminal behaviour then it needs to be dealt with legally but you need to offer them treatment, not for some airy fairy, let's-all-get-round-and-hug liberalism, but because it deals with the problem.'

Did Russell think that celebrities played an important role? 'Celebrity is a vacuous, toxic concept used to distract people from what is actually important!' But would Russell see himself as a role model? 'As the great [rapper] Tupac Shakur said: role is something people play, model is something people make. Both of those things are fake. What I want to offer people is truth and authenticity in the treatment to this illness.'

Now Chip was asked about celebrities. 'Who CARES about bloody celebrities?' Russell cut in.

He said that being arrested didn't deter him. 'Being arrested isn't a lesson. It's just an administrative blip.'

Keif noted: 'I think we are running out of time.'

'Time is infinite!' cried Russell. 'You cannot run out of time.'

But you can, of course. And then it was over and Russell, hat on, smile flashing like a neon sign, pranced out. 'Fanks for having us!'

3 MAY 2012

Bleeping Boris pedals on without a ******* gaffe in sight

*The day before his re-election as London mayor, fighting
against Labour's Ken Livingstone, even the Blond
Bombshell was showing signs of campaign fatigue.*

S O, I ASKED Boris, as he ricocheted down the street, a human vote-seeking pinball machine, are you keeping down the swearing today? 'Too bleep bleep right!' he cried, eyes momentarily darting towards me as he posed with two youngsters for a photo. 'Bleep bleep bleep bleep bleep!' he cried. Then he announced a change of plan. 'Make those asterisks! Seven of them!'

Boris must have begun the last day of the mayoral campaign by repeating this mantra: 'I must not ******* swear!' The day before, he'd been caught out on air. Ahead in the polls, his goal was to get through the day without a gaffe which, actually, is easier said than done on the streets of London.

'I must watch my language,' he tells a cab driver worried about illegal minicabs as he searches for a word for the problem in his super-sized vocabulary and settles, boringly, on 'scourge'.

It must be said that Team Boris was looking a tad ragged round the edges as the big white (actually off-white, which seemed fitting) battle bus pulled up outside Morrisons supermarket on the Uxbridge Road in Acton. Political walkabouts are fraught with madness. Boris's yesterday began with some advice from local resident Beryl, who is eighty. 'He needs to avoid this bit because that man over there is an alcoholic,' she said, pointing to a hooded figure, 'and he's going to vomit in a minute.'

To be honest, I'm not sure even vomit would have fazed him. To watch Boris in action is to see a tornado gathering strength. Here, all human life – brown, black, white, all shapes, sizes, ages – seemed to be whirling round a straw-haired man who was himself constantly in motion.

The big issues were jobs, police, fares and, inevitably, for all politics really are local, parking. It was as Boris was listening to a heart-felt rant on parking, that, suddenly, a man on a bike shouted: 'You Tory b******!' Boris opened up his arms towards him. 'My fellow cyclist!' he cried (though surely 'My fellow asterisk user!' would have been just as appropriate). The cyclist was so over-excited by that that he turned across the traffic, missing death by inches. 'Don't get killed!' cried Boris, voice fading away.

The whirlwind continued down the rather shabby street, adorned also by an Al Jazeera presenter, his back to the scrum, talking to camera: 'And still to come: is this the most popular Conservative in history?' Boris was waylaid by youngsters who wanted a 'team photo' and, after escaping, was gripped by a man holding a beer, extolling the virtues of the Bible.

So what day of the campaign was this? 'Day 1,000,' said Boris, eyes to the sky, running for his battle bus, which was now headed to Chiswick where the streets are leafier, the voters visibly richer. Instead of kebab shops, there are tapas bistros. But after what seemed days of handshakes and selfies, even Boris seemed to tire. 'I've said this 58,000 times,' he said, stopping suddenly and walking away. That few?

The Third Year

Gay Marriage and Europe

MAY 2012 — APRIL 2013

I T WAS THE mid-term year, the halfway mark, the year of living painfully. This was the year that Nick Clegg sang his 'I'm so so sorry...' song and Ed Balls became even more annoying. Lords reform died and the Leveson Inquiry ground on (and on) until it was finally over. Gay marriage turned out to the subject of not-so-gay debates. As ever for this coalition, debates and feuds over Europe provided the backdrop to the year, with the Euro-rebels making significant progress towards the holy grail of a referendum.

·   ·   ·

8 MAY 2012

Dave and Nick embrace tractor production

It was their second anniversary and you didn't need to be a marriage counsellor to guess that something in this relationship had gone wrong.

I THINK WE CAN safely say that the Dave and Nick bromance is over. Yesterday they renewed their marriage vows on the shop floor of a tractor factory in Essex and it just felt dire.

Whose idea was this? The only way is NOT Essex. The location was the windowless, noisy shop floor at CNH Tractors in Basildon, right next to a sign that said 'Cab Kitting Area'. One hundred blue-collar employees and four giant blue tractors – wheels six feet high – watched the two most powerful men in Britain as they struggled to remember why they ever thought coalition government was a good idea.

Their favourite word was 'difficult'. Their second favourite was 'tough'. Nick told us that the economy had had a 'socking great heart attack'. Then he told us that he was an optimist. It was incredibly heavy going: think of a tractor in a flooded muddy field, chugging and churning away at about 5 mph. That's our government.

We could see what the theory was. This is Britain's only tractor factory, producing 26,000 this year, up on last year. It all does seem a bit Soviet – tractor production up! – but everyone is always saying manufacturing is what put the Great into GB. But the problem wasn't the factory, it was Dave and Nick. They seemed to be on autopilot.

I have seldom seen two men look so out of place. Here they really were the only two metrosexuals in the village. Halfway through, Dave suddenly realised this and took his jacket off, widening his stance, hands on hips. Nick, jacket on, hair sticking up, looked totally European. After a while they gave up on first names and, like those couples who refer to each other as 'Mother' and 'Dad', reverted to 'Prime Minister' and 'Deputy Prime Minister'.

They trotted out their agreed lines without any visible signs of enthusiasm. Both now insist that House of Lords reform doesn't have to dominate the next year. Nick was emphatic that he cared far more about tax thresholds and apprenticeships than Lords reform. Dave, utterly passionless, noted: 'I think it is a perfectly sensible reform for Parliament to consider.'

Bizarrely, they pretended that François Hollande, the new socialist French President, agreed with their ultra-austerity plans. Actually, Dave isn't even calling it austerity any more. 'What you call austerity, I might call efficiency,' said Dave as Nick stood there, looking sadder than any optimist has ever looked.

I have seen these two many times out on the road at 'live and unplugged' events but this, frankly, seemed more like it was 'dead and recorded'. Usually they make an effort, looking at each other, mixing the serious and the humorous, helping each other. This time, it was by rote and detached.

'These are tough economic times,' said Dave. 'In the end we have produced some pretty chunky, clear policies that needed to be done. Of course I would like to be running a Conservative-only government. Nick would like to be running a Lib Dem government.'

Young marrieds, take note. This is not how you keep the magic alive. A mere two years ago Dave and Nick strolled down the garden path, birds singing, sun shining, bees buzzing. I suppose the danger signs were there last year when they spent their first anniversary at the handball arena in the Olympic Park. But tractors? Next year, who knows? Maybe it will be an abattoir.

Oh no! Minister takes a flying jump into horizon

The Defence Secretary had to resort to extreme measures
to make sure we had no idea that he had changed
his mind on which jets to order.

PHILIP HAMMOND CAME to the Commons to execute a tricky manoeuvre, a U-turn on a U-turn, which makes it an O-turn or, in this case, an Oh-no-turn. Ideally the Oh-no-turn should be attempted only under cover of total darkness and so, forced into the daylight, Mr Hammond had to resort to what the military call Extreme Verbal Camouflage.

What this means, to you and me, is that he made almost no sense.

The O-turn was over what kind of jets are going to be ordered for the two new aircraft carriers. Labour wanted jump jets, the coalition had cancelled that in favour of planes that use 'cats and traps', but now Mr Hammond had gone back to jump jets.

I tell you this on deep background. Cling to it.

This is Mr Hammond's version: 'We will switch the order for JSF aircraft from CV to STOVL, which we can do without delaying delivery.' The Defence Secretary, po-faced, explained that the 'horizon' had changed. So had the 'balance of risk'. Inter-operability was key. So is retaining optionality. Don't forget it.

He explained that the 'cats' (short for catapults and not lions and tigers) had to be a certain kind, the 'innovative electromagnetic version', which he called 'EMALS – the Electromagnetic Aircraft Launch System'. He explained that EMALS posed 'greater design challenges' than anticipated. What does it mean? I am not sure (and if I really understood, then I couldn't tell you without killing you afterwards).

Mr Hammond told us that fitting the cats to the Prince of Wales was going to cost a lot. I thought this was funny – Prince Charles with a cat in the middle of his forehead seemed just a bit crazy – but it was all part of Deep Camouflage because actually this is also the name of one of the carriers.

It seems that the STOVLs (that's 'short take-off, vertical landing') are now thought to be better. Plus, interoperability-wise, Mr Hammond is optimising the optionality. 'An emphasis on carrier availability,' he said, 'is the more appropriate route to optimising alliance capabilities.'

Mr Hammond was now so completely covered in verbiage that I couldn't see that he was even human. 'When the facts change,' he said, breaking into English for a moment, 'the responsible thing to do is to examine the decisions you have made and to be willing to change your mind, however inconvenient that may be.'

Labour howled, shouted, taunted. Bob Ainsworth, statesmanlike even with that bristle-brush moustache, said he had been Defence Secretary and the facts hadn't changed and, in fact, the coalition's original decision had just been wrong.

'I refute that last comment absolutely,' said Mr Hammond.

I can tell you that, in Deep Camouflage, that means 'Yes'. So here is my code-breaker analysis. Mr Hammond: We made a mistake. Labour: We know.

Now eat this paper. No one must know.

24 MAY 2012

Ed B puts in a vintage performance

There was great excitement over the news that our Prime Minister likes a glass or two of wine while chillaxing.

ED BALLS'S ORBITAL blue eyes were fixed on the Prime Minister during the entire thirty minutes of PMQs and his mouth never shut. 'Tell us about the recession!' the shadow Chancellor demanded over and over again, endlessly rhubarbing.

When the Prime Minister showed a spark of energy, the Balls arm went out, hand patting down the air, the epitome of fake solicitude. 'Calm down! Calm down!' he cattle-called.

Then there is Ed B's 'flatline' gesture to signal the stagnant economy and the 'shovel' gesture (digging yourself deeper). And yesterday Ed had added something new – a fruity little number as a sommelier might say – to his repertoire. 'Have another glass of wine,' he called. 'Chillax!' How Dave hated it! We are told in a new biography that Dave enjoys a few glasses at Sunday lunch and that he is seen as a bit too relaxed. I have to say that, at PMQs, he is more axeman than chillaxeman. Every week I can see Dave struggling with his inner Angry Bird. Yesterday I think he would happily have thrown a glass of Chardonnoying at Mr Balls.

It's been more than a year since the PM branded the shadow Chancellor 'the most annoying man' in British politics. Ed adored this. There is a rumour that he has had it embroidered on a cushion. After all, this is a shadow Chancellor who gives dinner guests something he calls the 'Cameron Dessert' which is, yes, Eton Mess. I wonder if Mr Cameron may start to serve Cham-pain Socialist to his.

PMQs was almost over – it was 12.27 p.m. – when Dave began to answer a friendly question about how he had restored stability to the public finances (these are VERY tough questions). 'I think you are right,' said Dave, who began to deliver his stock response about the wonders of deficit reduction. This had gained the UK 'hard-won credibility…' And then something inside Dave snapped. 'Which we wouldn't have,' he announced, 'if we listened to the muttering idiot sitting opposite.'

A huge grin enveloped Ed Balls's face.

'YEAH!' screamed the Tories. The Speaker began to shout 'Order' but this brought only more disorder. 'You will please withdraw the word idiot,' insisted Mr Speaker. 'A simple withdrawal will do.'

But of course the PM, often so gracious, could only be petty when faced with Mr Chardonnoying. 'I will replace it with the man who left us with this enormous deficit and this financial crisis,' he huffed, red-faced, Riesling to the bait once again.

15 JUNE 2012

Dave and Confused is tongue-tied

Our Prime Minister found himself babbling to the Leveson Inquiry until, finally, he had to phone for help.

DAVID CAMERON HAD obviously made a huge effort to look prime ministerial before the Leveson Inquiry, dulling himself down, speaking slowly, listening carefully to the chief inquisitor, Robert Jay (or 'Beardy' as he is known).

And then it all started to go wrong. Mr Jay, deadpan and wearing a ghastly orange tie, displayed a list of Dave's meetings with the press over more than four years. It appeared to be endless. Mr Jay noted that it had 1,404 entries – more than one every working day. Dave's cheeks (and, oddly, his forehead) flushed.

Mr Jay assumed the air of a surgeon, probe in hand, examining dead tissue in the body politic. What about this drinks meeting? What about that dinner? 'I remember the drinks,' said Dave. 'I don't remember the dinner.' (With 1,404 drinks, no wonder…) Dave had gone to Santorini to meet Rupert Murdoch. He'd met James Murdoch fifteen times. Yes, he was friendly with Rebekah Brooks, especially after she'd married his old friend and fellow Old Etonian Charlie Brooks, a Chipping Norton neighbour.

'How often did you speak to her by phone?' Mr Jay asked. Dave suddenly turned into a tongue-tied teenager. 'Not a huge amount but I always felt when I did ring that it was a lot less than Gordon Brown. I can't put numbers on it. Certainly in 2006, 2007, not necessarily every week.'

That was his answer? I called her less than Gordon Brown? Mr Jay, merciless, asked about 2008 and 2009. Dave squirmed. Yes, the 'level of contact' had gone up. Yes, he'd phoned more.

'But about how frequently?' demanded Mr Jay.

Our Prime Minister now morphed into a character named Dave and Confused. It was as if he was blindfolded, seeking answers by bumping into them. Had he seen Rebekah every weekend? 'I don't think every weekend. I don't think most weekends. But it would depend…'

Dave was babbling. 'Charlie and I played tennis together and all sorts of other things – which I'm sure we'll come on to, so that was why I was seeing more of her.' (Had Dave just referred, however obliquely, to Rebekah's police horse Raisa that he rode? Surely that was verboten.) Mr Jay revealed a cloying love text from Rebekah. Dave looked abashed as Mr Jay read out her invitation to a 'country supper' (isn't it all just so Chipping Norton?). The text gushed about his wife Samantha's charms before trilling: 'We're definitely in this together!' What, asked Mr Jay, did that mean? Oh, the agony. Dave muttered something about policies through clenched teeth, sighing with relief when Mr Jay moved on to the much easier questions about Andy Coulson.

When he came back from lunch, he had an announcement for the inquiry: 'Mrs Cameron keeps a better weekend diary than I do.'

I quite liked that 'Mrs Cameron'. Clearly there had been words. 'She reckons that we didn't see them more than on average once every six weeks. That is a better answer!' crowed Dave.

Lord Justice Leveson noted, drily: 'The great value of wives, Prime Minister.'

Dave nodded: 'Indeed.'

It sounded like something out of Jane Austen.

20 JUNE 2012

Why the Civil Service must be flatter

Sir Humphrey helps Francis Maude tell it like it isn't.

E ALL KNOW that Cabinet Office minister Francis Maude needs help when it comes to speaking English. He lives in a world of jerry cans and kitchen suppers. Yesterday he gave a statement on Civil Service reform. The only problem? It was written by a civil servant. Indeed, this, I hear, was his request for help:

Mr Maude: Sir Humphrey, I want to deliver a jargon-free statement on my brilliant Civil Service reforms.

Sir Humphrey: Yes, Minister, let me action that for you.

The result was there for all to hear. Mr Maude gave us more jargon than could fit into any jerry can. He began with an 'action plan' to 'deliver outcomes' but soon moved on to what Bob Dylan would call the harder stuff.

He bemoaned 'rampant gradism' and 'binary choices'. He talked milestones. He told us that 'digital by default should become a reality not just a buzz phrase'. (I suppose, over a kitchen supper, one talks of little else but 'digital by default'.) 'The Civil Service of the future will be smaller, pacier, flatter,' he announced. Ah yes, flatter. Like road kill, ironed hair, the Earth before Columbus made it round.

Mr Maude has also come up with the genius idea of naming and shaming the worst 10 per cent. I looked at Mr Maude reading out his statement, so pedestrian that he has his own personal zebra crossing, and felt this was a dangerous precedent.

Jon Trickett, the lugubrious Labour shadow, noted: 'In identifying the worst-performing public servants perhaps you might consider that you name and shame the poorest ministers? I can see one or two on the front bench now!' At this, Mr Maude threw back his head in an attempt to show he has a sense of humour, though he may have just given himself whiplash. Next to him, Andrew Lansley, the Health Secretary, looked entirely grim.

What, demanded Labour leftie John McDonnell, would be cut from their conditions? Mr Maude said civil servants hated being 'featherbedded and pampered'. (I'll bet they do.) 'Those conditions which are outliers, which are hard to defend, like the fact that as soon as you become a civil servant, you are entitled to six months' sick pay, are out of kilter!'

Tory MPs exhorted him to go further. Edward Leigh demanded: 'Are you really going to achieve where everybody else has failed and get less permanent secretaries who have got an Oxbridge degree in Latin, who can write a beautiful minute and are charming, and actually get people who can run a project?'

Finally the well-named Mark Reckless noted that Mr Maude says there should 'only' be eight layers of people between the top and the front line. 'Couldn't we be a little more ambitious?' he demanded. Mr Maude looked slightly pained, not to say flatter. Sir Humphrey, you have had your revenge.

22 JUNE 2012

Embodiment of a whisper who had no need of bombast

*Aung San Suu Kyi wasn't allowed trumpets
but then, she didn't need them.*

SHE IS SMALL and was made to seem even more so by the monumental grandeur that is Westminster Hall. Aung San Suu Kyi descended the cold stone steps, her white shawl wrapped over a colourful Burmese long dress, looking like the embodiment of a whisper. 'She's even shorter than the Speaker,' hissed a colleague. And indeed she was – and it was this that made it so moving.

She wasn't allowed trumpets – apparently only heads of state, not living icons, get those. But as we had waited the string ensemble located just under the glorious stained glass window had played Mozart, Pachelbel and Elgar. And now, as she floated down into the hall, they put down their instruments – voluptuous cellos curving on the floor – to give her a standing ovation. I looked above, at the stone angels above us in the incredible ceiling. Were they playing trumpets? I think so.

The blood and guts were provided by Mr Speaker's bombastic intro-duction, sparing none of the Burmese junta's gory deeds: rape and murder, forced labour, human minesweepers.

'Burma has become a beautiful but benighted land where fear runs through society like blood flowing through veins,' he intoned.

A better future, or a fervent hope for one, was embodied in this woman who had lived a perfectly ordinary life in Oxford before returning to her homeland and, over the years of house arrest, becoming a legend. To her left, on the raised steps, sat David Cameron and Ed Miliband, joined in the front row by Cherie Blair and, in a rare public Westminster appearance, Gordon Brown. To her right sat the saintly if faintly comical figure of the Archbishop of Canterbury. In front were rows and rows of MPs and lords; the sprinkling of celebrities – Annie Lennox, Jo Brand, Joanna Lumley – consigned to the very back with the media.

I would have seen much more on television – the flower in her hair, the look on Dave's face – but then I would have missed the way her voice, quiet, precise, her accent slightly misconstrued at times, penetrated that hall. This is a place where words can be cheap, not to say worthless, but everyone listened.

She has a nice, quiet line in humorous asides. 'I understand there was some debate as to whether I would speak here in this splendid setting,' she noted. 'I welcome that debate – it is what Parliament is all about.' This brought giggles (though not from the angels who were still smarting over the trumpet ban).

She talked about the rain (of course) and how she yearns for Burma to have its own rumbustious version of PMQs. (Did Dave look guilty? I hope so.) She set out the progress that has been made in Burma, the hunger for democracy so long denied. She is a practical politician, not concerned yet with votes so much as the ability to vote.

She talked of how poetry and the BBC comforted her during her dark days and how this is Burma's moment for change. I found it impossible, in this land where we believe fiercely in apathy and the right not to vote, not to be moved.

3 JULY 2012

Don't forget to nod if you don't agree

*Our Prime Minister embraces the double negative
to explain his new Euro stance.*

I F YOU ARE confused about David Cameron's stance on Europe, I can help. It's all about the double negative. Here is the Tory Eurosceptic Philip Hollobone yesterday: 'You are now not ruling out a future referendum on our membership of the European Union.' Dave nodded. Though actually, was that really wise? Doesn't nodding to a double negative just confuse things further? Plus, remember, two negatives don't make a positive (unless you multiply, but let's not go there…).

Dave couldn't have been clearer in the chamber yesterday. He used to not be in favour of some kind of referendum on Europe at some point in the future, but now he is no longer not in favour of not being in favour of a referendum at some point. Dave doesn't like the status quo and wants a 'fresh' deal with Europe and then we can have a 'fresh' mandate.

It sounds like a supermarket. If you are still confused, can I urge you to employ my own special (and soon to be patented) 'Yes! We have no bananas' method of understanding. So, previously, Dave's European policy could have been summed up as the 'Yes, we have no referendum bananas policy'. But the new improved post-weekend policy is the 'Yes, we have no no referendum bananas policy'.

Actually, it's a shame that Dave didn't sing it because that would have cleared things up immediately.

Ed Miliband didn't understand that it was all about bananas and insisted that, if it was a song and dance, it was the Weekend Hokey Cokey. Ed claimed that on Friday Dave had ruled out an in/out vote. 'But then – hey presto! – on Sunday, the Prime Minister hints he might rule one in,' said Ed. Then the government insisted that Dave hadn't changed his position. 'Three days, three positions,' said Ed. 'First it was no, then it was yes, and then maybe.' (Did Ed really just say 'hey presto'? Surely it was last used in public in 1972?)

Dave was withering in his response. 'I think you probably ought to give up the Hokey Cokey and stick to the Rubik's Cube.' (Fact: Ed can decipher a cube in ninety seconds and the Commons struggled for eighty minutes with Dave's Euro policy.) The Labour MP Huw Irranca-Davies, whose name could easily be a dance, tried to be helpful when he asked: 'Your referendum policy can be summed up as "no, but yes, but no, but yes". Are you likely to resolve this teenage dilemma before the next election?'

Dave frowned. He insisted that Vicky Pollard does not set our European policy. This was a surprise. But then, if she did, it might have been easier to understand.

5 JULY 2012

What's love got to do with it?
Just about everything

Barclays' Bob Diamond was supposed to talk about
rate fixing but, instead, he seemed smitten.

FOR SOMEONE MADE of the hardest substance in the world, Bob Diamond talks a lot about love. When asked, at the start of the Treasury Select Committee hearing, if he wanted to say something about what had happened (i.e., rate fixing, chaos, resigning), Bob nodded. 'Wow!' he said softly. 'I love Barclays!'

The committee of MPs tried not to stare. 'That's where it starts. I love Barclays because of the people! Sixteen years ago today, on 4 July 1996, I began at Barclays. It's been sixteen years of just tremendous enjoyment!'

Andrew Tyrie, the intensely geeky chairman, gently tried to guide Bob back to rate fixing. But Bob just kept telling us how great Barclays was.

Barclays was decisive, unbending, marvellous. 'I love Barclays!' he cried after only a few more moments.

I think it's safe to say that MPs were baffled by Mr Diamond and he by them. You could see them looking at him and thinking: 'But he was paid millions!' So, if money can talk, now we know what it would say ('I love Barclays!'). Gordon Gekko he isn't.

Bob is smaller than you'd expect, a picture of pure calm and pure control in wireless specs and black tasselled loafers. His cufflinks were little blue balls of fabric. He had a silver pen, a highlighter and a super-controlled way of moving his hands that shouted 'media training'. He also had a truly sinister policy of constantly referring to MPs by their first names.

Bob's message was amazingly simplistic. Barclays is wonderful (he loves it!) in every way. Indeed, Barclays was especially wonderful when it found out about the rate fixing because it immediately acted to stop it. This is what Mr Diamond called 'context'. 'Let me put some context on that,' he kept saying.

Why, he was asked, didn't he know that the rate fixing was happening? Bob blinked back. He was angry when he'd found out. 'There is no excuse for the behaviour. I stand for a lot of people at Barclays who are really, really angry about this. This doesn't represent the Barclays that I know and I love…'

At the word 'love', jaws tensed around the room. We knew what was coming. 'I love Barclays! Almost twenty-five years in financial services in the UK, I've developed great relationships. I just love my time here!'

There was a great moment when the Tory MP Andrea Leadsom fixed her gaze on him: 'Do you think you live in a parallel universe?' she asked. Bob blinked. 'Andrea,' he began, and she shot him a look of pure stiletto.

She asked about the rate-fixing traders. He said that they were fourteen out of thousands. 'What I am saying about Barclays – which is an amazing institution which I love – there are people, 140,000 employees, all impacted by these fourteen traders. And it is not OK. No one is saying that it is OK.'

Bob insisted that the real culture of Barclays was the opposite. What the traders had done had made him 'physically ill'. 'We talked about the "no jerk" rule. We were serious in Barclays, when people don't behave, they have to leave. Fourteen people! It was wrong.'

Bob the Very Rich Bulldozer continued relentlessly. 'One of the reasons I thought it was important to come here today is Barclays. Barclays is an amazing place...'

Labour's Teresa Pearce interrupted. 'Mr Diamond, you have told us repeatedly that you love Barclays, but from what you are saying you have not even met Barclays, let alone love Barclays. You keep saying, I didn't know, I didn't know.'

Bob ignored that. Diamonds, like love, are forever. What did these MPs know about it anyway?

6 JULY 2012

They're so vain, they probably think this debate was about them

If you ever wonder if Westminster is just a little bit self-obsessed, then you need go no further than this lamentable debate on the banks.

WHERE'S DANTE WHEN you need him? Forget the Inferno and its nine circles of Hell. Yesterday MPs invented a tenth circle just for us. The 'debate' on a banking inquiry was neither a debate nor about banks. It was a mud-slinging, cage-boxing, scream-fest between Ed Balls and George Osborne.

Ed was beside himself with fury, transported into something quite close to orbit. Why? It wasn't rate-fixing by the banks. It wasn't Bob Diamond's bonus. Oh no. It was that George Osborne had given an interview to *The Spectator* in which he said that Labour ministers, and Ed in particular, had questions to answer over the Libor scandal.

'Will you provide the evidence to substantiate the allegations you made about me?' screamed Ed. 'False allegations! Or will you withdraw and apologise?' George just laughed at that. Across from him, Labour's baying mob cried: 'Apologise! Withdraw!' The Tories bawled right back. It was Babel meeting Bedlam: a dystopia of contorted faces, thug-like cries, furious asides. I do hope the banksters out there were watching to get some tips on how to behave.

George, sinuous, scorpion-like, was the personification of a sneer. 'You were the City Minister – the City Minister! – during the Libor scandal...' His voice rose louder. 'I said you have questions to answer. That is precisely what I said. I want to know the answer to the question: which Labour ministers were involved? Answer that question!' But Ed Balls, a bulldog, if a petulant one, insisted that George had impugned him more directly. 'Where's the evidence? You should either put up or shut up! Present the evidence, apologise, that's your choice if you have any integrity in this house!'

'ORDER!' screeched the deputy Speaker. But these two did not want order, they wanted revenge, to have history on their side and to tear large chunks out of each other. Hilariously, they claim to be outraged by the banking culture. What about the Commons!

And the worst thing? They were loving it! Ed was playing to the crowd, taunting individual MPs, demanding that the Tories show humility. (I am not making this up.) At one point, the Tory Anna Soubry blew him a kiss as he promised her she could intervene. 'There's no need for that,' said Ed, blowing her kisses back.

I haven't seen George so happy in months. It's as close to heaven as he's been since the double-dip recession began. 'I have never seen the Labour Party and the shadow Chancellor so rattled about their time in office,' he chortled. Why had Ed not given a 'simple apology' for not regulating the banks? 'Just get up and say, "I was the City Minister and I am sorry!"'

But Ed had a better idea. 'I am asking you to apologise now. You have impugned my integrity!' he screamed. Oh dear. This was bordering on flounce. Surely the screaming had to stop at some point. Unless, of course, Ed was modelling himself on Violet Elizabeth Bott from *Just William*. 'If you had any integrity you should stand up now, withdraw the allegation and apologise!' George dripped disdain, his long elegant fingers pointing at Labour. 'The IDEA that I am going to take lessons on integrity from a man who

SMEARED his way through thirteen years of Labour government…' Honestly. They're so vain, they probably think this debate was about them. The bankers surely will.

18 JULY 2012

Apocalypse now for the hapless Mr Buckles

The Olympics was all set to be the big feel-good event of the year except for one man, the head of G4S, whose failure to recruit enough guards had forced the government to send for the army.

KEITH VAZ, THE Grand Inquisitor, loves a little bit of drama. Well, OK, a lot. Yesterday, after he and the Home Affairs Select Committee reduced the G4S chief executive, Nick Buckles, to something close to roadkill, Mr Vaz delivered this brutal summary.

'Unacceptable. Incompetent. Amateurish.' Mr Buckles looked so cowed that he could have been a Holstein.

The Great Vaz, speaking from a very great height, wasn't finished: 'Those words best express our deep concern about the way this has been handled. In the end, Mr Buckles, it is a matter for you to decide what you do about your future.'

Mr Buckles blinked. I could see him thinking: 'Is it over? Am I alive? Can I go home please?' What an extraordinary event it was. Mr Buckles was accompanied by a man named Ian Horseman-Sewell. As soon as I saw that name, I felt an apocalypse coming on. I wasn't wrong. Beforehand, we had wondered if Nick Buckles would buckle. But, soon it became clear that he had arrived, pre-buckled. By the end, he was as near to concave as a witness has ever been.

Mr Buckled was so hapless that it was hard to believe that he was the chief executive and paid £830,000 – except for that tan. He had the rich glow that only money can buy and the looks of a junior international playboy: slim-cut suit, foppish hair, expensive specs. Mr Horseman, the account manager for (not) delivering the Games contract, had a gangster-pinstriped suit with one of those awful Olympic badges. As a team, they looked very dodgy.

'Why are you still in post?' demanded the Great Vaz.

Mr Buckled whispered something about delivering the contract. 'It's not about me,' he said, adding that he was the right person to do this.

'My future is my third concern,' he added lamely.

He was made to flail himself, telling us how sorry he was. He was embarrassed, deeply disappointed, very sorry indeed. He'd first known that things were going wrong on 3 July when he was on holiday in the States (tan maintenance takes time). It was a 'very unique' contract because it was 'back-ended' with a 'massive pipeline'. It was all about 'cascade'.

David Winnick, the Labour MP who is beginning to resemble a Galapagos tortoise, attacked: 'Your reputation is in tatters.'

He muttered: 'I think at the moment I would agree with you.'

Mr Winnick shouted: 'It's a humiliating shambles. Yes or no?'

'I cannot disagree with you...' mumbled Mr Buckled.

The patented Buckled masochism strategy was working in that I almost felt sorry for him but, in the end, he was too weak. Vague. Limp. Unfocused. Tellingly, the only thing he seemed sure about was that G4S wasn't going to hand back its £57 million management fee despite the fact that little proper managing had gone on. The nadir came when he was asked about his statement that he wasn't sure if the guards they had recruited spoke English.

Why wasn't he sure? 'The question I was asked was "fluent English",' he noted. 'That was a question I didn't know how to answer. I didn't know what fluent English was.'

The Vaz: 'What do you think fluent English is?'

'I don't know.'

The Vaz: 'What are we speaking today?'

'I don't know.'

The Vaz: 'You don't know whether you are speaking fluent English?' At this, Mr Winnick boomed out: 'Fluent English is what we are speaking at the moment!' See what I mean by hopeless? Can Mr Buckled be for real?

4 SEPTEMBER 2012

I'd like to announce a death…

*The Deputy Prime Minister was furious as he
read the last rites for Lords reform.*

THE DEPUTY PRIME Minister came to the Commons yesterday more in anger than in sorrow. 'I would like to make a statement on House of Lords reform,' he said, pausing for a stagey rueful chuckle that he'd been practising it in the mirror. 'Or what's left of it.'

Mr Clegg had come to announce the official death of the Bill which, already, has had the longest funeral in history. Labour, who supported the Bill but joined with Tory rebels to oppose the programme motion (which timetables the rest of its stages), pretended to be disappointed about it.

Nick, on the shortest of fuses, immediately flipped. 'You really do get ten out of ten for spectacular insincerity!' he shouted at Harriet Harman who, suffering from flu, looked at him wearily and blew into her hankie. 'You had it within your grasp to be the friends of reform but turned into miserable little party point-scoring politicians instead!'

Wow. Coming from Mr Clegg that is almost a compliment. It's clear that he's been simmering away since August when he decided to kill the Bill rather than fight a guerrilla war to get it through. There were obvious signs of a summer of comfort-eating: the paunch growing into something quite close to a pot belly that even his metrosexual Euro suits cannot disguise.

Nick's whole demeanour was one of spectacular and flamboyant petulance: we are talking drama queen without the wig and make-up. 'One day, one generation of politicians is going to finally have to introduce a smidgen of democracy in the second chamber!' he ranted. 'We cannot continue as a country, as a parliament, trotting round the world, lecturing other countries about the virtues of democracy and not introduce it in Westminster ourselves!' (Can't we? I suspect Nick can.)

They say revenge is a dish best served cold but — and perhaps I should not have been surprised given the expanded waistline situation – Nick prefers to serve his steaming hot. He and the Tory rebels are in open warfare. 'You should comfort yourself,' murmured Bernard Jenkin patronisingly, 'you gave it your best shot.'

Nick rewarded this by twisting the knife, confirming he had ordered all Lib Dems to vote against the parliamentary boundary changes that Tories want so desperately. I am sure you can see how Nick does not do petty party point-scoring.

For once, Dennis Skinner, legendary sneerer, was the light relief. 'There is a silver lining,' he noted. 'The House of Lords survives and when the Liberal Democrats dump you as leader, you'll qualify for a peerage. Will you take it?'

For a moment, Nick looked like he might fudge it. But then I saw him mount that white charger and rear up before us. 'No I will not!' he cried. 'Call me old fashioned – it just sticks in my throat! I have campaigned all my life for the simple idea of democracy and that is what I will continue to do!'

He's writing history, if not Hansard. So make no mistake, Nick's the hero.

7 SEPTEMBER 2012

Pre-Posterous: why two Eds are better than one

Labour unveils its new big economic theory
with an absolutely terrible name.

THE TWO EDS launched the big New Labour idea yesterday. The future is not about New Labour or Old Labour or even New Old Labour. It's all about Pre-Labour. Yes, Pre! Like 'free' but better than that because it's pre-free.

The launch of Pre was at a conference called Quest for Growth. It was sponsored by a leftish think-tank whose logo is made up of two empty parenthetical brackets. Somehow, as I watched the Eds explain the beauty of Pre (not to be confused with any old nonsense like pi), those brackets seemed to say it all.

Ed M was on top geeky form. He told us that he had been inspired by how Tony Blair and Gordon Brown trawled around for fresh ideas in the '90s to create new Labour. For Ed, the Teenies are about doing the same thing. That's how he found Pre.

At first I was confused and felt the whole thing might be related to Pre, as in Pre-Posterous. But as I listened, and watched Ed M sway to and fro behind the lectern, noting that even his little white tufty bit of hair seemed to have moved farther to the left, I saw that he might be on to something here.

Ed explained that, in the '90s, New Labour believed in Re, as in redistribution. They wanted to give money to the poor through tax credits and benefits. But, in the cash-strapped Teenies, Re is never going to be enough. In addition to Re, we now must go one letter before and put the 'p' in for 'Pre'. 'The new agenda is that we need to care about the model of the economy we have,' he explained, 'and the distribution of income it creates.'

'There is a word for it,' he said. Yes, I thought, there certainly is. 'Not coined by me!' he added merrily. 'Predistribution!' The audience did not clap, at least not out loud. Instead, everyone looked extremely serious. Pre is all about furrowed brows. Now Ed asked the big question: 'Are you going to carry out predistribution as well as redistribution?' I looked around me. The jury may be out on that.

Ed says we must transform the pre-economy from low wage to higher wage. 'Think about somebody working in a call centre, a supermarket, or in an old people's home,' explained Ed. 'Redistribution offers a top-up to their wages. Predistribution seeks to offer them more: higher skills with higher wages.'

Wow, I thought. It's like magic. Or even voodoo except, of course, voodoo economics was from Ronald Reagan's days, which were so long ago that they were Pre-Historic.

Ed M was now joined by Ed Balls for post-Pre questions. There was a kerfuffle when they allowed a question from the *Daily Mail*. The man behind me harrumphed with outrage that anything so outlandishly right-wing should exist at the Pre-launch. 'You have been unflatteringly called the Two Eds,' asked Mr *Daily Mail*. 'Which Ed is in charge?' Ed M blathered on about how the two Eds were totally unified and focused on the future. Then Ed B stepped in: 'The thing that Ed should have said is, Two 'eads are better than one!' Let's hope so. They'll need them to explain the brave new world of Pre.

14 SEPTEMBER 2012

Maria's rhapsody in beige

*The new Culture Secretary inspires thoughts
of Julie Andrews and that song.*

I T WAS MARIA Miller's big day. Here she was, the woman plucked by David Cameron from the political equivalent of the chorus line to be a star. I had never really expected to see her rise above, say, Welsh Secretary. And now I know why.

It was not a huge success. At some point, I could hear Julie Andrews singing in my ear. 'How do you solve a problem like Maria?' If I could sum up her performance in one word, it would be 'beige'. If I needed two, they would be 'totally beige'. I fear that she may consider that a compliment. She was dressed top to toe in it. There are blancmanges out there with more colour than our new Secretary of State for Culture, Media and Sport.

The beiger (you may say that is not a word but it is now) she got, the more colourful the men around her became. Next to her (in deep-beige camouflage she was hard to see) was the Sports Minister, Hugh Robertson, who was Mr Olympics.

'May I record the congratulations of the whole House to everybody involved in London 2012,' trilled Hugh, which was a canny way of heaping praise upon himself.

'Especially Tessa!' piped up Labour's Chris Bryant.

Tessa Jowell, Mrs Olympics, beamed. But Hugh wasn't having that. 'Wait a moment,' he snapped at Chris. 'Slightly tedious, aren't you?'

I looked at Maria. Blank. I felt a desire to colour inside the lines. What was she thinking? Even the thought bubble was empty. She was asked what was going to happen after the Leveson report. The words, beige on beige, piled up. 'What we have to do at this stage is ensure that the inquiry runs its course,' she said. That's what I call an action plan.

Hugh, on the other hand, was having a ball. Tristram Hunt, Labour's handsome intellectual, was on the attack. 'Only a government of such awesome incompetence as this one could follow up the Olympics by abolishing the post of Minister for Tourism and Heritage! We know that the Tory Party did not like Danny Boyle's wonderfully progressive vision of British history, but did it really have to seek revenge by scrapping the post?'

Hugh, short and peppery, jabbed back. 'That is the silliest question I have heard in two and a half years! I loved the opening ceremony and, far from the Tourism Minister being abolished, he is standing before you!'

But Maria seemed determined not to stand before us until, finally, she had to, as is customary, give a little introduction of her department. I say 'little', but Maria embarked on a novel. Everyone exchanged looks of horror as she turned a page. Was it Book at Bedtime?

'Order!' shouted Mr Speaker. It was an 'abuse' to take so much time. She should be brief. 'That is the situation – always has been, always will be.'

'Thank you, Mr Speaker,' quailed Maria.

Oh, the horror of being told off by Mr Speaker! Maria withdrew further into her beigeness. For me, she was just an outline now, like one of those drawings on the floor in a murder mystery. A Labour MP asked about women in sport and the irrepressible Hugh jumped up to answer. Harriet Harman was going berserk, urging Maria to stand up and speak for her sex. But Maria could not. She had evaporated into thin air.

24 SEPTEMBER 2012

Nick's sorry, he's sorry, he's so so sorry

The Lib Dem conference in Brighton began with the deeply weird spectacle of the Deputy Prime Minister singing an apology.

I T WAS A sorry day in Brighton, rain pelting down, crocodile tears taking their revenge on the Lib Dem conference. The day began with Nick sitting on the Andrew Marr sofa giggling away as he watched himself on TV singing 'I'm sorry, I'm sorry, I'm so so sorry', Brighton's burnt-out old pier a black hulk in the background.

'It's actually very good,' hee-heed Marr.

'It's catchy!' giggled Nick.

Or was that 'It's catching'? Because something is in the air here.

The Lib Dem store had already sold out of Nick Clegg 'I'm sorry' mugs by lunchtime but, in response to demand, they were cranking up production of Nick 'I'm sorry' buttons. 'Very popular,' said the woman at the till. But she meant the buttons, not necessarily the man.

'Why didn't you apologise two years ago?' demanded Ronald, whose tie was the colour of egg yolk, as the Lib Dem leader, sorry, pop star (sorry, see, it IS catching) answered questions.

'I'll tell you why not,' said Nick, 'I'm not sure if anyone would listen then. There are people now who won't listen. There are people for whom it will never be enough.' (Was it just me, or did that sound like a new lyric? 'I'll tell you, I'll tell you…') Ronald called the broken tuition pledge a 'debacle'.

Nick, who gets more animated, more boyish and more engaging when a crowd isn't with him, began to gesticulate wildly. Was he going to sing? 'I was asked a question by a journalist this afternoon – "Are you going to apologise for the apology?" Which I thought was getting a little bit over the top!' I think two people giggled at that. Nick dug in, flooding us with words, telling us that if he'd done it during the 'heat of the protests' then his apology would have fallen on 'entirely stony ground'.

'Of course people will now mock and sneer,' he said, which could be another lyric, if not the major refrain, of his recent political career.

A woman took the microphone: 'We were going to be the party that wasn't going to break promises and the first thing we did was break a promise. That is what people find so difficult to forgive.'

She got a big clap for that. Was this a Q & A or a therapy session? Nick pointed out, as if it were news – which it might actually be here – that the Lib Dems hadn't won the election. 'I'm flattered that people think that we should take decisions, that we won a mandate to govern on our own. We didn't! We didn't! No one has struggled with this more than I have.' (I looked at him and, like everyone in the hall, heard that in song: 'We didn't! We didn't!' I tell you, it really is catching.)

But then, because they are Lib Dems, they moved on to the tiny fine print of the Communications Data Bill. There was a hilarious moment when a man demanded that Nick rein in Danny Alexander: 'He's been more right wing than Peter Osborne!' (I'm sorry, I'm sorry, it's George, not Peter…) One man, when talking about forests, said that you would have to be God to regenerate them. 'As a human being…' said Nick, which was, in the circumstances – I'm sorry, I'm sorry, I'm so so sorry – not really necessary.

4 OCTOBER 2012

Welcome to Britain's newest One Nation cult

Ed Miliband launched One Nation Labour in his speech
the day before and, just twenty-four hours later,
it was already impossible to avoid.

I BRING YOU NEWS from inside Britain's newest cult, One Nation, which has taken over the Labour conference with alarming speed.

Yesterday, in a mass gathering addressed by Ed Miliband, whom they call The Leader, hundreds of believers displayed all the signs that they have 'drunk the Kool-Aid'.

The indoctrination rally, under the guise of a question and answer session, was in the main hall, whose blue set was now emblazoned with the words One Nation.

'You will see on the backdrop behind me the phrase One Nation,' said The Leader. 'I think you heard it forty-seven times in my speech yesterday. One Nation is incredibly important to us.'

The followers asked how One Nation would treat trade unions, the disabled, students – and, well, just about everything. The Leader explained the role of education: 'It is about preparing young people to become citizens of One Nation.' Everyone nodded. Were their eyes glazed? Ed, as The Leader, seemed different. Already there are signs that a personality cult is forming around this tall, bendy man with the bog-brush hair with that strange Harry Potter-esque bit of white in it.

The day before, Ed had told us about his elder son's desire that One Nation be a land that included flying dinosaurs (yes, I know it's strange, but it's a cult).

Now we heard about his younger son, Sam, aged two. 'He was watching my speech on TV with his grandma. My wife told me this story – and I don't know if it's true because he can't properly speak – but she claims that after fifteen minutes he suddenly said "One Nation".'

The followers laughed. The Leader could do no wrong. They jumped up and down, desperate to get his attention, waving flags, umbrellas, random pieces of clothing. 'Don't take it too far, this waving of clothing. We want to keep this clean!' instructed The Leader.

One woman said she was a great-grandmother. 'You don't look old enough,' said The Leader, adding: 'Flattery will get me everywhere.'

The great-grandmother admitted: 'I gave you a kiss at the south-east conference!' The crowd giggled. Soon another woman, this time from Wales, after asking how Europe was going to fit into One Nation, revealed that her friend had also been kissed by The Leader the day before. 'I am jealous,' she announced.

The Leader guffawed, his big cartoony teeth glinting against the lights. He wasn't wearing a jacket and, under his shirt, you could see he was wearing an undergarment. He seemed an unlikely sex object but, then, I haven't drunk the Kool-Aid.

The Leader urged his followers – or 'Comrades' as he called them at one point – to help him write the One Nation manifesto. But One Nation was not just about policies, it was also about the spirit of the country. 'That is why One Nation matters,' he said, 'One Nation matters…' I looked around me. Everyone looked hypnotised.

8 OCTOBER 2012

A tale of two egos and a sorry story

Grant Shapps, who also goes by the name of Michael Green, made an unforgettable debut as Tory Party chairman.

GRANT SHAPPS TOOK to the stage in Birmingham yesterday to strut his stuff as the new Tory Party chairman. I was on tenterhooks to see if he would appear as himself or as his alter ego, Michael Green. It is an amazing fact that Mr Shapps, using the alias of Michael Green, wrote a self-help book called *How to Get Stinking Rich*. And no, I haven't made this up.

So would it be Mr Shapps or Mr Green on stage today? My hopes were cruelly dashed by someone named Mr Swaddle (how do they find them), who insisted on introducing Grant Shapps as, well, Grant Shapps. Some mistake surely, I thought, as the man cantered on to the stage, managing to avoid the set which consisted of two huge cardboard trees emblazoned with the Union Jack.

He stopped and looked out over the hall, which was bedecked with no fewer than six banners that shouted: BRITAIN CAN DELIVER. (After years of lower case, upper case is back.) Yes, I thought, well maybe Britain can deliver, but can Grant? Or even, for that matter, Michael? Short and stocky, blue eyes blazing, his suit trousers too long, Grant/Michael looked like a used car salesman who had wandered into the wrong showroom.

He began, possibly on the advice of Michael, by telling us something about himself. He'd campaigned in four elections, knocked on thousands of doors, delivered millions of leaflets. 'But I've got to tell you,' said Grant, 'it's not always as glamorous as it sounds!' Boom boom, boom crash…

Undeterred, Grant ploughed on, giving us way too much information about himself, taking us through all his triumphs until, finally, he arrived at the reshuffle a month ago when he was called to Downing Street to see the Prime Minister. 'Grant,' said Grant, impersonating Dave. Thank God, I thought, at least the PM doesn't think his name is Michael.

Grant unveiled his cunning plan for a Tory victory in 2015. The gist? Tories must stop being so shy.

'Why are we the shy Tories?' he demanded. (I think Michael would have approved of that one: no one got stinking rich by being shy.) Grant made fun of Ed Miliband's speech last week, saying that there was one thing he forgot to say. 'In fact it was just one simple word – Sorry.' Thankfully he didn't try to impersonate Ed. But Grant wasn't finished: 'But for Ed and Labour, sorry really does seem to be the hardest word.' He paused and, utterly shameless, giggled: 'In fact, there's an idea – he could even have set it to a song.' Nooooooo, I thought.

Surely this has to end? But now he began to impersonate Boris. I was grateful when it ended. Next time, I do hope Michael Green comes instead.

9 OCTOBER 2012

We are still all in this together, insists George

*It was the Tory conference dominated by someone who wasn't there:
Andrew Mitchell, the Chief Whip, at the centre of a storm over whether
he called a Downing Street policeman a 'pleb', didn't attend as he
didn't want to be a distraction. Actually, a weary conference would have
welcomed a bit of distracting from the Chancellor's austere vision.*

GEORGE OSBORNE SEEMS almost to relish his new role as the Fifth Horseman of the Apocalypse. Yesterday was his gloomiest exhortation yet. Some would call his speech serious. I would say that it was like going to the dentist without the pain relief.

His message was clear. The George Osborne signature plan of sado-monetarism IS working, just slower than anticipated. More pain, less gain. That is the situation. 'Let the message from this conference be clear: we will finish the job we have started!' he cried. The hall, full of loyal Tories desperately trying to find something to make them feel better about it all, looked on wearily.

I could almost hear them saying, as one, 'Oh, do we have to? Can't we have a bit of fun?' To which the answer is: no. There was not one feel-good moment in this speech.

George noted that three years ago he'd said we were all in this together. 'It wasn't just a slogan,' he said. No one clapped. 'We need an effort from each and every one,' he said. 'We are still all in this together.' But, looking around me, I don't think anyone wants to be.

George was dressed in black. Now we knew why. George paraded his bogeymen. First up is anyone who doesn't have aspiration. We've all got to get some of it, and pronto. 'We will be the government for people who aspire,' he said (for a moment, I thought he said expire). He has a new plan for aspirers: they get rid of their rights and get shares instead. 'Workers of the world unite!' cried George, his horse rearing up, hooves flashing, just because he can.

Then there are benefit scroungers, who are well and truly back on the dartboard. 'Where is the fairness, we ask, for the shift-worker, leaving home in the dark hours of the early morning, who looks up at the closed blinds of their next-door neighbour sleeping off a life on benefits? When we say we are all in this together, we speak for that worker!'

But the biggest hate figure of all is Ed Miliband, the man who stole Disraeli. 'It is risible', sneered George, 'to believe you can become a party of One Nation simply by repeating the words "one nation" over and over again!' He had talked to Ben about it: 'You can imagine Benjamin Disraeli's disappointment. Moments after the joy of being told that there really is reincarnation, he discovers he's coming back as Ed Miliband!' Cue laughter and applause. After all, who needs One Nation when you can have One Condemnation?

31 OCTOBER 2012

Winter of discontent over Richard III

MPs go to war over where the king found under a car park should end up.

MY GRAVE, MY grave, my kingdom for a grave! I wouldn't go so far as to say that Richard III has been haunting the Commons, but let's just say that we are feeling his presence here in Westminster. Lately rarely a day passes without mention of what's going to happen to the bones found under a car park in Leicester.

RIP? We should be so lucky.

It's more a wrangle of the roses than a war, though, as it happens, the MPs involved are Labour, which of course usurped the rose under the reign of King Tony. Basically, it all began when the Justice Ministry decided that, if the bones belong to Richard III – and how many skeletons have an arrow in the backbone, scoliosis and a 'mortal battlefield wound' in the skull? – the king will get a funeral.

But where would it be? John Mann insisted the answer wasn't York or Leicester but Worksop. Leicester's Jonathan Ashworth noted that since Richard had been in Leicester for 500 years (albeit under a car park, which, let's face it, lacks a certain majesté) then he should stay in Leicester.

But Hugh Bayley, from York, noted gently that it was not 500 years but 527. 'Despite that passage of time, he is still very well regarded in York,' he noted, to giggles.

'Is he still on the electoral roll?' asked one Labour MP.

Mr Bayley restrained himself from claiming the bones. 'To argue on the floor of this place over his mortal remains is more like medieval cathedrals fighting over saints' relics,' he said.

Yesterday, though, an agitated Mr Ashworth was back in the Commons, raising a point of order. He noted that, over the weekend, the Justice Ministry had said that, should the bones be the king's, the plan was to re-inter him in Leicester Cathedral.

That was seen as 'very exciting' in Leicester. Mr Ashworth said: 'Last night, however, the department appeared to backtrack. When asked, it refused to repeat the words.' He added ominously: 'No one would want to accuse the government of now U-turning on Richard III.'

Oh dear. U-turning on Richard III. Doesn't that sound painful? I imagine that, since the poor guy was under a car park, he's seen his fair share of U-turns. But still, not a good image.

Mr Ashworth wants Helen Grant, who is new to the job of Justice Minister and may wish after this she had never taken it, to come to the Commons and explain.

At this point, Labour's Chris Bryant, who is rarely quiet for longer than a few minutes, interrupted. 'A hearse, a hearse, my kingdom for a hearse!'

Mr Speaker intervened. In the Commons, by tradition, royals are not really to be commented on. 'I think his late majesty has been dead for long enough to evade our normal rules,' announced Mr Speaker (rash, or what?) who then added that, sadly, this was not a matter for him.

So Mr Ashworth must live to fight another day. I tell you, the Battle of Bosworth Field has nothing on this.

1 NOVEMBER 2012

Reckless by name and ruthless by nature

The Euro rebels take on the government over cutting the EU budget.

I T WAS KNOWN as the Reckless amendment, named after its author, whose first name was Mark and not, disappointingly, Utterly, and it demanded that the EU budget be cut. Yesterday, at PMQs, David Cameron, red in face, if not in tooth and claw, insisted that a cut was, indeed, what he wanted.

'YEAH!' shouted the Tories. But, added Dave fatally, it might have to be a freeze instead. Oh dear. The Eurosceptics would not like that. Only a cut would do. There is no negotiating on that.

Mr Reckless watched the Prime Minister from the bar of the House, his face impassive. What he saw was a chamber that had been hit by the parliamentary equivalent of the devastating Hurricane Sandy, strewn with debris (and, potentially, careers). The most incredible sight of all was Labour, the party of Euro largesse, taunting Dave for not being tough enough.

'The whole country will see through what is rank opportunism,' Dave snarled at Ed Miliband.

'When it comes to opportunism, this Prime Minister is a gold medallist!' Ed screamed right back.

So began a day of rumour, innuendo and braggadocio (though Eurosceptics won't like that – too Italian). As it turned out, PMQs was a mere amuse-bouche (too French) for the main event, the debate that went by the Euro-name of 'Multi-Annual Financial Framework'. It is to this that Mr Reckless had attached his wrecking (or, if you prefer, 'recking) amendment. The man speaking for the government was Greg Clark, the Financial Secretary, new to the job and almost pathologically polite. Mr Clark, MP for Tunbridge Wells, need I say more, is almost the epitome of the word 'spiffing'. 'The PM deserves the support of the House as he goes in to bat for Britain!' he said.

Chris Leslie, for Labour, was so sanctimonious that I felt queasy as he explained why he was rising above party politics to vote with the rebels. 'Our goal is to stand up for the taxpayer!' I examined his nose. It wasn't growing. What would Pinocchio (sorry, Italian again) say?

Now arose Mark Reckless. He painted a picture of the EU that was so dissolute, so licentious, so venal that it was as if Hogarth's Gin Lane had somehow become Greed Lane. EU officials were overpaid, under-taxed, over-indulged. While we in Britain were cutting, in Brussels it was gluttony a-go-go (I paraphrase). 'If you think the EU has too much money, its budget is too large and needs to be cut, then support my amendment!'

He made no concession to Dave about a mere freeze instead. Maybe Mr Reckless should change his name to Mr Ruthless. Other MPs stood to agree with him. I began to think that the government might lose this one. And now arose Bill Cash, not so much superstorm as super-bore. The EU was living 'on another planet'. Lucky EU, I thought as he began to gesticulate wildly. 'There is no turning back!' he cried. 'We have to say no!'

The Commons listened with respect. That in itself should have been a harbinger. The rebels won, 307 to 294. As the result was announced, a hearty cheer went up. The front bench sat there, faces blank. At the back, Mr Reckless allowed a tiny smile to play about his lips. Ruthless indeed.

13 NOVEMBER 2012

I'm an attention-seeking Tory MP (please don't), Get Me Out Of Here

When Tory MP Nadine Dorries headed for the jungle to eat bugs, her colleagues were only too happy to help.

NADINE DORRIES ALWAYS said that Westminster was the real jungle. 'When they asked me: would you go into the jungle with snakes and rats?' she told the viewers of *I'm a Celebrity … Get Me*

Out of Here! on the first night, 'I thought "It's Westminster. I work there. How hard can it be?"'

How hard can it be? Oh Nadine. How idiotic can you be? Actually, no need to answer that. Before she went into the (real) jungle, I always thought of Nadine as an outspoken, sometimes brave but often foolhardy MP with a penchant for publicity. I never thought she really deserved her nickname of Mad Nad. Now I am having a reassessment.

Nadine is not the most popular of MPs, but even she might not have realised how much her Tory colleagues were going to enjoy her 'humble in the jungle'. In particular, the Communities Secretary Eric Pickles is relishing (sorry) it, claiming that he has the number 'on speed dial' to vote for her to undergo the ghastly Bushtucker Trial. Indeed, the whips are sending 'get out the vote' messages to MPs to 'Vote Dorries'.

The Tory whips have had a few setbacks recently (the Euro rebellion vote, the Chief Whip resigning over 'plebgate') but they triumphed on the Mad Nad Bushtucker Trial vote. Thus, last night, Nadine and someone named Helen Flanagan (soap actress, looks great in a bikini) had to undergo a task called 'Bug Burial'. This involves being in a closed coffin with thousands of bugs.

Nadine claimed not to be surprised: 'I fully expected this because I'm an MP and MPs are a conduit for public anger.' Not to mention the whips. Plus, there's her constituents, who must be just a bit perplexed by having an MP who is 'working from the jungle'. And Dave and George, whom Nadine once called 'arrogant posh boys'. They might have had a little vote too.

One of her fellow jungle celebs – someone named Hugo from something called *Made in Chelsea*, sorry to sound like a High Court judge – tried to encourage her: 'Nadine, you're going to win this. Just think how many witty comments [you can make] when you do go back into Parliament. You can say "I've been in a coffin full of bugs and nothing compares to the crap that comes out of your mouth."'

At this, Nadine concurs: 'That's a good line.' Despair. No, Nadine, that is not a good line. It is ludicrous but, it must be said, not quite as mad as the Bug Burial. As Mad Nad stood there, wearing bug-proof goggles, looking at her 'coffin', even she was reduced to silence. (Helen made the sign of a cross and said she was going to be sick.) In the Westminster 'jungle', the ultimate punishment is for an MP to be put on a tedious committee that examines every word of an immensely boring Bill. In Australia, they cut out the middle man and just dump maggots in your coffin.

The goal was to stay in the coffin for ten minutes. Helen lasted a few seconds. Nadine, jungle veteran of the green benches, stayed put. After two minutes, as so often happens in politics, the maggots were joined by 3,000 cockroaches. Then more maggots and 5,000 crickets. 'You're going to bury me if you put any more in,' said the woman in the coffin underground.

She lasted four minutes before shouting, 'I'm a celebrity, get me out of here!' Later she said it was the most horrific experience of her life. Westminster will be pleased.

30 NOVEMBER 2012

A warning shot and he moseyed into the night

The Leveson Inquiry, which cost £5.5 million and produced a 1,987-page report, ended with an extremely strange press conference.

I T MUST BE said that Lord Leveson has a unique version of how to give a press conference: take no questions and then go to Australia. Inside the Queen Elizabeth II Conference Centre, the other event of the day was a British Society for Heart Failure conference. It seemed right.

The press conference was in a huge windowless blue room. It felt like we were on a deep-sea dive. The music was beyond 'chill' – the kind they play to calm down violent types. The room seemed mostly full of lawyers. I felt like hiding my notebook.

Lord Justice Leveson, or Brian as we call him at Westminster, sat on stage by himself, reading out his statement in a voice of doom. Behind him was a darker blue shadow of himself. He began by praising the press. I waited for the 'but'. I didn't wait long. Basically, and I paraphrase, which I suspect Brian may not approve of, he wants us to have some sort of statutory (but independent) underpinning because it will make us stronger.

He had an Oscar moment where he thanked all the lawyers in the room (it took some time). He ended with this:

> I believe that the report can and must speak for itself. To that end, I will be making no further comment. Nobody will be speaking for me about its contents, either now or in the future. The ball moves back into the politicians' court. They must now decide who guards the guardians.

At this he stood up and did a little bob of a bow at us. Most of the room burst into applause. The journalists, who were not applauding because we never do, looked confused. Brian headed off stage. 'Did you enjoy it, Sir Brian?' shouted a hack. Sir Brian broke into a canter. And so did we, as we headed back, across the road to the Commons. We had to skirt a scrum around Max Mosley, who has made something of a career of fighting the press over coverage of his S&M activities. Robert Jay, the inquiry's star lawyer, rushed by, paparazzi snapping away.

Back in the House, the politicians were fighting over the ball that Sir Brian had given them. Everyone could agree on only one thing: that we must all think of the victims, such as the Dowlers and the McCanns, who have conducted themselves with immense dignity throughout. Then, having said that, it was a bit of a free-for-all.

Ed wants to legislate right away. Dave wants to wait and think before 'crossing that Rubicon'. And Nick? Well, Nick had to have his very own statement to explain that, actually, he agreed with Ed. He's not going to share his ball with Dave on this.

I think they need a referee but it's not going to be Brian. He's out of here.

12 DECEMBER 2012

Devil's in the detail: Miller gets stuck in a quad lock

The Culture Secretary embarks on a year of consultation over same-sex marriage with a statement that is greeted by cries of pain.

OH THE FURY, the fury! Culture Secretary Maria Miller outlined her proposals for same-sex marriage to the Commons yesterday to what can only be described as Old Testament wrath. 'Do you feel that you are competent to act as God? To change and challenge the redefinition of marriage between one man and one woman?' demanded the Rev Willy McCrea from the DUP. Maria said it would be 'inappropriate' to answer though I can't think why a simple 'No' wouldn't have sufficed.

She was challenged by MPs from all parties, but most of the cries of pain came from her own backbenchers. 'I congratulate you on delivering consultation results reminiscent of a Liberian presidential election,' Stewart Jackson said. 'These proposals are a constitutional outrage. There is no electoral mandate for these policies!'

Ms Miller said that, somehow, somewhere, over a rainbow possibly, we had all known that the Tories would do this as it had been hinted at in some obscure attachment to the manifesto. She insisted that churches would be protected from having to carry out the ceremonies by something called a 'quadruple lock' which, basically, seemed to be that no institution would be forced to carry out a gay marriage.

'I was up late last night reading the Conservative manifesto,' spat Peter Bone, waving the little blue book before throwing it down with a 'thwack'. He did the same with the Labour and Lib Dem manifestos. 'In those political bibles, there is no mention of redefining marriage! It isn't even hinted at!' Maria told Mr Bone that she respected his views. 'I think you should be celebrating this development,' she chirped, saying that she hoped the quad-lock would appease him. He glowered.

Matthew Offord, from Hendon, told her that same-sex marriage was a slippery slope to polygamy. 'Are you aware of the campaigns now taking place in Canada to legalise polygamy, since marriage was redefined there in 2005?' Maria was clinging to the quadruple lock as if her life depended on it.

Tory David Burrowes, normally so mild-mannered, attacked: 'Now that the State wishes to redefine marriage, will it redefine adultery and non-consummation?' Ms Miller burbled: 'Again, that is an important detail.' Adultery as a detail. For once, she didn't mention the quad-lock, though surely it could be used for chastity belts.

Another Tory, Andrew Selous, noted: 'This country will be passing a law that is directly contrary to what Jesus said about marriage in Mark chapter ten and Matthew chapter nineteen.'

Maria told him about the quadruple lock. Houdini, where are you? You must free Maria from this quad-lock obsession.

8 JANUARY 2013

Nick and Dave embark on DIY government

Dave explains how to seal the deal at the very top of government.

DAVID CAMERON AND Nick Clegg chose to 'celebrate' two and a half years of government yesterday with a joint press conference at No. 10 with matching wood lecterns with little retractable signs that carried the less than joyful words: 'Coalition Government: Mid-Term Review.'

Nick Robinson of the BBC, who plays a quasi-official role as the coalition marriage facilitator, asked: 'Some say your marriage is stronger than ever. Others say you are planning a divorce. How would you sum up the state of your union?' Dave and Nick looked uncomfortable. Dave made a little chin-wobbling smile/grimace at the word 'divorce'. Both looked like they wanted to skedaddle.

'I hate to spoil the party,' said Dave, 'but let me put it like this, "We are married, but not to each other"!' Nick was looking at him steadily. 'You know,' Dave barrelled on, 'this is a government, not a relationship. It's a government about delivering for people.' (Or not, as the case may be.) This would have been a good time to shut up but Dave couldn't stop. 'To me it's not a marriage. It is, if you like, it's a Ronseal deal, it does what it says on the tin.'

Nick's face had that expression that married couples will recognise as one of carefully constructed blankness. Dave had just compared their relationship – the most powerful, crucial relationship in the nation – to a tin of wood preserver. Surely this took winter gardening tasks, not to mention product placement, to an entirely new realm. After all, what Ronseal Shed and Fence Preserver actually says on the tin is: 'Colours, Waterproofs and Preserves Against Rot and Decay'. It says nothing about boundary changes and House of Lords reform.

Dave was warbling on about what it says on his and Nick's tin. When Dave stopped (just before moving on to wallpaper), Nick chirped: 'Ronseal deal. You could call it the unvarnished truth.'

The joke fell to earth (or, perhaps, the deck, as this is Ronseal) with a thud. We all groaned. Dave, though, looked straight at Nick, laughing, almost silently, his lips stretching out to the point where they disappeared entirely.

A little later the couple were asked about it again. Where, to paraphrase Kylie, had the love gone? Dave looked fed up now. Why couldn't we grasp that it wasn't about love? It was about woodworm! It was time to forget the real deal and embrace the Ronseal deal in the glorious new year that is DIY Britannia 2013.

23 JANUARY 2013

Moggday warning of dire events

Jacob Rees-Mogg, the Member for the Nineteenth Century,
adjusts his monocle and launches an ultimately doomed
attempt to delay Nick Clegg's Royal Succession Bill.

THE TALL AND ungainly form that is Jacob Rees-Mogg arose to emit something quite close to a cry of pain. 'The two front benches are pushing through an act of political correctness not gone mad but simply not thought through!' he insisted, his voice as reedy as a stately bassoon. 'This seems to me to be an INSULT to the nation, our sovereign and indeed to Parliament.'

Oh the despair! The Mogg, as he is known, gave a magnificent speech, arguing that the Bill to outlaw royal male primogeniture must be given much more time for debate. 'It is being rushed through. Why? Once you've got the two front benches in agreement you could rename the days of the week if you felt like it!' MPs looked alarmed. For Nick Clegg had proposed this Bill, and surely the man who thought we'd all embrace AV is not above the idea of renaming Tuesday (Cleggday? Nickday?). Actually, if I could rename yesterday it would be Moggday. This man may be forty-three but, in his heart, he lives in the 1800s. I wish he'd just be done with it and wear a stove-pipe hat, a watch fob and a monocle – or at least pince-nez.

The Mogg's main concern is the consequences of removing the ban on heirs to the throne marrying Catholics. 'I speak as a Catholic myself or, quite happily in the terminology of the Bill of Rights, as a Papist and a member of the Papist religion, which I find no shame in being called! I rather prefer it to the more politically correct phraseology of "person of the Roman Catholic religion", which is rather middle management speak,' he said. This brought 'hear, hears' from the Tory benches.

Mr Clegg said that the law on Catholics was from another age when they were banned from virtually everything, including owning a horse worth more than £5. Those worried about what religion any royal children would be brought up as were missing the point.

The Mogg did not agree. He wanted to discuss the ramifications of that but MPs had other more historical topics in mind. Sir Alan Beith jumped up from the Lib Dem benches. Mr Rees-Mogg had gone from being an eloquent proponent of 'things as they are' to wanting to remove the Act of Settlement, the Act of Union and the Glorious Revolution of 1688 (at this the Mogg looked thoughtful, as if he remembered it well). 'What has turned you from a man of conservative instincts to the radical firebrand in such a short time?' he demanded.

The Mogg said the answer was simple: this Bill. 'Once you start fiddling,' he said, 'you have to do it properly.'

At this, Labour's Chris Bryant, a former vicar, nodded thoughtfully. 'You are a true Tory,' he noted. 'Some of this legislation is Whig legislation and you are not happy about that.'

Ah yes, those dastardly Whigs. I wonder what they would have made of the events of Moggday.

24 JANUARY 2013

Hail the all-conquering Dave!

The planning for the Prime Minister's speech on Europe had a 'spin-the-bottle' feel to it but, then, something amazing happened.

DAVID CAMERON'S GREAT Euro Address was, if not his finest hour, then certainly his finest forty minutes as Prime Minister. It helped that expectations were low. The speech had been months in the making. As he explained last month: 'This is the tantric approach to policy making. It will be even better when it does, eventually, come.'

No one believed him, of course. Even the scheduling had a 'spin-the-bottle' feel to it: it was Tuesday, no Thursday, then Friday in Amsterdam and then amid feelings of Dave-jà vu, it was fixed for Wednesday in the City at the break of dawn. You think I exaggerate. Sunrise in London was 7.52 a.m. yesterday, just eight minutes before Dave. This was a continental breakfast without the Continent (though, somehow, I noticed, those mini-croissants got through the Europhobe cordon sanitaire).

The speech was in the Bloomberg basement, in what may have been an underground car park before it was turned into a 'venue'. Low ceilings, round walls and aquarium lighting made it feel as if we were all underwater. Behind Dave was a 'Britain and Europe' sign: I couldn't help but notice that on TV the final 'e' in Europe kept disappearing into his right ear.

But, amazingly, it was, to use a favourite Dave word, a 'proper' speech that was 'properly' (pronounced by Dave 'proply') done. It laid out why the EU had to change and what he wants for the New Settlement (capital letters essential). The country will be able to vote on this in an in/out referendum. The speech's only indulgence was to paint Dave as a heretical hero. 'In its long history, Europe has experience of heretics who turned out to have a point.' Guess who? If Dave is going to be a heretic, he needs to get a good robe and mess up that concreted quiff that serves as his hairdo.

Back in the Commons, for PMQs, his backbenchers treated him as a con-quering hero too. It was so adoring that I thought we were going to have to send out a sickbag alert. This, for instance, was Crispin Blunt: 'Pitt the Younger said that "Europe is not to be saved by any single man".' But, Mr Blunt said, rather bluntly I thought, what did Pitt know? He hadn't heard Dave's speech. Dave was Europe's single saviour.

Dave the Saviour ducked his head. The likes of Bill Cash and Gerald Howarth lavished even more praise on him. It must be said that, if I were Dave, this would scare me quite a lot.

30 JANUARY 2013

Boundaries are broken for man who wasn't there

The Tories were furious when, as payback for wrecking
Lords reform, the Lib Dems refused to allow
constituency boundary changes.

T HERE WAS A Nick Clegg-shaped hole on the front bench for the debate on boundary changes, and Tory MPs weren't happy about it.

'Do you have the powers, Mr Speaker, to call on the Deputy Prime Minister to come to this House?' demanded Tory backbencher Micky Fab (aka Michael Fabricant), his straw-coloured tresses looking even more distressed than usual at Mr Clegg's absence.

'No I don't!' insisted Mr Speaker, who was having a fine old time in his huge Alice in Wonderland chair. Actually, make that Malice in Wonderland, for what I saw yesterday was the parliamentary equivalent of extreme sport. Forget bungee jumping, this was bungee debating.

'Do the Lib Dems not do principle on the twenty-ninth of the month or is it just on Tuesdays?' harped Micky Fab to Tory delight.

So this is what divorce looks like. I can report that there is no fury like that of a political party scorned. The Lib Dem backbenchers sat there, faces of concrete, sulking for Britain. The Tories had betrayed them over Lords reform and now they were going to see what that felt like. This was not so much tit for tat as spit for spat.

The Tories were on their high horses, waving the sword of truth, always worrying, insisting they were the ones with principles here. On the sidelines, Labour cheered the hatefest with schadenfreude gusto.

There is some irony in the fact that the Lib Dem position was put forth by the closest thing they have to a lord, the ex-lord John Thurso or, to give him his full name, John Archibald Sinclair, 3rd Viscount Thurso. He insisted that to vote to postpone these changes was the only fair thing to do. Tory Sir Peter Bottomley disagreed, insisting it was unfair to continue with such unequal constituencies. 'What do you think Jo Grimond would have said if he'd watched what is happening now?' he demanded.

Viscount Thurso suddenly looked very lordly indeed.

I had the great privilege of listening to Jo Grimond on many occasions. He met his wife in my grandparents' house and proposed to her. Laura was, indeed, godmother to my sister. I feel certain that if he was in the circumstance we are in, he would support his Liberal colleagues. One has some small advantages in life!

One does indeed.

Some Tories insisted on referring to Mr Thurso as their 'noble friend'. This brought more uproar. 'Are there any noble members here or are we all common?' demanded Labour's Kevin Brennan. The Speaker tried to bring calm, saying: 'All members of this chamber are equal.'

Could it get more absurd? As this is politics, the answer is yes. First the Tories demanded to know what the Chartists would make of it all and then Penny Mordaunt recruited Edmund Burke to her cause, quoting him about MPs needing to use their judgement.

'We cannot be on auto-pilot in this place,' she insisted. 'We must do what we believe is right.' That is why she had voted against the 'constitutional car crash' that was Lords reform. But the Lib Dem stand on boundary changes was pure self-interest. 'Edmund Burke did not say that we owe our constituents our spite, pettiness and self-interest!' Yikes! I looked over at Viscount Thurso to see if Burke had told him something different. 'The Liberals have exchanged their legendary sandals for flip-flops!' cried Ms Mordaunt, though I am pretty sure that Edmund Burke didn't wear flip-flops at all.

6 FEBRUARY 2013

Angry and moving but not a bit gay debate

At one point the historic debate on gay marriage was sidetracked into wondering whether it would mean that siblings could marry.

T HE GAY MARRIAGE debate was anything but gay. Indeed, out of the dozens who spoke, only one MP came even close to something approaching joy. Otherwise the debate was fraught, intense, angry, accusatory, occasionally eloquent and often moving. And that's only the Tories. Here, then, were the stand-out moments of the day:

The gayest MP: Step forward Yvette Cooper, the normally rather stern Labour leader-in-waiting who seemed high on confetti. 'Call us hopeless romantics!' she cried. 'We all love the idea of a wedding, we all support the idea of a strong marriage and, clearly, we all like a good party!' She beamed. Everyone looked puzzled. Party animals they aren't.

God's vote: Tony Baldry, who is a Church Commissioner and therefore God's representative in the chamber, explained that he was voting against because even the Almighty feared the power of the European courts. (I paraphrase.)

Where's Dave? Who knows? Maria Miller, the Culture Secretary and dogged if nothing else, was joined on the front bench by a menagerie of ministers, none of whom could be described as big beasts. Dave has a funny way of leading from the front.

Orwellian moment: Roger Gale said that it was impossible to redefine marriage. 'It is Alice in Wonderland territory, Orwellian almost,' he insisted, announcing, bizarrely, that a civil union Bill could be created to apply to brothers and sisters. Forget Alice, this was Roger in Wanderland.

What would Elton say? Nick Herbert, the former police minister, who is gay, made a rare joke, saying that the marriages of millions of straight people would not be threatened by this. 'What will they say? "Darling, our marriage is over: Sir Elton John has just got engaged to David Furnish"?' (Did I see Yvette throwing confetti at this?)

I'm a celebrity... Nadine Dorries, well and truly back from the jungle, was opposed because, as gay couples would not have to vow to be faithful, they could not use adultery as grounds for divorce. 'If I was a gay couple,' she said at one point, which seemed unlikely.

Understatement of the day: The Tory blonde bombshell Margot James said that the gay marriage row showed that the modernisation of the Tory Party 'was not yet complete'. I felt that you didn't need to be Sherlock to have worked that out.

Favourite moment: Stephen Timms, Labour MP for East Ham, said that marriage was really about having children. At this Lyn Brown, the Labour MP for West Ham, arose: 'You were at my wedding. I was not young,' she noted. 'Are you telling me that my marriage is less valid?' She glared at him. He quailed.

The best speech: The winner, by some way, was the Tory Mike Freer, vibrating with intensity as he explained why, for him, this was deeply personal.

> I am a member of this Parliament. I sit alongside you in committees, in the bars and in the tea rooms. I queue alongside you in the division lobbies. But when it comes to marriage, why are you asking me to stand apart and to join a separate queue? I ask you: if I am equal in this House, give me every opportunity to be equal.

Lonely hearts moment: Guy Opperman, a Tory, says that the Commons is on 'a journey'. And so it seems, is he. 'I am not married. I have yet to find the woman who would want to marry someone such as me – but she is out there, Mr Speaker, I promise you.' Who needs internet dating when you can just advertise via Hansard? Go Guy, aged forty-seven, barrister, GSOH and looking for love.

12 FEBRUARY 2013

Where's the beef? Not in the lasagne...

The Environment Secretary knew exactly who to blame when
supermarkets discovered horsemeat in their lasagne.

OWEN PATERSON, ENVIRONMENT Secretary, is a bit of a nay-sayer. Or, as the subject yesterday was horsemeat, make that a neigh-sayer.

'You've got a nerve!' he shouted in his stentorian way at Labour. 'You wouldn't think that this is their system that we've inherited!' Well, he has a nerve, too. Nothing was his fault. The food safety system was invented by Labour. Food regulation was the responsibility of Europe. The testing was done in Ireland. The abattoirs were in Romania. And the lasagne, well, I think we all know that lasagne is very much (whisper it) Italian.

'You completely miss the point,' he shouted at Labour's Mary Creagh, who had dared to intimate that he might have been a bit slow off the mark. 'The retailers are responsible for the quality and content of their food! That is laid down in European law!'

Where, Labour kept asking, was the beef? Clearly, it was not in the lasagne. 'Some beef products haven't even come into contact with a cow, except maybe sharing a field with one!' foamed Andrew Gwynne.

Ben Bradshaw cut through the neighing. 'You say there is no evidence of criminal activity in this country but can I remind you that inaccurate labelling is illegal? Why has it taken you three weeks to summon the retailers?' Mr Paterson was reduced to a tiny whinny: 'You are right that inaccurate labelling is an offence, but we have to establish what is in these materials and who is responsible for the label. In the Findus case, the material has been withdrawn!' The material? Is this is a new way to talk about food? Will we soon be asking each other: what material is on the menu?

Behind him, Tory MPs were displaying herd tendencies. 'Can I congratulate you on your decisive action,' insisted Cheryl Gillan. There was, for me, a most satisfying moment when an MP named Angie Bray did, actually, bray her approval.

Tory MPs urged us all to eat British beef (they didn't mention lasagne). One spoke of 'contaminated' food. Mr Paterson took them to task: 'I didn't use the word "contaminated". This was "adulterated".'

So, if I've got this right, Mr Paterson thinks food is 'material' and, if it is something else entirely than it should be, it's 'adulterated material'. Where, indeed, WAS the beef?

But now one brave Tory was not afraid to call a horse a horse. Jacob Rees-Mogg, doffing his top hat and squinting through his monocle, said: 'My constituents, because of European failures, are getting DISGUSTING food. Will you consider emergency legislation to allow us to stop importing disgusting food?' Mr Paterson wondered what the legal definition of disgusting might be. Well, here's a tip: adulterated material might be a good start.

5 MARCH 2013

Angels of a sort dance for all to see

The lawyers in the House were quite close to heaven as they debated why they were debating the secret courts amendments.

I'D LOVE TO tell you what the debate on secret courts in the Commons was about, but the presence of so many lawyers in one place made it all rather murky. 'Some say that we are angels dancing on the head of a pin!' cried Sadiq Khan, for Labour, during a rare foray into normal language. 'I disagree!'

Well, as Mandy Rice-Davies might say, he would, wouldn't he?

First of all, Mr Khan probably doesn't like the idea of himself in little pink fairy wings, though, actually, I think they would add to his gravitas. Secondly, he's a human rights solicitor: it's in his nature to disagree.

Mr Khan is not opposed, just wary, and so he had arrived clutching yet more amendments to amend the other amended amendments to this Bill. I quickly gathered that it was vital that none of Mr Khan's argument about secret courts (which the lawyers call CMP or Closed Material Procedures) be easily understood.

At one point he tried to speak to us plebs about how this could help judges. 'It's for Parliament to add to their toolkit the option of a CMP after exhausting all the other things in their toolkit!' he announced. So now we had angels dancing on the head of a pin, carrying toolkits.

Up popped Ken Clarke. 'I do think an ordinary intelligent person from the outside world having listened to this debate would be quite baffled. It has seemed to me for some time that we are in complete agreement!'

Lawyers looked at him in horror. How dare he say such a thing! What was the point of having wings if they were going to stop amending amendments and just agree?

'I think that I'm in agreement with the Labour Party and the Liberal Democrats and, I hope, my own...' said Mr Clarke, doubt suddenly creeping in to his voice. Caroline Lucas, the Green MP, insisted that she was not in agreement.

'I respect your sincerity,' said Mr Clarke. 'You are a representative of those who are just against the whole policy. I have met such people outside. I mean, to use a sort of frippery, some of my best friends are human rights lawyers!'

Mr Khan shouted: 'NAME THEM!'

I loved that reference to 'outside', as if it were another universe entirely. There was an embarrassing moment when Andrew Tyrie, a non-lawyer, wanted to know why it was that the lawyers were so opposed to this Bill.

Mr Clarke explained that it was in their nature. 'I am left in wonder of admiration at their ingenuity at producing an endless procession of amendments, so that every time their principles are adopted, a fresh set of amendments are produced introducing new concepts.'

These lawyers were, he said, 'grasping at straws'. My, I thought, what busy angels they are: tool-kitted, straw-grasping, dancing like mad. No wonder it's secret.

20 MARCH 2013

I, a humble flea, jump for my life

*The week before, the Prime Minister had withdrawn from
the post-Leveson, cross-party talks and backing a draft
royal charter for the press. The day after it was passed by the
Commons, it became clear who might be the first victims.*

YOU LEARN SOMETHING every day. Yesterday, for instance, there
I was, minding my own business, watching Max Mosley, of orgy
fame, as I have so many times before, wax lyrical on press control.
Mr Mosley was appearing with two members of the campaign group Hacked
Off before the Culture, Media and Sport Select Committee.

Then, suddenly, Labour's Jim Sheridan burst into life. 'What concerns
me are the parasitical elements within the press who abuse their position in
here' – by which he means Parliament – 'in terms of hiding behind their pen
and calling people names.'

Yikes. My fellow sketch-writers and I looked at each other from behind
our pens. Was he talking about us? 'That's the so-called brave people,' Mr
Sheridan continued, his Glaswegian accent as thick as porridge. 'I don't understand why they are allowed to come into this place and behave in the way
that they do.'

I felt as big as, well, a flea (though one with a pen). I think we know
where I'd be if Mr Sheridan, who later confirmed that he was referring to the
sketch-writers, ruled the world, though, I guess, post-Leveson, he just might.

And there I was thinking this was about freedom of the press. Now I
know it's about freedom of the parasites. And it's only day one, post-statute.

So Max was looking extremely chipper (a flea writes). This must be the
fourth time that I have invaded his privacy by sketching him. Usually he gives
us the gory details of his S&M parties but this time he was more concerned
about victims of the press.

Philip Davies, Tory Rottweiler, was attacking Hacked Off and Mr Mosley for claiming to represent the Dowlers and the McCanns when, in reality, they were actually backing the Hugh Grants of the world – i.e. famous people who dislike newspapers.

'When there are breaches of the law – which there have been – some of us can attack,' Mr Mosley said in his quiet, almost velvety voice. 'Most of us can't because we haven't got the money. Your sympathies are obviously clearly with the sort of people who wrote stories about the Dowlers, the McCanns and so on. Well, sorry, we don't agree!'

Mr Davies: 'I thought you were a lawyer.'

Mr Mosley, surprised: 'I am.'

Mr Davies: 'Well, you know that what happened to the McCanns was illegal. What happened in terms of phone hacking is illegal. Don't please start pretending we need laws to make something illegal that is illegal.' Mr Davies demanded the witnesses 'be straight' about whom they were representing. 'Don't accuse us of not being straight!' Max fumed. 'You have absolutely no right to do that. In my case everything that could have happened to me has happened. My interest is to make sure it doesn't happen to other people.'

Angie Bray, a well-named Tory, asked him who needed representing in the fight against the press.

'The public,' Mr Mosley said. And that's you, is it? 'The fact is that somebody has to voice…' Mr Mosley began, adding that 75 per cent of the public want Leveson implemented. 'Is that wrong? Is it wrong to try and get politicians to do what the vast majority of the public want?' I may just be a flea but I am not sure that the vast majority of the public see Mr Mosley as one of them. Just saying.

28 MARCH 2013

Thunderbrother gets tired of being a puppet

David Miliband decided it was his turn to head off to save the world.

FIVE. FOUR. THREE. Two. One. Thunderbrothers are Go! To Primrose Hill, then, to watch David 'Brains' Thunderbrother mount an international rescue mission to save his reputation. It may look like a Georgian terrace in one of the most desirable parts of London but, inside, behind that door, interrogators were putting on the pressure as to why he was leaving his Thunderbrother.

'We are taking a job,' said David Thunderbrother, breaking into a bit of royal speak. 'We are not emigrating.'

No one believed him. David knew he had to be more convincing. He put on his red tie and went out to be photographed. He didn't take his trademark banana. Now that he was moving to New York, he was going to carry around big apples instead.

A series of Lady Penelopes ushered in the interrogators named Adam, Nick, Tom etc. The sketch-writers were banned. After all, this was a serious international rescue mission and not funny in the least. Brains sat in front of a piano and tried to look relaxed and not like a puppet in a retro TV series.

So, Nick (or maybe Adam) asked: 'Why are you leaving?' David explained that, as a Thunderbrother, it was important to make a difference. 'I hope that you feel that I came into politics to try and make a difference and now I'm leaving politics to try and make a difference in a different way.'

That raised eyebrows (puppets have eyebrows too).

So why was he leaving again? 'I'm British. I love Britain. I'm committed to Britain. I'm passionate about the Labour Party. But I've had to make a choice,' explained David.

Ah, choice. Very New Labour. Now that he was leaving, was New Labour dead? 'That is very flattering,' said Brains, suppressing a grin. So why was he leaving again? He didn't like being seen as a distraction while his brother Ed was leader. 'I didn't want the soap opera to take over,' he explained. Though, as this was sci-fi, not to mention Primrose Hill, which is nowhere near *EastEnders*, he really needn't worry.

Brains now asked himself a question. 'Has it been hard for me to accept that I can best help the Labour Party by giving not just the space between the front bench and the back bench to Ed but the space between the front bench and 3,000 miles away?' he mused, before answering himself: 'Yes, that's hard for me, but I think it's right…' So why was he leaving again? 'It's very, very unique to have two brothers fighting a leadership election. We are two brothers who fought a leadership election, but we don't fight each other.'

No one believed him. David said he'd told his Thunderbrother all about his new job. Had Ed tried to make him stay, showering him with job offers? David said Ed had been 'very respectful'. So that's a no, then.

David explained what it meant to be a Thunderbrother. 'We were brothers before the leadership, we'll be brothers after the leadership election, we are brothers now.'

Hmmmm. What was he talking about? 'Brothers are for life,' he announced. To which you can only say: F.A.B.

11 APRIL 2013

Personal, poignant and political with a hand-bagging thrown in

MPs gathered (or stayed away) for the bouquets and brickbats session to remember Baroness Thatcher, who died on 8 April at the age of eighty-seven.

DAVID CAMERON GAVE an almost perfect speech of remembrance yesterday, saying that Lady Thatcher was a politician who made the political weather. And in this country the weather could never be anything but unpredictable. 'They say that cometh the hour, cometh the man. Well, in 1979 came the hour, and came the lady. She made the political weather. She made history. And let this be her epitaph: she made our country great again.'

The Tory benches were more than full, spilling into the two usually reserved for the Lib Dems who were, yesterday, a bit thin on the ground.

The Labour side was about half full. The bench usually reserved for the awkward squad, including the class warrior Dennis Skinner, was empty. That, in itself, was a statement: sometimes you don't have to say a thing to shout your feelings.

Ed Miliband struck a measured and respectful tone, quoting Mrs T from an early 1965 speech to the Townswomen's Guilds: 'In politics if you want anything said, ask a man. If you want anything done, ask a woman.' The Commons, still male-dominated but with many of the new Tory women very much inspired by her, laughed. Soon Conor Burns, the man who spent many a Sunday evening with Mrs Thatcher in her later years, gave the most personal tribute of the day to his 'mentor and protectress'.

From the balcony, Sarah Brown looked down, representing Gordon, apparently, who wasn't in the chamber. Just down from her was Jonathan Aitken, the disgraced former Cabinet minister who found salvation in prison. The Strangers' Gallery, where the public watches from behind glass, was full to start with but, by the time the first female MP was called to speak, almost two hours into the debate, was half empty.

Over in the Lords, the debate was windier, with the notable exception of Lord Tebbit, aka the Chingford Skinhead, always pointed and now stiletto sharp. 'My regrets?' he asked, noting that because of commitments made to his wife, injured in the Brighton bombing, he had felt unable to return to government with Mrs T. 'I left her, I fear, at the mercy of her friends. That I do regret.'

In a scene Shakespeare would have appreciated, the stooped white-haired Lord Howe of Aberavon, whose resignation triggered her downfall, watched from a nearby bench.

Back in the Commons, Labour MPs began, slowly, to talk about the darker side of Thatcherism. Much to my amazement, it was Glenda Jackson, who may have won two Oscars but usually bores for Britain in the Commons, who let rip, castigating the 'heinous social, economic and spiritual damage wreaked upon this country'. Glenda, who seemed to be channelling Elizabeth I, whom she has played, derided her idea of womanliness: 'The first prime minister of female gender, OK. But a woman? Not on my terms.'

The Tories hated it but it was a real hand-bagging which, again, is a tribute, though of another kind.

19 APRIL 2013

For war tales with a soothing touch, send for the Ironing Lady

There was only one way to get back to 'normal' after Lady Thatcher's funeral...

IT WAS THE morning after and in the Commons we did not have so much the Iron Lady as the Ironing Lady. I refer to Maria Miller, the Culture Secretary, a woman whose aim is to make everything flat, smooth, dull. Her other nickname is Beige, but I am worried that this may be too interesting.

What, she was asked, about the shambles of superfast broadband in rural areas? Andrew Selous, a Tory whose name Mr Speaker always warbles mellifluously, as in sa-looooo, was worried about villages in his constituency. 'I am pleased to tell you that the programme in Bedfordshire is green-rated,' said Mrs Beige. Green-rated? What can it mean? Is this the digital equivalent of shovel-ready?

What, she was now asked, was she doing to increase tourism? 'The campaign launched by a partnership between the GREAT campaign and VisitBritain will deliver 4.6 million inbound visitors.'

Inbound visitors? I do hope they are green-rated. Kerry McCarthy, the Labour MP who is as close as we'll ever get to punk in the chamber, asked about Britain's musical heritage. 'Liverpool is the most obvious example because of the Beatles, but we should also remember Manchester during the heyday of Madchester and the Hacienda,' she noted.

I am not sure Maria knows about Madchester. A tiny furrow appeared in her forehead until she frantically ironed it away. 'Many of our cultural institutions are going abroad to present a positive image of this country's cultural and arts sector,' said Mrs Beige. What was she on about? Did she think Madchester was a cultural institution that was on its way to Spain?

She went on: 'But it is campaigns such as the GREAT campaign that can pinpoint cultural assets which reside not only in the South East and around our capital city but throughout the United Kingdom.' She had completely lost me now. I do hope that no inbound visitors encountered that sentence. If she has an ability, it is to turn every topic, no matter how interesting, into mush.

The subject of the centenary of the First World War came up. Beige said that the government would 'deliver a four-year programme' to mark it. There was £50 million for a 'framework'. MPs made a series of rather gentle points until Jonathan Edwards, of Plaid Cymru, stood up. 'The First World War was caused by a complete foreign policy malfunction based on the imperial ambitions of the elites of the time!' he announced. 'It resulted in the deaths of 30 million soldiers and 7 million civilians. Surely it would be more appropriate to commemorate the end of the war, rather than to replicate in 2014 a jamboree reminiscent of the jingoistic nonsense used to drum up support for the slaughter.'

Passion alert! Maria wasn't having any of that. 'The tone of your intervention is not quite what I would like to hear,' she said, her mouth a disapproving moue. 'We should ensure that we mark the entirety of the First World War from its beginning to its end, as it had a considerable impact on every community.'

A considerable impact. The Ironing Lady had done it again. Against all odds, she had made the First World War sound like a fender bender.

The Fourth Year

Bingo, Badgers and More Europe

MAY 2013 — MAY 2014

I T WAS A year where it was impossible to avoid Europe. Nigel Farage and UKIP claimed it was now a post-fruitcake party and set about trying to win the 2014 European elections. Ed Miliband made a shocking pledge on reducing electricity bills and the Tories relaunched themselves as the workers' party with a Budget aimed at bingo and beer. This was all against a backdrop of small events such as the badgers moving the goalposts, Syria and the worst floods since Noah.

· · ·

6 MAY 2013

Blue Baron seizes yet another Euro moment

The year began with the Tories banging on about Europe and, specifically, why the Queen's Speech didn't mention a referendum.

COMETH THE HOUR, cometh the Baron. I speak of the eponymous John, Baron of the Eurosceptics, and leader of yesterday's Great EU Referendum rebellion.

'Seize the moment,' he cried, rejecting saying carpe diem as too close to Rome and, therefore, the EU.

I looked at the Baron. He is fifty-three and was, I suspect, born fifty-three. For a Tory politician, he looks quite normal. Grey, serious, principled; he is righteousness itself. If he rode a horse, and I don't think he's ruled it out, it would be a black stallion and he would be carrying the flag of truth (no golden stars).

'Seize the moment!' he again told his own front bench. Actually it was hard to seize anything for there is no aspect of the EU referendum debate that is real yet. The referendum itself won't materialise until 2017, if then. And yesterday's debate was about something that did not exist in the Queen's Speech: i.e. any mention of the referendum. The rebels had no chance of winning the fight to put down an amendment and, to keep with the 'touch the void' theme, the Prime Minister was not on the front bench but in New York.

Instead, George Osborne was there, listening to the Baron's plea. I must report that George did not seize the moment. Seize the pen, possibly, but not the moment. He did allow a tiny grimace to scud over his face like a small cloud. Was it an emotion or merely indigestion? We will never know.

The Baron urged him to join the rebellion. 'You could claim, quite rightly,' he told George, 'that the situation is not of your making. Blame me! Blame us as a group!' The Baron explained his cunning plan: with George (and Dave, if he existed) on side, the amendment would, somehow, pass. With such a mandate, the Liberals, as he called them, could not deny time for paving legislation.

'Let the media knock on their door and ask questions!' he cried.

I quite like the idea of knocking on the Liberal door.

'Knock knock,' we'd say.

'Who's there?' Nick Clegg would answer.

'Questions on the EU.'

'Ask me in 2017!'

Indeed, earlier yesterday, at PMQs, Harriet Harman did, essentially, that. 'If the Prime Minister were here today,' asked Harriet, which is quite a big 'if' these days, 'would he be voting for the government or against the government, or would he be showing true leadership and abstaining?' Mr Clegg, effectively, told her to come back in 2017.

The main thing we learnt yesterday was how seriously the Baron and his fellow believers are taking all this. 'This matter is more important than party politics!' he cried. Around him, scattered on the benches like confetti, Euro-rebel followers nodded. They were not wrecking their party, they were saving it. The Baron explained this was a 'golden opportunity' to give the electorate a say on the EU. 'We should be bold of heart, seize the moment and do what is right by the electorate and the country.' They lost, but the Baron will live to fight another day.

17 MAY 2013

Eurovision comes to Westminster

I observe the strange and obscure ceremony that chooses who will get to sponsor a Private Member's Bill, thrust into the spotlight this year because of Europe.

ELCOME TO EUROVISION, Westminster-style. I speak of the arcane ritual known as the Private Member's Bill ballot yesterday. For starters, it is not a ballot at all. It's more a raffle, with a bit of bingo thrown in and also darts, as in when they bellow 'One Hundred and Eighty!'

Our Master of Ceremonies was Lindsay Hoyle, the Deputy Speaker whose sense of fun and Lancashire accent are proving a huge hit these days. He had a glamorous assistant, of course. Tall, thin, dressed as a penguin with a white bow-tie, his real name was David Natzler and he was Clerk of Legislation but, of course, we started to call him Debbie.

'ORDER ORDER!' shouted Mr Hoyle. Next to him Debbie opened a battered black dispatch box which looked like something from a boot fair except it had EIIR on it. Inside was a nest of bits of paper, just the right size to be Chinese takeaway fortunes except, instead, they all had numbers.

The Eurovision set was extremely grand, as befits a ceremony of such constitutional importance to our nation. Committee Room 10 overlooks the Thames with red wallpaper of such deep flock that it could be described as padded. At one end was a huge painting entitled Alfred Inciting the Saxons to Prevent the Landing of the Danes. Even the art was Eurosceptic.

The 'audience' was made up mostly of Tory MPs desperate to have their number picked so they could introduce an EU Referendum Bill. But the snag was that it wasn't good enough to just picked. There would be twenty numbers picked, with the last plucked out first, but only the top few had a hope in hell (technical term) of securing a debate.

Lindsay boomed: 'Number twenty!' Debbie, after rummaging, almost tremulous, trilled: '214!' Lindsay consulted the oracle that was his cross-numbered list of MPs. 'Dr Matthew Offord!' he boomed. We all looked blank. Obscure doesn't even begin to cover it.

The next number picked was '212'. Lindsay did not like that. 'I think we better shake 'em up,' he ordered. Debbie fluffed the bits of paper a bit.

The countdown continued with Lindsay getting more and more enthusiastic. 'Sir Malcolm Bruuuuuuce!' he cried when the Lib Dem nabbed a slot. When he got number thirteen, he noted: 'Unlucky for some!' Through it all, the Euro-sceptics examined their lists with the urgency and focus of people conducting brain surgery. You have to admire the sheer tenacity of the Euro-obsessive.

'The excitement and tension is growing!' boomed Lindsay, as we approached the great moment. Number three was Tory Jonathan Lord, a Euro-rebel, and number two was a Labour MP.

'Shake 'em up!' cried Lindsay as the big moment arrived. 'The winner of the day is…' 'One hundred and ninety-nine,' announced Debbie.

'Oooohhhhh!' cried the audience. Lindsay flipped through his list. 'James Wharton!' We looked at each other. Who? But within minutes, we were being flooded with information about Mr Wharton. He was the young (aged twenty-nine) Tory from Stockton and a Eurosceptic. His majority was tiny (332) and he had made the news for being linked with a company that sells stone statues of giant penises.

Sorry, but it's true. It may not be in the best taste but, then, this IS Eurovision.

5 JUNE 2013

Nick passes the hot potato to Little Chloe

The Deputy Prime Minister remembers, just, that he is in charge of the register for lobbyists.

NICK CLEGG IS so brave that, at first yesterday, he allowed Chloe Smith to handle the hot potato that is the lobbying register. 'The government have repeatedly made very clear their commitment to introducing a statutory register of lobbyists,' warbled Chloe, aged thirty-one, whose greatest fear, never realised to date, is that she might say something interesting.

Ah yes, I think we all know how strong that commitment has been. Only two weeks ago, in his great Why I Still Love the Coalition press conference, Mr Clegg told us that the lobby register was going nowhere fast. But suddenly, what with the nasty media entrapping everyone, the register is back on the agenda.

Sometimes, in politics, the emperor has no clothes and sometimes the clothes have no emperor. When it comes to Mr Clegg and the lobbying register, both are true. Nick, who promised in 2010 to launch the biggest programme of constitutional reform since 1832, has so far managed to consult like mad on the lobbying register and then park it – with Chloe.

Yesterday, at his departmental questions, Mr Clegg was asked about the House of Lords, another reform gone wrong. He said some 'housekeeping' in the Lords was needed. Man your dusters! These 'minor technical housekeeping changes' include 'kicking out crooks'. So, yes, for Westminster, that is very minor indeed.

Just as the DPM was explaining why nothing is his fault, Bernard Jenkin, the Tory Europhobe, demanded: 'Why did you answer this question [on Lords] and not the one about lobbying, which has been in your in-tray for three years?' Nick took his pinny off and looked sad. 'In the spirit of coalition harmony, of course,' he said, employing his special ironic face (which also looks sad, as you ask).

He was asked about lobbying and, this time, he answered. Why had it taken so long? 'We are working flat-out to cross the 't's and dot the 'i's on this package,' said Nick. Can I note that there is one i and one t in the word lobbyist – how long can it take?

But now, Andrew Turner, the Tory MP for the Isle of Wight, who always appears as if he is just visiting from Mars, stood up. 'What is a lobbyist?' he asked. 'WRAP – Wight Residents against Asphalt Plant – is a group of constituents who are against an asphalt plant on the River Medina. Are they lobbyists?' Nick assured Mr Turner that asphalt haters were not to be the focus of his attention. 'I stress again that we should not regard the word "lobbyist" as a bad term,' said Nick. Honestly. This really could take some time.

12 JUNE 2013

O tell me the truth about love...

*Michael Gove is overcome with emotion as he explains
yet another attempt to revise GCSEs.*

YESTERDAY, IN THE Commons, as he was explaining his latest attempt to revise GCSEs, the Education Secretary had a Cupid moment. Labour's maverick Diane Abbott was on her feet. I was sad to see that she was not wearing her leopard maxi dress, my favourite. When Diane wants to be – and it's not that often – she can be eloquent. Yesterday, she seemed inspired by Mr Gove's attempt to boost core subjects, such as English and maths.

Some people claimed, she noted, that obtaining rigorous qualifications in core academic subjects was not in the interest of working-class and black and minority ethnic children. 'On. The. Contrary,' said Ms Abbott, rocking back and forth. 'Precisely if someone is the first in their family to stay on past school leaving age, precisely if someone's family does not have social capital and precisely if someone does not have parents who can put in a word for them in a difficult job market, you need the assurance of rigorous qualifications!'

Diane sat down and stared at Mr Gove. For once, he seemed quite lost for words. Then, suddenly, he blurted out: 'I am in love!'

Diane, horrified, flapped her hands in front of her face as if warding off an attack of bats.

Mr Gove, who is nothing if not persistent, as his four attempts to revise GCSEs show, looked moon-faced. 'I mean, you are absolutely right,' he chortled, his voice going all squeaky on the word 'right'. I looked over. Diane was still warding off the imaginary plague. 'And if I had been a member of the Labour Party, I would have voted for her to be leader!'

Oh my goodness. Tell me the truth about love? For a politician, I'm not sure it gets deeper than backing their leadership bid.

Mr Speaker looked over. 'I hope you can recover from that,' he said drily. I'm not sure she did. She left halfway through.

But what was this? Chris Bryant arose to denounce Mr Gove's assertion that he had a Hegelian approach to policy making: 'Thesis, anti-thesis and, then, synthesis.' (Most of us just call that messing things up but, for Mr Gove, it's Hegelian.) Mr Bryant now let rip: 'But what I really do not understand is why you think that learning vast quantities of "The Wreck of the Hesperus" or "The boy stood on the burning deck" or *If* will make young people better equipped for the work environment.'

Mr Gove insisted that that was not the goal. It was important that all children got a chance to appreciate beauty – in thought and in the written word. He added: 'I know that you appreciate beauty in many spheres of human endeavour…'

Mr Bryant muttered: 'Truth is beauty, beauty truth!'

Mr Gove looked thrilled. 'You are quoting Keats now!' Then he added that he, too, liked poetry. 'I was delighted when John Cooper Clarke, one of my favourite poets, said that our approach to the teaching of poetry was absolutely right only last week!'

Fact: John Cooper Clarke, the 'punk poet', whose hair makes him look as if he's been electrocuted, wrote a poem called 'T***'. Perhaps now he will write another one about twits.

19 JUNE 2013

Breezy Dave gets his summit down to a 'T'

*It was the G8 summit at which, we learnt afterwards,
President Obama had called George Osborne 'Jeffrey',
later admitting that he got him mixed up with R&B singer
Jeffrey Osborne. But what else, actually, did we learn?*

THE G8 ENDED with Dave on the banks of Lough Erne, a breeze ruffling his hair. Well, OK, so the wind was doing a little more than ruffling. But, still, unlike Monday's press conference that was in a tent with a fake backdrop, it was real and raw. This was cinema verité.

'I know that some people wonder whether these summits really achieve anything,' said Dave.

He then gave us a list that, indeed, did make me wonder. It's all to do with what Dave calls 'The Three Ts' – i.e. tax, trade and transparency. It was, to use another T, a bit technical.

It seemed to me that Dave was glossing over what the summit had actually accomplished. Here, then, is my list:

No ties: They used up so many other Ts that there was no T left at Lough Erne for ties. Were they banned? Held hostage? In quarantine at the airport? Even in the 'family photo' – and truly these leaders make the Addams Family look entirely normal – no one had on a tie. And yesterday, once again, as Dave stood before Lough Erne, hair ruffling, there was no tie.

Wild swimming: At 6 a.m., Dave went swimming in Lough Erne. It was very Putin-esque. Indeed, at Dave's press conference, I wouldn't have been surprised to have seen Vlad the Swimmer striking out behind him. Dave said jumping into a freezing-cold lake was a great way to start a day of tough talking and he revealed the 'guilty secret' that he loved a dip in a Cumbrian lake. Can this really be true? I have seen the water feature in No. 10's back garden: it's not exactly wild.

The spouse-less summit: Sam Cam, who probably was the one who banned the ties, wasn't there. None of the wives or, indeed Herr Merkel's husband, made the trip, except of course First Lady Michelle and the two First Daughters. But yesterday they decided to hang out in a pub with Bono. 'We talked about everything and nothing,' said the rock star. As you do.

Launched Northern Irish cuisine: The first evening Dave told the advisers to get lost and took the tieless ten (the G8 plus the two Euro-trash leaders) for an 'intimate' dinner that featured a 'traditional' Irish bar. They ate Kilkeel crab, roast fillet and braised shin of Kettyle beef, Antrim new potatoes and crumble with Bushmills whiskey custard. Sadly, I could find no report on Guinness consumption.

How to drop a bomb: Dave waited until after the summit and his press conference on the bank, hair ruffling, to tweet this: 'Now #G8UK is over I can reveal a bomb was found in Lough Erne. It was American from World War Two. Apparently they had a practise [sic] mortar range here!' Yikes, that really was wild swimming then.

27 JUNE 2013

George could have an L of a time with my A to Z of cutbacks

I get into the spirit of 'all in this together' by bringing you my austerity alphabet.

G EORGE OSBORNE SAYS that we are all in this together and so, in the spirit of the age of austerity, I offer you my A to Z of the Comprehensive Spending Review. And, yes, as you ask, the alphabet has been cut, like everything else:*

A is for Abuja: It's a big winner, George says, at the very nexus of our high-growth market embassy network. You read it here first.

B: sorry, efficiency savings mean B had to go.

C is for civil servants, who will no longer get automatic pay rises for longevity. 'Automatic progression pay is antiquated,' says George. And, incidentally, not cheap.

D is a slacking consonant, had to go.

E is for English, which got a huge boost with George launching his 'English for Dole-Seekers' classes. I could actually hear UKIP's Nigel Farage cheering when this was announced although, of course, his surname may be illegal soon.

F is for the future, which George is in favour of: 'Britain was once the place where the future was invented. We can be that country again.' To be honest, it seems a bit fanciful.

G is for global race, which we must win (see 'F'), though it seems unlikely as President Obama doesn't even know George's name and thinks it's Jeffrey.

H is for Hague, as in William, who is 'the best Foreign Secretary we've had in a generation'. A generation is twenty-five years (unless George is cutting that too) and that means he's rubbishing Geoffrey Howe, Douglas Hurd, John Major, Malcolm Rifkind, Robin Cook, Jack Straw, Margaret Beckett and David Miliband.

I: all vowels from here are cut.

J is for the Joker, as in Batman, who George seems to be channelling with his white face and black hair, not to mention that sneer and cackle combination.

K is cut because 'c' is more versatile.

L is for learning. George is a huge fan of 'brilliant' Michael Gove and we are going to pay for more free schools (go figure)...

M is for museums, which will remain free, at least until Friday.

N is a poor man's M and so out.

O: please see I.

P is for Pickles, as in Eric, the Community Secretary, who got a big hug from George (sorry about that mental image) for slashing his department by 60 per cent and abolishing twelve quangos. 'He's a model of lean government,' said George to giggles as the horizontally challenged Pickles beamed.

Q is for quango, and on the bonfire.

R is for railways, as in HS2, which George says is transformative but for which his backbenchers use other words that cannot be printed in a family newspaper.

S is for single parents, who must now start 'preparing' for work even as the child is in utero.

T is for thermometers, which are essential kit for oldsters who must now prove they are living somewhere as cold as Britain to get the winter fuel allowance. To which we can say: hasta la vista.

U: see I and O.

V is for visas, which are going up, because foreigners can pay.

W is for Waterloo, which is a huge winner with George promising to restore the battle site by the 200th anniversary in 2015. Wellington will be pleased, as will Belgium.

X isn't fit for purpose.

Y is now categorised as a vowel.

Z is for Zippy, a loud but funny character in the children's programme *Rainbow*. Yesterday, Ed Balls, the shadow Chancellor, said that our Prime Minister was 'Zippy' and also christened the Chancellor as 'Bungle', a bear who is always picking a fight.

* By cutting ten of the twenty-six letters I have achieved efficiency savings of 38.5 per cent in the alphabet.

4 JULY 2013

Dave launches into a 'Len-a-thon'

*The Prime Minister seems to see the leader of
the Unite union wherever he goes.*

I FEAR THE PRIME Minister has a bit of an obsession with Unite leader Len McCluskey. Some have said it is a man-crush, but it's actually more flattering than that. He hates him so much that he can talk of nothing else. For David Cameron yesterday, every topic at PMQs led directly back to Len.

Ed Miliband asked why class sizes at schools had gone up.

'Your questions are written by Len McCluskey!' shouted Dave.

Ed insisted he was speaking for parents up and down the country.

'You go up and down the country speaking for Len!' insisted Dave.

Ed Balls shouted something at Dave who shot back: 'I know you are paid to shout by Unite, but calm down a bit!' Calm down? Dave, you can't be serious. How can anyone be calm as long as Len McCluskey exists? Yesterday, Dave, on his Len-a-thon, was about as serene as a poltergeist in a crockery-smashing competition. There seemed to be nothing in which Len, an evil mastermind right out of Bond, was not involved.

A Labour MP asked about the increased use of food banks.

'It's Len's fault!' trumpeted Dave (I paraphrase).

A Tory MP asked a planted question about voter registration. Dave launched into a mini-speech on Len and Labour Party selections. 'Votes are being bought, all done by one man, Len McCluskey!' A Labour MP asked about the economy. 'You are a member of Unite,' noted Dave, 'so you have to stick to their script. What a sad day for democracy.'

Ah, so Len was responsible for democracy as well. But I don't know why I was surprised, for Dave soon revealed that unemployment was all Len's fault too. What about the poor take-up on the Green Deal? 'Is that Len McCluskey's fault as well?' asked a Labour MP. I think we know the answer to that.

After a while it got a little embarrassing. Len, Len, Len. I got the feeling that Len, like Zelig, was present at most of the key events in recent history. If Dave is Harry Potter, then I think we all know who Voldemort is (you may think it was Lord Voldemort but, actually, it was Len Voldemort all along).

I was surprised that Dave did not blame the explosive violence in Egypt on him. Surely it has Len's fingerprints all over it. It was all slightly alarming, and not just for me. I just happened to see the Prime Minister and his wife after PMQs.

'So who is Len?' asked Sam, teetering in six-inch Louboutins.

'Who is Len?' asked Dave, incredulous. 'The real question you should be asking is who ISN'T Len!' 'OK. Who isn't Len?' asked Sam, perfect hair swinging just so.

'Ed is Len. The other Ed is Len. They are all Len!' said Dave.

'Do you think you are working too hard, darling?' asked Sam. 'You seem a little obsessed.'

'OBSESSED?' shouted Dave, then carefully lowering his voice and feeling the back of his head to find his moving bald spot. 'What gives you that idea? Did Len tell you that?'

5 JULY 2013

Dangerous bats in belfries have them rolling in aisles

*Bats may be one of God's creatures, but MPs
want them to stop going to church.*

I T HAS ALL gone slightly bats in the Commons. If I was a pipistrelle hanging out, upside down, in a belfry, I'd be worried. I fear the wrath of God is nothing compared with the wrath of Sir Tony Baldry, Tory grandee and church commissioner. Sir Tony, our very own Baldrick, is a man of considerable girth and almost as many opinions. He was wearing his Garrick Club tie, something he likes to do when answering Church questions just in case the issue of women bishops comes up.

The bats question came from David Nuttall, a favourite of mine as he is a Tory who puts the nut into nuttiness. 'As a churchwarden, I know that many members of parochial church councils live in fear of bats taking up residence in their church buildings, because of the damage bats cause and the difficulty they have in removing them because of EU rules.'

I knew that, if the question came from Mr Nuttall, the EU would have to be involved for it is Satan in bureaucratic form to him. Sir Tony agreed that an increasing number of bats were indeed roosting in churches. 'The present situation is simply unsustainable,' he insisted, pointing out that the church of St Hilda's in Ellerburn had spent £29,000 so far in 'bat mitigation' with no resolution in sight.

MPs were starting to flap. Sir Tony has, in the past, made it clear that he is not anti-bat in general.

'As far as I am concerned, bats are part of God's creation. Indeed, there are three specific references to bats in the Bible.' But bats in the Bible are one thing, bats in the belfry, aided and abetted, not to say protected, by the EU habitats directive – quite another.

I looked over to see if Labour bat-lover Madeleine Moon was in her place but, sadly, she was not. Who would defend the bats? Up arose Labour's

Kerry McCarthy, timidity itself. 'I must say I rise with some trepidation,' she squeaked, noting that Sir Tony had been 'explosive' about her pro-bat stances. Would Sir Tony try to bring the bats and the C of E together? Sir Tony's short answer was 'No'. 'You and the Bat Conservation Trust seem to think that this is an issue which somehow can just be managed. I have to keep on saying to her that this is NOT an issue that can be managed.' He did, actually, look as if he might explode. 'Churches are not field barns!' He has had many letters from clergy distressed by having to clear bat faeces and bat urine off the altar and communion table every Sunday. 'That is not acceptable!'

I wondered if the churches had thought of simply boring the bats with long sermons or, perhaps, even marrying them, after which ceremony the bats would never be seen in church again. That certainly seems to work with humans. But Tory Anne McIntosh wants something more practical, for St Hilda's is in her constituency: 'It is a matter of urgency that the congregation can reclaim their church from the bats.' MPs tittered. Sir Tony agreed. 'Absolutely!' MPs were laughing openly. 'This is not a joking matter,' Sir Tony said sternly. 'This is serious.'

MPs put their serious faces back on. As I said, if I were a bat, I'd be worried.

6 JULY 2013

Rare sighting of a Dodo-like creature: Tory Unitedous

There were raptures as James Wharton presented his Private Member's Bill on the Euro referendum.

IT WAS LIKE a dream. Actually, it may have been one. Yesterday, at 9.33 a.m., I entered the Commons and found Tory MPs, packed into their benches like sardines in suits, to be totally united. I stared. This was something truly rare, like seeing the dodo for the first time since the seventeenth century.

I knew that I needed help to identify this strange creature. So I rang the expert. Sir David Attenborough, a man used to seeing strange phenomena, raced over to Westminster to help.

'Ahhhhhh,' he whispered to me, words susurrating as we were peering through the fronds of a plant he brought along to make us feel out in the wild. 'This is the rarest of species. Indeed, many live their whole lives without seeing Tory Unitedous.'

We readjusted our binoculars as a cheer filled the chamber, both tribal and powerful. Tory Unitedous was welcoming a fledgling to its ranks, the young James Wharton, the 29-year-old who, by sheer chance, had won the mysterious oddity that is the Private Member's Bill ballot and thus was given the honour of presenting a Bill promising an EU referendum in 2017.

'It is an honour to introduce a Bill that has at its heart the heart of our democracy,' began James, tall and unmistakably of the Tory tribe, his black hair slicked back. 'Power should reside with the people. In introducing the Bill, I speak for many in the House, but I speak for millions more outside.'

Sir David nudged me as Nadhim Zahawi rolled to his feet. Mr Zahawi is so loyal that once he almost won my coveted Lickspittle of the Year competition.

'Often, with Tory Unitedous, the limelight is irresistible,' whispered Sir David.

Lusty cheers resounded for Mr Zahawi, who looked almost entirely happy. He asked Young James: 'Have you received representations from the leader of the Labour Party, Len McCluskey, on what he thinks the position should be on this important issue?' Oh my! How Tory Unitedous shrieked with laughter! For, of course, Len is not leader of the Labour Party but of its financial backer, the Unite union. James said that he hadn't heard from Len or, indeed, Ed Miliband, and returned to his theme, noting that the last referendum on Europe was in 1975. This, by the way, was before Young James was born: 'How things have changed: politics has moved on, and the EU has moved on.'

A new roar filled the room as Dennis Skinner, the Labour dinosaur, stood up. Sir David looked almost in awe as he peered down at the legendary Beast of Bolsover. 'I voted for a referendum in 1975,' rasped the Beast. 'Sadly, the country did not follow my advice, or we would not be doing what we are doing today. However, the Bill is deficient in one respect: it does not ask for a referendum until 2017. What we need is a referendum before the next election!'

Young James rocked back and forth. 'I wish more people had listened to you in 1975,' he said, to immense Tory merriment. The vote, in the end, was 304 to zero. As we watched the MPs voting, still amazed, Sir David whispered to me: 'This was the day that Tory Unitedous roared.' We may not see it again.

9 JULY 2013

Theresa Maynia sweeps over centre court in SW1

It was Wimbledon but, in Westminster, it was game, set and match to the Home Secretary.

THERE IS MURRAY mania but, in the Commons yesterday, there was just plain Theresa Maynia. The Home Secretary came to the chamber clutching a trophy with her name etched upon it. 'Last year, I said the right place for a terrorist is a prison cell, the right place for a foreign terrorist is a foreign prison cell,' she said. 'Today, Abu Qatada is indeed in a foreign prison cell.'

This brought huge cheers. Theresa allowed herself a tiny turning up of the red lips. I wouldn't go as far as a smile. Still, for once, the Ice Queen seemed a little warmer. And, just like at Centre Court the day before, David Cameron had come to watch her before heading back to welcome Andy M himself to No. 10 to meet the likes of him and Ed Miliband (there is a downside of winning Wimbledon).

The Maynia fans encompassed most of those on the Labour benches including Hazel Blears, who chirped: 'It took twelve years to deport Abu Qatada and it only took Andy Murray seven years to win Wimbledon. The whole country will be very pleased!' I am not sure about that 'only', but Mrs May again battled against the desire to smile. She explained that it wasn't just her (I love that), but also ambassadors, officials and James Brokenshire, the Security Minister, who was by her side, looking about twelve, his bog-brush hair positively pogo-ing with happiness.

Andrew Griffiths, a Tory, chortled: 'I'm not sure what gave me greater pleasure on Sunday: watching Andy Murray's victory or the news that Mr Qatada was leaving on a jet plane!' Even the Great Vaz, the all-seeing, publicity-seeking missile that is the chairman of the Home Affairs Select Committee, was full of praise. 'I know you have worked extremely hard over the last few years to secure this result. In fact, you must have felt since becoming Home Secretary, to coin a phrase, that there were three people in your marriage.' Mr Vaz beamed at this bizarre 'joke' (sic). Ms May grimaced. I examined her face closely. It was not a smile.

Even Labour's awkward squad were asking for her autograph. 'On this leftie side of the gangway,' said Ronnie Campbell, speaking for Dennis Skinner too, 'we are delighted that this evil man has been sent back to where he belongs. But I get worried because I watched him swagger on to that plane and I just wonder if he's got a secret way back. Do you have all the doors covered?' Mrs May insisted that the country was Abu Qatada-proof.

The gushing became so bad that, by the end, I feared that an emergency plumber had to be called to the chamber.

10 JULY 2013

Is this a New Ed we see before us...?

*The Labour leader's speech on party reform was so
'massive' that I wondered if it was really him at all.*

CARPE DIEM, IN the Labour Party, is so often carping diem. But now Ed Miliband has changed all that. The Labour leader, who has been so lifeless that there was a theory that he was part of some sort of embalming experiment, has suddenly come alive.

'We are going to seize the moment!' cried Ed who, being Ed, then actually seized both of his hands together in front of him, strangling what was left of the limited air in the room.

The room, just off Fleet Street, was packed for Ed's Seize The Moment moment. I must admit that I hardly recognised the man in front of us. Passionate. Risk-taking. Massively (his new favourite word) over-excited. I peered more closely. I have long suspected that there is a secret third Miliband brother. Was this him? I wondered if a DNA test was necessary. Like Richard III, we needed to be sure. But even if it was – and I have asked for a strand of hair for analysis – it wasn't the Ed I knew. This Ed had verve and brio (no, not Biro). One journalist referred to him as 'New Ed'. Not Red Ed, then, but, possibly, Ned.

New Ed wants something called New Politics. In this great revolution, trade union members will get to choose for themselves if they want to be members of the Labour Party. You may think that a tad basic but, for Labour, letting people think for themselves is radical. He also wants to reopen talks on party funding and thinks MPs should be MPs and not do other jobs (don't tell the Lesser Spotted Gordon Brown).

But what, he was asked, if the unions don't want to change? Ned looked stern. 'Let me be clear about this. I will set a very clear direction. I'm saying very clearly today I want in no uncertain terms to change the way that is done. That is a massive, massive change to the way the Labour Party works.'

I hope it's clear that this is massive massive. 'I don't think anyone should be in any doubt about my determination to get this done.' His hand gestures had grown into arm gestures now and I feared we were moments away from a full arabesque.

Ed explained again how massive massive it was. 'So Falkirk happened,' he said, referring to Unite trying to rig the vote to select a candidate. When these things occur, he said, you have a choice. You can deal with it as a one-off. 'Or you can seize the moment!' he cried. 'I have seized the moment in making a big change. I think that is the right thing to do. Look, Tony Blair said this morning this is a change that he wishes he had made.'

When I heard the words Tony Blair, I knew how massive massive the change was. Red Ed hardly ever mentioned TB. But TB is New Ed's New

Best Friend. 'When the moment arises,' said Ed, seizing the air again in front of him, 'the question is do you actually take action? And we are taking action!' But, asked a journalist, have you gone far enough? Ed looked frustrated. 'Tony Blair says this is a transformational extraordinary moment!' So there you have it: massive massive. And here's another massive thing: Ed might want to be Prime Minister after all.

16 JULY 2013

Playing croquet with flamingos would be easier than this

There are times when reality is so strange that only fantasy can make sense of it. This happened when MPs tried to figure out how the Duchy of Cornwall worked.

I BEGAN TO SUSPECT almost immediately that the script for the Public Accounts Committee's encounter with the Duchy of Cornwall had been written, not by J. K. Rowling under a pseudonym, but by Lewis Carroll. Let's call it Margaret in Wonderland, and it was just like the Mad Hatter's tea party, but not quite as sane.

The first thing MPs wanted to know was whether the Duchy of Cornwall, the estate that provides Prince Charles with his income, which was £19 million last year, was a legal entity.

A bespectacled smoothie named William Nye (who was, indeed, nigh on impossible to understand) pursed his lips. It seems not. Yes, it could be sued, but it wasn't a legal entity.

'It MUST be a legal entity!' shouted the chairwoman, Margaret Hodge. Mr Nye demurred, softly, smoothly, velvety.

The next point of interest was whether the Duchy was a corporation in all but name. That brought more lip pursing from Mr Nye. It was a private estate, not a corporation.

But did it not have a chief executive? Mr Nye demurred: 'The closest thing to a chief executive is the Secretary and Keeper of the Records.'

So, said Margaret, would he describe himself as chief executive? 'He would describe himself as the closest thing to a chief executive,' insisted Mr Nye.

I felt that playing croquet with flamingos would be easier than understanding Mr Nye. To be fair, it's his job (principal private secretary to the Prince) to live in a different world, but he did seem to think in circles. The Duchy paid no corporation tax because it paid no corporation tax. Ditto for capital gains tax. He seemed utterly unflappable.

The Labour MP Nick Smith began to talk about ducks (don't blame me, blame Lewis Carroll). In the real world, he claimed, what looks and quacks like a duck is a duck. So if the Duchy looks and behaves like a corporation, then surely it is, indeed, a duck? Mr Nye explained, softly, smoothly, that the Duchy was, in fact, a swan. (I paraphrase.) It was a private estate but not like other private estates. I looked over at Margaret. I think she had to stop herself from shouting 'Quack'.

This brings me to Austin Mitchell, the veteran MP for Great Grimsby who did once change his name to Haddock. He was wearing American stars and stripes braces. This would be confusing if I had not known Lewis Carroll was involved. Mr Austin growled, for that's how he talks, even if he was once a fish: 'So it's not a corporation but behaves as if it IS a corporation. But wouldn't it be better if it were just taxed as a corporation instead of some kind of medieval anomaly?' Mr Nye did not even blink. 'Well, it's true that it is medieval in that it was founded in 1337, but I think it has moved into the twenty-first century.'

The subject turned to marmalade.

Why, demanded Mr Mitchell, did Duchy Originals not have to pay tax, when Mr Mitchell's marmalade had to: 'It is superior quality!' Mr Nye explained, softly, smoothly, that Duchy Originals was nothing to do with the Duchy of Cornwall except, of course, the word 'Duchy' and the fact it uses the Duchy badge.

Yes, well, that makes perfect sense. Croquet anyone?

30 AUGUST 2013

You're a disgrace, Gove shouted at backbenchers. His wife tweeted: 'Losers'

The result of the vote on what to do in Syria
seemed more an accident than a plan.

N O ONE COULD believe it when it happened. The whole debate, taking place with MPs recalled from holiday so abruptly that they still smelt of suntan oil, had felt moribund. It had seemed like a pre-game debate about Syria and the post-game analysis about Iraq. Then, at the very end, eight hours after it had begun, all that changed.

'ORDER!' cried the Speaker, John Bercow, at 10.30 p.m.

The tellers lined up. 'The ayes to the right 272,' it was announced and everyone knew what that meant. 'The noes to the left, 285.'

David Cameron looked straight ahead, shocked, humiliated. He had been defeated by thirteen votes. Suddenly none of the clichés seemed quite good enough to do justice. The government had lost on the most unlikeliest of statements, a motion that had been watered down until it only hinted at reprisals against Syria, calling for a 'strong humanitarian response' to the use of chemical weapons.

'Go now!' came the shout to Dave from the opposition benches.

Ed Miliband, just as shocked, jumped up to make a point of order. This was his moment – though it was hard to believe given his wooden performance earlier – and he wanted to make sure that, in light of the vote, the government would not use the royal prerogative to use military action in Syria.

David Cameron, so angry he just glared, assured him that the government would not do such a thing. 'I get that,' he spat.

It was chaos. 'You're a disgrace!' shouted a furious Michael Gove at Tory backbenchers as others insisted that the vote must be rerun because some government MPs had been 'in a meeting'. But the vote would not be rerun. Everyone had known there would be a vote at that time. There was no excuse. Mr Gove's wife tweeted: 'Pathetic losers who can't see past their own interests.'

You really couldn't make it up. From the beginning, the whole thing had seemed something of a sham. MPs had been recalled from the summer break but I am not sure, as they took their seats, they really knew why. The original idea, perhaps, had been to ask for a vote on military action against Syria's use of chemical weapons. But in the end, they 'debated' two motions: one government, one Labour, that did not seem that different other than the call for a strong humanitarian response.

But, still, Labour did not hide its feelings from the start.

'This House has been recalled, I believe, in order to give cover for possible military action this weekend,' noted Labour's Dame Joan Ruddock primly, immaculate in royal blue.

David Cameron insisted that this was not the case. 'I wanted the recall to debate these absolutely vital national and international issues!' This brought loud rumbles of disbelief. The PM's speech teetered on passion but in general settled for resolute irritation aimed at the opposition. He told us that this debate wasn't about intervening in Syria but to show our abhorrence of the use of chemical weapons. And, throughout, he had the appearance of someone whose original speech had been stolen.

'I am saying this is a judgement!' he insisted. 'We all have to reach a judgement about what happened.' But I concluded – and, as the vote shows, I was not the only one – that Dave has, clearly, already reached his judgement on what had happened in Syria.

Ed Miliband's performance was anything but impressive. 'We need to be clear-eyed,' he insisted, repeating this as if a stuck record. Indeed, at that moment, Ed seemed to have devised his very own geektastic foreign policy. At its heart was something called a 'sequential road map'. Surely a map is a map, but not, it seems, in the Miliband household. He doesn't own an A–Z, instead he has devised an A–B and then a B–C. I started losing the will to live when he said: 'The fifth point of our road map…' I felt that we were lucky to escape without an organogram and a free pocket pen protector.

Labour's Jim Sheridan oozed his approval for Ed's 'measured approach'. 'We must understand from previous conflicts that war is not some sort of hokey-cokey concept. Once you're in, you're in.' Ed nodded approvingly: 'That is why there must not be a rush to judgement.' Rush? At this rate, it seemed a hopeless crawl.

The Tory grandee Sir Malcolm Rifkind noted, drily, that Ed didn't seem to realise that the government had agreed to his request to wait for the UN. 'We and the country can only conclude that you are incapable of taking "yes" for an answer,' he said.

Later, it seemed all the more incredible that what, earlier, had seemed to be Ed M's tedious sat-nav escapade had ended at such an incredible destination, a defeat for the government.

13 SEPTEMBER 2013

Putting a price on One's head

Labour says the Lib Dems put the lick into lick-spittle as it is announced that the Royal Mail is to be sold.

I T IS ONE of my beliefs that the Queen often watches the Parliament channel just to catch up on news about Oneself. Yesterday she would have tuned in to hear about the sale of the Royal Mail, which, of course, she has already put her stamp on.

'Philip,' called the Queen, getting out her Tupperware box filled with chocolate digestives, 'come watch with me and the corgis. It seems that a man named Fallon has put a new price on my head.' Prince Philip picked up a digestive and peered at the fleshy face of the man named Fallon, as in Michael. 'But they can't put up the price of a stamp again or you'll need a mortgage to send a letter,' he grumbled.

The Queen shook her head, the crown wobbling dangerously. 'No, not stamps. They're selling the Royal Mail, all of it, even the bit with One's head on it.'

Now Philip shook his head. 'The Not-So-Royal Mail then.'

The corgis began to bark at the TV, where Mr Fallon was talking glowingly about how the Royal Mail would be 'floated' so we could all own a bit of it. There were 'no plans' to change the universal service. The Post Office was separate and would not be affected. Postman Pat, and his black and white cat, thought it all marvellous too. Or, I think he said that last bit: hard to tell with all that barking.

Next up was his Labour shadow, the obscure Ian Murray, who branded it a 'fire sale' and insisted: 'The minister cannot see the woods for his own ideological trees.' What, I wondered, was an ideological tree? It must, like the corgis, be barking.

Mr Murray said this privatisation, the biggest since British Gas, was opposed by 70 per cent of the public. Even Mrs Thatcher, he noted, refused to do it.

'The government is playing politics with the Queen's head!' burbled Mr Murray, which made the corgis bark even harder and the Queen reached up to readjust her crown. (Indeed, Mr Fallon kept saying the price of stamps had been capped though, obviously, he meant crowned.)

I think it's safe to say that Labour detested the sale. 'I am not surprised that the minister is the person bringing this forward – Domesday for Royal Mail is reality – but when someone gets old they will do anything to get into a ministerial car,' sneered Michael Connarty. Mr Fallon, who looks as if he never walks if he can ride, wore a contented frown.

But now, what was this? Dennis Skinner, ardent republican, was on his feet, facing down the man named Fallon. 'Do you recall that in the late '80s we had a wholesale privatisation of almost all the public utilities with the exception of this one? And it was under what Mrs Thatcher called the "share-owning democracy". And what happened to that?' he sneered.

'Almost without exception EVERY single public utility is now owned abroad and RIPPING the British consumer off. The only difference between now and then – those lick-spittle Lib Dems have joined the Tories to privatise it!' At the words 'lick-spittle Lib Dems', there was a cheer, though, surely, even when it's privatised, you'll be able to lick stamps and not lick-spittle them.

21 SEPTEMBER 2013

Laugh? They almost pulled the fridge out

I was there, watching the quaffing and laughing, for the great Godfrey Bloom 'sluts' moment.

IT WAS A joke. Yes, it was. I was standing next to Godfrey Bloom MEP, he of 'Bongo Bongo Land' and other egregious views. Still, in his defence (I can't believe I typed that), it was just a joke.

The speeches had just started at the UKIP Women in Politics event, after a considerable amount of champagne quaffing. Well, it was lunchtime and UKIP is a party fuelled by booze. Looking round, there actually seemed to be more men than women. Indeed, the first person I had spotted was Neil Hamilton, disgraced Tory, UKIP stalwart and total blast from the past. One hand was occupied leaning on a cane, the other held a glass of fizz.

'You may ask how this happened,' he beamed, cheeks glowing. 'I had an accident in bed with my wife!'

Boom Boom! I race off to find Christine, celebrated battleaxe, who denied the story. As she is talking, I become fixated on her ears, from which dangled large silver pound signs with little diamonds. UKIP bling. Somehow I knew it was inevitable.

Back to the sluts. So, Godfrey was over in one corner, wearing one of those awful UKIP purple and yellow ties. He was billed as a star attraction and, despite his outspoken views that women should do more housework, clearing behind the fridge and all that, he clearly had the status here of a highly indulged pet.

'Laydeez!' cried MEP candidate Janice Atkinson. 'Is there anyone in this room who doesn't like being called ladies?'

A man shouted: 'Me!'

Laugh? They almost cried. (This is normal for UKIP.)

Janice is passionately against all-female shortlists. 'If we get to Brussels next year,' she cried, 'we are not tokens. We are not mandatory gender women!'

Another non-mandatory gender woman, Lisa Duffy, the party director, told us that, actually, she'd joined UKIP for the men, not the women. But then she suddenly looked over at Godfrey, admitting she was not living up to his ideal that women should do more housework.

'Godfrey would like me to clean behind the fridge,' she said to giggles, 'but I don't think I have ever pulled my fridge out!'

Godfrey chortled: 'Shame on you! Shame on you!' Lisa wasn't fazed. 'Since I joined UKIP, I rarely do any housework at all. I've given up on ironing completely!'

Lisa, who said she'd gone all 'goosebumpy' during Nigel Farage's speech that morning, launched into an impassioned defence of not having all-female shortlists. 'We don't highlight women in UKIP, we highlight everybody in UKIP. We are all working hard to get our country back!'

The next speaker was MEP candidate Jane Collins, who noted that she had been Godfrey's campaign manager in 2004. 'And I too have never cleaned behind my fridge!' she cried.

At this Godfrey interrupted: 'This place is full of sluts!'

Laugh? They certainly did. Jane added: 'I too don't do an awful lot of housework. But I do hold an HGV licence allowing me to drive some of the biggest trucks in the country. So I can definitely drive and park my car better than Mr Bloom!'

Cue more hilarity.

We had a final blast from Janice, who does look a bit like she is channelling Mrs T, making fun of the Labour Party and 'Harriet Harmaninsta as in feminista'. She told us about something called the EU's Women's Rights and Gender Equality Committee. On hearing this name, Godfrey did one of those exaggerated shudders, like a D-actor in a schlocky horror movie. Which, of course, he might be. Still, it was only a joke.

25 SEPTEMBER 2013

You can't do better than this for political theatre

*The Labour leader in his conference speech goes wild as he
unleashes his grand plan for controlling the price of electricity.*

FRIENDS, AS ED Miliband must have said a hundred times yesterday, it was wild. For about an hour, the Labour leader paced his small
white triangle of stage in Brighton, a pipe-cleaner man in a suit, no
notes, no autocue, gesticulating, gurning, shouting and then almost whispering. Showman, evangelist, comedian, game show host. This was Ed as we
have never seen him before.

It was a teeth-first event. I swear they are getting bigger. And whiter.
He began by saying that he wanted to thank someone. Then, suddenly, he
interrupted himself: 'Not Justine!' Then he added, looking over at his wife.
'Actually I WOULD like to thank her. Round of applause for Justine please!'

They clapped like mad. Now he added: 'Not my mum!'

Were we going to have to clap for her, too? It seemed that Ed had already
run out of significant women in his life. The woman he wanted to thank was
named Ella Phillips, who rode past him on her bike and then fell off. 'I helped
her up and afterwards she called me something that I have never been called
before. She said I was an action hero!' He gazed out, at the Labour conference, with his encircled panda eyes. 'Why are you laughing?' he asked, which
they loved even more.

The teeth were blinding me. 'I was pretty pleased about this until something dawned on me. Ella was concussed.' More laughter. 'Ella, if you are
watching, THANK YOU! You made my year!'

It was pure political theatre and, actually, quite close to a circus act. Truly,
I would not have been that surprised if a lion had suddenly arrived on stage,
jumping through a blazing hoop. I looked up but, sadly, no trapeze. Roll up,
roll up, see the Amazing Memory Man, Ed the Mnemonic Miracle!

The speech owed a debt to gospel with every 'verse' ending in this refrain:

'Britain can do better than this. Britain can do better than this. We're Britain! We are better than this!'

Ed was taking the action hero thing seriously. He and his teeth are freezing electricity and gas bills, extending the vote, creating jobs and apprenticeships for Britons (We can do better than this!). He has been talking to people all over Britain (Better than this!). Market traders, women in front rooms, an angry man who refused to tell him his name, a scaffolder who lives nearby who asked him if he had a bodyguard and, in the end, convinced him he had to do something about energy bills.

Now Ed shouted at the audience: 'Do the Tories get it?' There was a lacklustre response, more gerbil than lion.

'I DIDN'T HEAR YOU!' shouted Ed. The audience roared back.

'That's better!' cried Ed. (Britain, better than this!)

Ed said that next week, at the Tory conference, David Cameron would be doing a 'lap of honour' for doing such a great job as PM. 'No doubt, he'll be taking off his shirt and flinging it into the crowd, expecting adoration, like he did recently on holiday. Maybe I should make this promise while I'm about it. If I become Prime Minister, I won't take my shirt off in public!'

This got another roar. 'But anyway, back to David Cameron. He's on this lap of honour. COME ON! That is not worthy of a lap of honour, that is worthy of a lap of SHAME!'

Friends, it was so crazed that I almost didn't want it to end. Almost. Next time, I hope he brings the lions too.

Life of Brian is one full of respect

*Lord Justice Leveson comes before MPs to
tell them, er, respectfully nothing.*

WITH RESPECT, CAN I warn you that there is no lack of respect in this column. You see Lord Justice Leveson, as he was, and Sir Brian Leveson, as he must be called now that he has had a promotion, came before MPs full of respect but without any answers.

'With great respect,' he announced, 'I'm not saying anything.'

The Culture, Media and Sport Select Committee tried to look respectful. The judge, light bouncing off his pate, fringed by a halo (as I think he would see it) of white, moved his black eyebrows up and down. Sir Brian, who arrived with an entourage of four women, is a bit of an eyebrows man, I think.

Brian, as I have always called him, throughout his long inquiry, turns out to be kind of an odd guy. Here is a man who spent fifteen months and £5 million of our money examining the subject of press regulation. He produced a 2,000-page report last November at a strange press event in which he refused to take questions. This, then, was our chance to find out what he thinks.

MPs fished for his views on the warring plans for a royal charter. One MP, almost begging, insisted that the people of Britain needed his views. 'I think they know what I think,' said Brian. 'I think, with respect, that all of you know what I think.'

MPs looked as if they wanted to bang their heads on their desks.

One MP ventured that maybe Sir Brian thought it a bad move to move ahead on the charter with the support of the press.

'With great respect,' said Sir Brian, 'I haven't said that at all.'

He began to quote great chunks of his 2,000-page report. He seemed particularly partial to Section J2. But K was also very popular. MPs glazed over. Sir Brian quoted himself more.

Tracey Crouch, a super-sporty and very sharp Tory, asked Sir Brian why he had never taken questions. 'With great respect, I couldn't do more than I did,' he insisted, noting that he'd produced a 2,000-page report, a 51-page summary, an eight-page executive summary. 'Nobody could be in doubt about what I thought.'

But, Tracey noted, the press would have had questions.

Sir Brian noted that he spent his life passing judgment in courtrooms and, after his verdict, he never took questions.

'With respect…' ventured Tracey.

'With respect,' countered Brian, 'that is how I feel about this report!' Suddenly, I felt over-respected. What a shame that Aretha Franklin couldn't just pop up from behind him and belt out: 'R-E-S-P-E-C-T! Find out what it means to me!' But instead it was left to Tracey. 'With respect, Sir Brian, it's not a judicial decision in a case of X versus Y, it's about the future of the press.'

Sir Brian, he seems to know everything and nothing about the press at the same time, wasn't having it. He believes that his report speaks for itself, even though it never touches on the idea of a royal charter. He does not believe that he could, as an expert, weigh up the pros and cons, and have a view. 'With great respect,' said Brian. 'I couldn't have done more than I did.'

Which just goes to show that Brian doesn't understand what Aretha's singing about at all.

8 NOVEMBER 2013

Intelligence chiefs are outstanding in a field

*We were all searching for a haystack in a needle
when the top spies came to Westminster.*

MY MISSION, WHICH I chose to accept, was to spy on the spy chiefs in their first ever open session at Parliament. The operation, known by the code word Haystack, took place in the Boothroyd Room at Westminster. I gained early access to the room, securing a window seat. The blinds were pulled behind me. Outside, ordinary people (OK, tourists) were going about their business. But here, at Spy Central, we were on time delay.

Yes, time delay! I have never been on time delay before and I can tell you that it is exactly like normal except that, for a delicious few moments, you know what no one else knows. I looked around at my fellow time-delayers (others had secured access, I can't tell you how – I'd have to kill you). We were special.

The super spies entered the room. Even with a time delay, they looked disappointingly normal. Andrew Parker, the head of MI5, looked just like the birdwatcher that he is. The guy from GCHQ, Sir Iain Lobban, was a dead ringer for every other middle-aged man in Britain. Only Sir John Sawers, the head of MI6 – the man known as C – looked like a spy: tall, dark and handsome in a lantern-jaw sort of way. 'We are not sending agents like James Bond into the field and hearing back from them in two months,' C said, explaining how the spy services worked now.

What did it mean? I wished that I had invested in a decoder ring.

The committee, made up of shadowy MPs and peers, some of whom must be sleeper agents as I haven't seen them in years, asked how spies operated when listening in on ordinary Britons.

The man from GCHQ said he liked to think of this in terms of haystacks. If you think of Britain as an 'enormous hay field', then the spies were out there looking for enemy needles or fragments of needles. 'We do not disrupt the hay,' he said.

I pondered this. How I yearned for Dame Judi Dench, who is surely the top spy in the world, to pop up and explain. For some reason (probably the time delay), I remembered that camels can go through eyes of needles. Surely it was all code.

C told us that spies were not 'crystal ball readers'. It wasn't, he said, as if the start date for the Arab Spring had been in a safe somewhere in Cairo. If it had, we would have known about it. But it wasn't. So we didn't. (Also, and this may be crucial, Egypt may not have many hay fields, but it does have camels.) The birdwatcher told us everything that spies do is legal. C said that if there was ever a question about the legality of the hay field, then he woke up the Foreign Secretary. There was condemnation of *The Guardian*, the enemy within, for telling secrets. 'Our adversaries are rubbing their hands with glee,' C said. 'Al-Qaeda is lapping it up.'

Now Sir Iain, who must have some sort of bucolic tendency, returned to the hay field and how that means that ordinary people mustn't worry about being spied on. 'I've got haystacks,' he said. 'I've got needles.' But if he found a needle, he just looked at the actual needle: 'I do not look at the surrounding hay.'

Does that sound plausible? And can you see that he didn't even mention the camels? You notice these things on time delay.

22 NOVEMBER 2013

All sensitive badgers should look away now

The humans argue over who moved the goalposts
when it comes to eradicating TB.

I BRING YOU NEWS from the world of Mr Badger. There he was, all set in his sett, watching the Parliament channel yesterday, while Mrs Badger was down the tunnel-way, making a cup of tea when, suddenly, the distinctly human face of the Environment Secretary filled the screen.

'Mrs Badger!' he cried. 'Come and see. It's Owen Paterson, the man who thinks that badgers move goalposts!'

Mrs Badger waddled in. 'Move goalposts! Ha! Why you barely move out of your chair!'

But she could hardly be heard for Mr Paterson, who shouts his sentences in a stentorian way, was badgering – a verb that badgers object to, by the way – Labour for not agreeing with his cull that is aimed at stopping the spread of TB in cattle. 'From a sedentary position,' he barked, 'the chuntering goes on!'

And it was. 'Follow the science!' Labour MPs shouted.

'We ARE following the science!' barked Mr Paterson. He was following the science from Australia ('which is TB-free!'). He was following the science from New Zealand. He was following the science on white-tailed deer from Michigan. (I had an unpleasant vision of Mr Paterson in a deer-stalking cap, following the herd, something that politicians are quite good at, of course.)

Mr Paterson was almost spitting his words now. He was following the science in Ireland where TB was decreasing. 'And the average Irish badger is 1kg heavier because they are healthy!' he shouted. 'We will end up with healthy badgers and healthy cattle.'

Mr Badger glanced down at his portly stomach. 'That man needs to calm down,' said Mrs Badger.

But now Labour's Kerry McCarthy, the badger's best friend, if you do not count the tiresome Brian May and his hair, noted that only 60 per cent of the farms in the west Somerset cull zone contained cattle. 'Why are you culling badgers on farms without cattle?'

Mr Paterson sniggered. 'Well, you must understand that badgers move around.'

This brought more giggles. I felt that a goalpost wasn't far away.

Mr and Mrs Badger looked at each other. It was always unnerving listening to humans talk about them as if they knew it all. Of course Mr Paterson did once have two pet badgers named Baz and Bessy (humans can't resist names that begin with Bs for badgers). Anyway, as everyone knows, Mr Paterson considers himself to be an expert on everything.

'When they are "super-excreters" and they move on to cattle farms, sadly they are very effective transmitters of this disease,' he now explained. 'That is why we are addressing the disease not just in cattle but also in wildlife.'

Mrs Badger turned to Mr Badger. She didn't like the sound of 'super-excreter'. 'Shall we turn it off, dear?' she asked. 'The news is so depressing these days.'

But as Mr Badger lumbered up, shadow minister Huw Irranca-Davies started to berate Mr Paterson for not following the science. He noted that nearly half the board of Natural England had challenged the badger cull extensions. 'Is it not clear that you are a complete stranger to evidence-based policy and a master of moving the goalposts?'

Mr Badger harrumphed. 'I'd like to see that,' he said, turning off the TV. 'Humans!'

29 NOVEMBER 2013

Ominous smoke signals from Plain-Speaking Jane

The government has the jitters over a policy that seems to have been written on the back of a fag packet.

THE GOVERNMENT IS on the fag packets again. On, off and now on again. Its policy on plain packaging for cigarettes is beginning to resemble Nick Clegg's attempts to give up smoking.

The Public Health Minister had to be dragged to the Commons to explain what was going on. Her name happens to be Jane Ellison and although she is no Plain Jane, she is, most definitely, Plain Packaging Jane. 'We have been consistent in a desire to take an evidence-based approach to public health,' she said, pretending the on-off-on policy was entirely rational.

'A Crosby-based approach!' shouted Labour MPs.

Jane did not look up. Somewhere over at Tory central office, the election strategist Lynton Crosby's ears were burning. At Westminster, Labour believe that Lynton has almost mythical powers and the fact that he is a partner in a firm that has advised a tobacco company is enough for them to believe it's all a plot.

'Only a government as shambolic as this one could U-turn on a U-turn,' said Luciana Berger for Labour, who was furious. I couldn't help but notice that she was wearing high heels so green they needed mowing. Is the Theresa May shoe fetish rubbing off on Labour too?

'I thought that was a rather disappointing and naïve response,' said

Plain-Speaking Jane. 'The government have held a consultation, but we have not had a review before.' (I feel a fact-finding mission, a task force and a stocktaking cannot be far behind.)

Behind her, Tory backbenchers were not entirely supportive. 'Idiotic, nanny state proposals such as the plain packaging of tobacco are what we expect from the Labour Party!' sneered Philip Davies. He expected Conservatives to stand up to the 'health zealots': 'If they could, they would have everything in plain packaging.'

Jane, short, with dark, bobbed hair and spectacles constantly in transit down her nose, displays alarming signs of being almost normal for a politician. Now she said something nice to the ever rude Mr Davies.

But another fellow Tory, David Nuttall, was equally disdainful: 'Will you reassure me that this is not the thin end of the wedge and you will not look for evidence to support the contention that selling children sweets in brightly coloured packets contributes to childhood obesity and seek to ban such packaging?'

I imagined a world where everything even remotely sinful – even Luciana's green shoes – would come wrapped in brown paper. Perhaps that might give it a bit of allure. 'Let's nip down the shop and buy some plain packaging,' we will say to each other after a long week at work.

The Tory Robert Halfon loves to wear brightly coloured suits. I couldn't imagine he'd be in favour of plain anything. 'I confess that I enjoyed a Henri Wintermans Café Crème after breakfast this morning on the way to work,' he announced. At first I thought this was a coffee – which surely is another candidate for plain packaging – but it turns out to be a cigar.

I was feeling the need for a fag break, or at least a fag packet debate break. But now John Pugh, who is a Liberal Democrat, asked: 'What exactly is the downside of plain packaging, apart from fewer fags being sold?'

As Jane opened her mouth, Philip Davies could be heard, sniping from the rear towards the Lib Dem benches: 'A left-wing nanny state wallah like you would not understand.'

I fear that Mr Davies will be forced to wear plain packaging very soon indeed.

10 JANUARY 2014

Desperate Dan ganderflanks around the woods

The government consults, ahem, stakeholders over its strategy on trees.

WE HAD A new word in the Commons: ganderflanking. It's old Wiltshirese for aimless messing around. A Swindon MP wanted to know if it would be 'in order' to describe what goes on in the Commons. I felt like shouting 'Yes!' This led Mr Speaker to muse on the idea of purposeful messing around.

Well, it was environment questions yesterday and, frankly, it was ganderflanking a-go-go. It began with a simple question about trees that wasn't, for a change, planted by the whips. 'What steps are being taken to safeguard trees from disease?' asked the ubiquitous Tory Tony Baldry.

Dan Rogerson, the new Lib Dem minister who looks like a feather down pillow with little wire specs, arose. He is, in parliamentary terms, a sapling but, still, that is no excuse. 'We are working with stakeholders to develop a new plant health strategy,' he murmured, 'which will set out a new approach to the biosecurity for our plants.'

If I were a tree, I would be very afraid. I had a brief vision of Desperate Dan, as he will inevitably be known, bending over a new tree, talking to its stakeholder. Dan said that there were new restrictions on the import of sweet chestnut and plane trees. I wondered if it might be more effective to restrict the views of his boss, Owen Paterson, sitting next to him, on ancient woodlands and bulldozers.

But what, asked Tory Philip Hollobone, was the tree most at risk? 'We are, of course, concerned about ash, although ash dieback is a disease that takes several years to progress,' Dan murmured, 'and we are obviously concerned about larch as well.' I liked that 'of course' and 'obviously'. To say that Dan was wooden was an insult to trees, not to mention stakes.

Labour's Barry Sheerman arose: 'You will know that this is the 150th anniversary of the death of one of our greatest poets of the countryside, John Clare.'

Dan looked a bit more desperate.

'John Clare wrote a great deal about diseased trees – there was a plague of oak disease in his lifetime – and he was a great defender of the English countryside,' Barry said. 'What do you think John Clare would have thought of giving up our ancient woodland and replacing it with new growth?'

Dan looked stunned. 'I, uh, thank the, um, uh, right honourable gentleman for bringing a cultural dimension to our proceedings,' he flannelled. 'I share his concern, and that of John Clare, for ancient woodland, and that is why the guidance is very clear.'

Hmm. I tried to imagine a poem as lovely as a tree but knew it wouldn't contain the word 'guidance'.

Mr Speaker ganderflanked: 'Not for nothing are you known as culture vulture Sheerman!'

Mr Paterson said how to balance 'offsetting' and preserving ancient woods. (What would John Clare do with the word 'offsetting' except, possibly, cry?) 'As someone who has planted an arboretum,' shouted Mr Paterson, 'the idea that I am going to trash ancient woodlands is an absolute outrage to me personally!'

Ganderflanking indeed.

6 FEBRUARY 2014

Cameron's macho 1st XV gets kicked into touch

Ed Miliband popped the woman question at
PMQs, much to Team Dave's irritation.

THEY SAY THAT behind every great man there is a great woman, but next to David Cameron at Prime Minister's Questions yesterday sat fifteen men. Not a bad number, if you want to play rugby. There were no women. I'm not sure Dave noticed, but you have to account for the fact that women are often called away to make the tea (or, in Theresa May's case, anti-terrorist legislation, which is almost the same thing). Anyway, this was rugger! Dave wanted a rufty-tufty scrum on unions and strikes.

That, at least, was the cunning plan. The session began with a planted question from a senior Tory backbencher (why do they do it?) about Bob 'Brazilian' Crow's Tube strike. Dave crowed, a verb banned in the RMT, or so I hear, that he condemned the strike. 'I hope the Leader of the Opposition will stand up and condemn it unreservedly now!'

Ed Miliband unfolded himself, never a quick process, to a tidal wave of Tory noise. And then Ed asked about the floods. The wave froze in mid-crest. The Tories had to look serious about the floods. Dave threw some money at the problem and told us he was chairing a Cobra meeting.

Then, in mid-flood, Ed suddenly popped out of the water, twirling like a synchronised swimmer (which, let's face it, is really not rugby). 'The Prime Minister said that in 2014 he was going to lead the way on women's equality. Can you tell us how that is going in the Conservative Party?' Chaos. Labour jeers filled the chamber until Mr Speaker screamed: 'ORDER!' Dave, avoiding the women question, embarked on a desperate soliloquy on the Bellwin scheme for funding local government.

'A picture tells a thousand words,' chuckled Ed. 'Look at the all-male front bench ranged before us. The Prime Minister says that he wants to represent the whole country. I guess they did not let women into the Bullingdon Club either, so there we go!' I could almost see ministers looking at each other furtively, wondering who had been in charge of token woman placement that day.

Ed, twirling away now, said there were as many men who went to Eton or Westminster in the Cabinet as women. Dave explained that of the full members of the Cabinet who are Tories, 24 per cent are women. 'That is not enough!' he said. 'But this party is proud of the fact that we had a woman Prime Minister…'

Ed now turned to Dave and said: 'You mentioned Mrs Thatcher. Unlike you, she was a Tory leader who won general elections!' Ed told us that Bernard Jenkin, the Europhobe, had written about inadvertent sexism in the Tory Party. Apparently, according to Bernard, Dave had greeted a top businesswoman at a reception by asking: 'Where's your husband?' Actually, I didn't think that was so bad. It's so much nicer than: 'Where's your policy?'

12 FEBRUARY 2014

Action Man Dave is pumped up and primed for action

How bad were the floods? So bad that David Cameron, now known as the Duke of Wellingtons, called a press conference.

THE FLOOD WATERS finally reached Downing Street yesterday with shocking results. The first sign that we were seeing the tremendous power of the tidal surge was when Dave called a press conference. It is the wettest winter in two and a half centuries, which, by coincidence, was the last time Dave called us in.

'My message to the country today is this: money is no OBJECT in this relief effort,' he said, blazing blue eyes matching admiral blue suit. 'Whatever money is needed, it will be spent.'

These are words that we have never ever heard him speak before. We've had years of austerity this and austerity that. Now, suddenly, our slice'n'dice government has gone into loadsamoney mode. Dave threw thousands and thousands of pounds at almost everyone: homeowners, business, transport.

What, he was asked, did he mean by saying money was no OBJECT? 'Money is no OBJECT!' he said explanatorily. 'We will spend what is necessary. We are a wealthy country.'

Was it Dawlish that did it? The PM was there yesterday, looking at the ruined train track, in his action man hi-vis orange jacket and blue hard-hat. Elsewhere in the country, flood victims were finding it hard to avoid politicians. Ed Miliband managed to submerge his wellies in Purley-on-Thames while a Tory MP accused him, as the cameras rolled, of seeking a 'photo opportunity'. Then there was the Defence Secretary, Philip Hammond, a man rarely seen on foot because he loves his Jag so much, looking a bit like a stork in wellies as he got a telling off in Wraysbury. I suspect he'd rather be in Afghanistan. (Is Mr Hammond the latest stand-in Environment Secretary? There was no sign of Eric Pickles yesterday.) The PM has gone into ultra-action mode. He has cancelled his Middle East trip next week (by which time there will probably be a hosepipe ban in place). He's chairing Cobra almost constantly. He's put a Major-General in charge of the military effort. He's wearing hi-vis gear to the breakfast table. Dave was extremely pumped up about everything, including our new pumping strategy. Money is no OBJECT on pumping either.

He was asked about whether he agreed with Eric Pickles's less than enthusiastic comments on the Environment Agency leaders. 'The hardworking staff have done a brilliant job!' cried Dave. I noticed he was careful to always add the word 'staff' when he praised the Environment Agency. Yes, he was asked, but what about the leaders? 'Now is not the time for resignations,' he added. 'This is not a time for people to leave their posts. This is a time to knuckle down.' (Storm clouds ahead, obviously.) The other big Dave message? 'There are lessons to be learnt and those lessons will be learnt,' he said more than once. We are a wealthy country when it comes to how many times we say that lessons must be learnt. Repetition is no OBJECT.

Dave hasn't looked so purposeful in ages. 'As is so often the case, in the toughest of times, we are seeing the best of Britain!' he cried. Then he strode out. There was a job to do. There were hard-hats to wear and money to spend. There was Cobra. There was, finally, after weeks and weeks, a sense of urgency.

26 FEBRUARY 2014

Workers of the party, unite … you have nothing to lose but your white ties

The Tories announce that they are on a moral mission to be the party of the workers. What, I wondered, would Marx say?

THE TORY PARTY relaunched itself as the 'workers' party' yesterday in a rebranding exercise that was close to genius. I tried to go but, obviously, being a mere worker bee myself, I was banned. Nor was the event televised. I began to wonder if the Tories had just made the whole thing up.

The workers' party. Hmmm. I tried to imagine how the Tories would do that. 'The people's flag is deepest blue,' they would sing, vowels perfectly rounded, happy smiling moisturised faces glowing. Everyone held up one arm and, in their clenched fist, I could see iPhones. They served tiny faggot canapés. The manifesto would ban white ties.

The new proletariat was launched at Tory HQ by Grant Shapps, the party chairman. Sadly, his alter ego, the elusive Michael Green, author of such e-books as *How to Get Stinking Rich*, was nowhere to be seen. Grant looked fetching in his 'worker' overalls. He arrived carrying a wrench, because all workers do. The event may have not been televised but we did get a copy of the speech.

'The Conservatives are the workers' party and we are on your side,' said Grant, wrench now safely tucked into his tool belt (all workers have tool belts). 'That's the message we have to get across to people.'

Grant explained that it was a 'moral mission' to be the party of working people. I wondered if he would be announcing the reopening of a pit, though he wasn't wearing a headlamp which, for the Tories, would be a key accessory detail.

Usually Grant's speeches rotate around one central theme which is, er, Grant. Yesterday he talked about someone else. 'Imagine a young kid growing up in inner-city London – just a few miles from here,' said Grant. 'His mum and dad are working, but not very rich, trying to pay the bills. He quit school at sixteen and struggled to get on. So let me ask you something: what did the Conservative Party have to offer someone like that?'

I imagined the question hanging in the air as Arabella and Tarquin furiously googled 'quit school sixteen, inner city London'. Grant banged his wrench on the lectern: 'I'll tell you! That young man's name is John Major and the Conservative Party made him Prime Minister!'

Sir John began as only he could. 'Golly!' he said, looking out at the 150 workers there.

I last saw Sir John in the autumn when he came to the press gallery to make a speech (or, as we call it now, dominate the evening news). 'If we Tories navel gaze and only pander to our comfort zone we will never win general elections,' he noted then. 'All the core vote delivers is the wooden spoon.'

Ah yes, the wooden spoon. Yesterday Sir John endorsed a new apprenticeship scheme. 'Golly!' he said. 'What a nifty idea!' Everyone clapped and took selfies. For yesterday the Conservatives went beyond the wooden spoon as they embraced the hammer and the honey-sickle.

28 FEBRUARY 2014

Über-Mutter shows how to give away nichts

We all gathered to hear Angela Merkel, she of the quantum chemical strategy, tell it like it is.

I T WAS A grand event and you have to wait for those. Thus the press sat along one side of the Royal Gallery in the House of Lords, watching Die Welt go by. Even by the standards of this magnificent building, the gallery is awe-inspiring, its arched doorways flanked by gleaming golden statues of kings and queens. The murals are vast, the stained glass kaleidoscopic, the wallpaper ultra-flocked.

MPs filed in, Europhiles and Eurosceptics mingling as one. David Cameron, who is both phile and foe, not the easiest of roles, was almost the last to arrive. I asked two German journalists next to me what German sketchwriters, if such a group exists, would call Frau Merkel. They eyed me gravely and said: 'Über-Mutter.'

Über-Mutter. I liked it. At the press conference that followed, a German journalist noted that Frau Merkel had been treated almost as a queen. She wasn't (her BMW really can't compare with a Cinderella coach). But she was, most definitely, given the respect accorded the Über-Mutter of Europe.

Everyone stood as she entered, her suit Margaret Thatcher blue. 'Like a visit from the Pope,' I heard a peer mutter about the Mutter.

I braced myself for Mr Speaker's introduction and obligatory 'joke', the appearance of which seems, like the constitution, to be an unwritten fact of parliamentary life. As he began, I noticed that he has begun to inflate his 'r's so that 'very' becomes 'veddy'. (If only Hansard could record such things.)

'The Chancellor is an unusual politician in many regards,' he announced as Angela with a hard 'g', as Dave calls her, looked on, her face giving nichts away. 'Relatively few MPs have doctorates, and those who do have them overwhelmingly in the social sciences. The Merkel doctorate, by contrast, is in a hard science, mainly physics, and involves to be precise, and I quote…'

He took a breath that those of us who are swimmers recognise as the gulp before diving down to traverse the length of a pool underwater, then blurted: '…investigation of the mechanism of decay reactions with single bond breaking and calculation of their velocity constants on the basis of quantum chemical and statistical methods.'

Strangely, the crowd of eminent parliamentarians burst into applause.

'Now that title probably sounds snappier in German,' said Mr Speaker to more giggles. 'Possibly even one veddy long word!'

Über-Mutter looked on, her face unreadable. She began her speech in English, just slightly inflected, and told her version of a joke, about when she came to London for the first time in 1990.

'We walked through Hyde Park looking for Speaker's Corner which, especially for us East Germans, was legendary, the very symbol of free speech. I hope that it's not an insult to you, members of the British Parliament.'

More laughter. In English, so she could control the exact words and not leave it to the translator, she noted that there were special expectations for her speech.

Some say that she is going to pave the way for fundamental reform of the European architecture. 'I am afraid they are in for a disappointment,' she said.

Others are expecting the opposite, how the rest of Europe is not prepared to pay almost any price to keep Britain in the EU. 'I am afraid these hopes will be dashed too.'

And so she walked the tightrope, an unlikely but deft funambulist.

Surprised? You shouldn't be.

She is an Über-Mutter after all.

1 MARCH 2014

Welcome to UKIP, post-fruitcake

Nigel Farage lets rip at his mini-conference in Torquay,
his eye on the prize of winning the Euro elections.

I SUSPECTED THAT I'D found the UKIP conference in Torquay when I saw a man in the car park dressed in a three-piece, wine-red corduroy suit, accessorised with obligatory £1 UKIP badge. They do like to do dapper at UKIP. But it was the man with the fruitcake that clinched it.

'Have some fruitcake!' urged Herbert Crossman, beaming with pure happiness as he handed me something crumbly. 'The only fruitcake here is on the tray!' This is not quite true, but as someone who has covered UKIP for many years I can report that yesterday's shindig at the Riviera Centre in Torquay was, definitely, UKIP's first post-fruitcake conference.

The party leader, Nigel Farage, has spent the past year ruthlessly culling the party of (most) of its major screwballs. 'We've got rid of them!' he shouted yesterday. Badgers aren't the only thing endangered here. The transformation of UKIP to NewKIP is almost complete.

Of course, more than any other party, this one IS its leader. Nigel Farage, rhymes with barrage, arrived on the stage festooned with signs that said 'Love Britain, Vote UKIP', his marvellously cartoony rubber face morphing into a look of wonder as he gazed out at the crowd.

'NIGE!' a woman near me cried. It was a riveting performance and, as I watched him, I saw that 'Nige' is a party leader with more than a touch of the demagogue about him. The speech was a barnburner and at the core of it was a message on immigration delivered with the precision of an Exocet. 'The fact is that in scores of our cities and market towns, this country, in a short space of time, has frankly become unrecognisable!' he cried.

How they loved it! Every one of the 700 or so people crammed into this hall clapped. 'It's a fact that in many parts of England you don't hear English spoken any more. This is not the kind of community we want to leave to our children and grandchildren.'

I looked around. The faces of the NewKippers were rapt.

'Did you see the immigration figures yesterday?' asked Nige to a room of despairing nods (the figure showed a large increase, almost all from Europe). 'If the Eurozone goes as badly over the next few years as I believe it will, we face the prospect of the largest migratory wave that has ever come to this country and we have three political parties who are not prepared to do anything.'

It was UKIP, he said, that had made it possible to debate immigration. 'Remember ten years ago? You couldn't talk about it. If you did, somehow, you were a terrible, bad person. We proved the point. It is not extremist to talk about immigration, it is responsible and right!' He made forays into other subjects – quangos, floods and the foreign aid budget to name a few – but then exhorted his groupies (sorry, audience) that the message for the next eighty-four days (he knows, he ticks off every day until the Euro elections) must be about Europe.

'This is the moment that we waited for!' he barked, his voice overpowering the microphone and the room. 'This IS it! This is the big one for UKIP. Together we can achieve something remarkable in these European elections. We can top those polls.'

He received an instant standing ovation. As he toured the room, pressing the flesh, I could almost smell how much he wants to win.

18 MARCH 2014

Hammond lost in fog of war against plain English

I grapple with the 'bespoke entity' that is the Defence Secretary in search of a clear sentence.

I FEAR THAT PHILIP Hammond remains at war – with the English language. The UN has asked me to be an official observer of this increasingly hard-fought battle and so yesterday, at Defence Questions, I was at my post. It didn't take long to spot the first incursion.

The Defence Secretary was trying to explain the new body that is going to be in charge of defence equipment and security. The name for this, and I think that only he could have thought it up, is DE & S Plus. It sounds like a sort of Marksmen & Spencer outlet for plus-sized types.

Mr Hammond tried to put us right. 'We have agreed that this will be established as a bespoke central government entity from 1 April.' The word 'bespoke' stopped me. I have only heard this applied to hotels and clothes. I feared that DE & S Plus was going to get lots of calls from larger ladies seeking kit that has nothing to do with war.

Mr Hammond 'explained' (I am sorry to have to put that in quotes but the situation was escalating) that DE & S is a vital part of the 'Whole Force' concept. This sounded intriguing, like some sort of new organic cereal, but turned out to be the idea of the military working with civilians at the MOD.

His voice, which almost purrs, like the Jaguar cars he loves, now became ever so slightly animated. 'They are not pen-pushers as some of our media would have us believe,' he said, 'but vital components of our defence infrastructure.'

I was, more or less, lost now. The fog of war is never foggier than when

Mr Hammond is speaking. He told us about an 'envelope' of resources. (I suspect this just means 'money'.) 'There will be an overall envelope of resources for operating costs which will be subject to a downward trajectory over time, representing efficiency.' (My secret translation code ring tells me this means the budget is being cut.)

There was some talk of the Crimea but Mr Hammond let others handle that. There is no need for plus-sized bespoke entities there yet. Instead he fielded a question about the military and the floods. 'We want to make sure that the defence budget is neither advantaged nor disadvantaged,' he said. 'That implies a full marginal costing recovery regime.' (I do hope the Somerset Levels are taking note.)

But possibly the worst moment came when a Lib Dem asked about conflict prevention (their pet subject and, if you were in coalition with the Tories, it would be yours too). Dr Andrew Murrison, an understrapper, said that the MOD was a 'full partner' in delivering the 'building stability overseas strategy'. This meant, he said, that the MOD used a 'multi-departmental approach to prioritise UK activity in upstream conflict prevention.'

As this nonsense filled the room, my head fell to the table with a thud. Mr Hammond, the mist swirling around him, had won again.

20 MARCH 2014

It's a full house for George

It was the bingo and beer Budget for, yes,
hardworking families. I joined the game…

IT ALWAYS TAKES a while for the Chancellor to get to the point when he is delivering a Budget and it is quite easy to get a bit bored.

'Rabbit!' the Labour hecklers kept shouting as Mr O made his way through his speech.

I peered down at the chamber but could see no rabbits being pulled from the hat, yet. Actually I did see a four-legged object, but it turned out to be a frog heading for George Osborne's throat. 'We are all in this together!' chortled the Chancellor. The frog jumped in at the 'together', as well it might.

Soon I began to realise what this Budget was all about. This is the way I call it then:

Kelly's eye: It's about bingo. 'Bingo duty will be halved to 10 per cent to protect jobs and communities,' Mr O said. This was a huge relief: the country has worried about little else for months. Everyone shouted 'house', just because they could.

Me and you: It's about booze. Mr O is scrapping the alcohol escalator duty. It's about time. I was tired of seeing all those bottles of wine going endlessly up and down, hogging all the space.

Cup of tea: We are getting a new pound coin that is Brechtian. 'It will blend the security features of the future with inspiration of the past,' the Chancellor said. That seems unlikely. Anyway, it's taking the shape of the threepenny bit. 'Threepenny Opera!' shouted a Labour heckler.

Knock at the door: It's all about us. 'If you are a maker, a doer or a saver, this Budget is for you.' Surely most of us are at least one of these. But I wish he'd gone the whole way and name-checked candlestick makers. They need a boost.

Man alive: It's all about patriotism. We are giving money to celebrate in 2015 the 800th anniversary of the signing of Magna Carta. Did I see David Cameron flinch? Remember when, on the David Letterman show in America, he didn't know what it meant?

Half a dozen: It's about potholes. There is going to be £200 million made available and councils will have to bid for it. Like an auction, apparently, for holes.

Lucky seven: It's all about graphene. You may not know about graphene but those of us who follow the Chancellor's speeches know that the new super-strong wonder substance is his absolute favourite thing. It is a 'great British discovery' and now it will have its own headquarters.

Garden gate: It's about garden cities such as the new one in Ebbsfleet, which is an old quarry. So not really that green at all but it sounds better than 'Quarry Cities'. Plus, Mr O announced, garden cities are going to get their own prospectus. Can there be a higher honour?

Doctor's orders: It's all about air passenger duty. He said that now you pay less tax travelling to Hawaii than to China or India. Those of us who tend to staycation in Derbyshire wouldn't know.

David's den: This bingo call apparently refers to No. 10, as in the Prime Minister and so, appropriately, I can reveal it's all about politics. But you knew that.

And the rabbit? It's all about savers and pensions and, on first hearing, quite baffling. So it wasn't just one rabbit but a whole bunch of little rabbits. But then everyone knows that rabbits, even budgetary ones, multiply.

21 MARCH 2014

Balls brings House down with bingo banter

The shadow Chancellor needs to apply for an Equity card after his hardworking comedy act.

IT WASN'T A speech so much as a comedy act. Ed Balls began by holding up a piece of paper with the Tory 'bingo and beer' poster on it. He read out the slogan: 'Bingo! Cutting the bingo tax and beer duty to help hardworking people do more of the things they enjoy.'

He flapped the paper some more, just for the fun of watching George Osborne try to ignore him. 'How patronising, embarrassing and out of touch that is! The Tory Party calls working people "them" – them and us. Do they really think that they live in a different world to everyone else?' Mr Balls twirled. He pointed to George Osborne and noted that it is said that the Chancellor had not known about the poster. 'Pull the other one, I say!' cried Ed.

'But it gets worse!' he cried. 'I hear that the Prime Minister did not properly understand what the Chancellor was saying. Apparently when he told the Prime Minister that he wanted to cut taxes for bingo, the Prime Minister thought he was referring to an old school chum: 'Hurrah, another tax break for millionaires. Bingo, Bingo!' This brought guffaws. Even George was in danger of giggling. Mr Balls, who needs to apply for an Equity card immediately, turned his attention to the future of Grant Shapps, the Tory Party chairman who released the poster, noting that No. 10 had now said they had 'full confidence' in Mr Shapps.

'That's the end of him then!' shouted Mr Balls, noting that it has been reported that Mr Shapps is now on a tour of northern cities to see how the other half live.

'I wonder how it's going,' said Ed. 'Can you imagine?' He pretended to be Mr Shapps: 'Goodness me, the houses even have indoor toilets up here!'

Mr Balls kept throwing the pages of his speech around him until he was surrounded by what seemed large pieces of confetti. He began, almost balletically, to throw them behind him, leaving his team to catch them. He teased George about his leadership ambitions, his new, non-foppish haircut, his 5–2 diet and estuary accent. It was, trumpeted Ed, a re-branding.

Various Tories tried to steer Mr Balls back to the subject at hand. 'If we can just sort of gently return to the Budget?' asked Sir Edward Leigh. But Mr Balls would do no such thing. 'What a mess!' he cried. 'A right old Eton mess!' Everyone groaned. As for Ed, I think he almost bowed.

27 MARCH 2014

Farage reaches the big stage at long last

Nigel faces Nick in a debate about Europe that, disappointingly, was about Europe.

THE THING TO remember is that Nigel Farage was almost the winner by just showing up. Of course, his press team claimed that he was very relaxed about it all. 'He's been to the pub,' they announced. He was sweating. And nervous. And the reason is that he is a man who has spent a lot of time talking politics – to very small audiences (think snug bar). This wasn't just a highlight. It was the apex. Here he was, the man with the face like a cartoon frog, standing next to the Deputy Prime Minister. Finally, after years and years, he had arrived at the centre of political debate, if only for one night.

And what a night! I am typing this from a 'Spin Room' – a place with ten huge arches, interspersed with giant floor-to-ceiling columns topped with curly golden scrolls. There are more than 100 people in here, from around the world. And if that doesn't impress you, what about this: Kay Burley, the Queen of Sky, is here! Nigel is now so big that Kay has to be here for him.

Around me are about ten televisions, all with Nick and Nigel on them. They and the audience are in a room below us. We aren't allowed to see them: it makes it much more exciting for us if we are banned. The LBC set is so bad that it's almost good: bits of garish red and blue icebergs looming behind them, like some sort of food-coloured shipwreck.

I am sorry to tell you that the debate over Europe was, indeed, about Europe. I had hoped for something else. Still, at least they properly don't like each other.

'By the way, I don't agree with Nick!' said Nigel, in one of the few moments where he wasn't angry.

Nick, who tried desperately throughout the hour not to turn his body towards Nigel, looked pleased.

They didn't just disagree. They were on separate poles. They kept coming up with 'facts' that the other insisted were 'not true'.

Nigel kept sounding patriotic. Nick tried to sound reasonable. For Nigel, all things are about Europe. Asked about gay marriage, he denounced the European Court of Human Rights. Nick found that absurd: 'Why is UKIP dogma so strong…' Nige hit back: 'I'll tell you what the dogma is, I believe the best people to govern Britain are the British people!'

If Nick won the battle, and I'm not even sure of that, then Nigel won the war. The leader of UKIP, the buffoon with the pint of beer, had finally arrived on the main political stage – and he didn't fall over.

4 APRIL 2014

Art of apologising without saying sorry

Maria Miller touches the void as she gives a personal statement on getting her expenses wrong.

WE LIVE IN the era of the non-apology apology, and yesterday Maria Miller took that particular tautological phenomenon into an entirely new realm. Her 32-second non-apology apology for overclaiming expenses on her mortgage in 2009 was so perfect, so empty, so totally void, that I can only conclude that it was something else entirely. Perhaps, say, a work of art entitled: The Non-Apology Apology. Indeed, I fully expect it to be entered for the Turner Prize.

Actually, and rather irritatingly, I now owe Maria Miller an apology. I have always accused her of being beige in word and deed and believed that, if you cut her, her blood would run beige. She was in the Cabinet because she was a woman and a safe pair of hands. She ruled, Queen of Beigeness, over the areas of culture, media and sport, turning all she touched to blancmange.

But her non-apology apology was brutalist beige and, therefore, not beige at all. It took the genre to a new high or, in this case, low. She arrived in the Commons just as the excellent Jane Ellison was taking some flak from the Tory backbenchers over the fact she is minded to bring in plain packaging for fags. Maria made her way up to the hinterland that is the backbenches. She had a single sheet of paper in her hands. When she sat down, her leg jiggled. She had eye bags and was wearing black and white (she has had to burn her beige wardrobe for obvious reasons).

There is a tradition in the House about 'personal statements' which is that your best friends surround you in a 'doughnut'. I can report that Maria had a power doughnut. She was accompanied by Anne Milton, who used to be a Health Minister and is now a government whip. They arrived together, walking by three other government whips. Actually, we were awash with whips. I counted at least six in the Commons during the non-apology apology, which is a record.

Sir George Young, Chief Whip, sat on the other side. Moments before Maria stood up, Jeremy Hunt, the Health Secretary, sprinted from the front bench to sit beside Sir George. To the other side of Anne Milton was the lantern-jawed Gavin Williamson, who just happens to be David Cameron's parliamentary private secretary.

Maria, appropriately, was the empty bit in the middle. She arose and deigned to say seventy-nine words. I have seen blinks that lasted longer. First, she noted that Labour's John Mann had made an 'allegation' and that the Commons Committee on Standards had dismissed it. The subtext was clear: I'm innocent! She continued, her words marching, lady-like, pinkie fingers extended, into the air: 'The committee has recommended that I apologise to the House for my attitude to the Commissioner's inquiries.' Again the subtext was clear: I am doing this because I was told to. Then she added: 'And I, of course, unreservedly apologise.' She emphasised the words 'of course' and 'unreservedly'. They were in italics and not bold. As words, they were empty vessels, little Marie Celestes bobbing by. There was not one ounce of 'sorry', scintilla of contrition, proton of penitence to be seen.

She walked out, head held high, off to write a cheque to us for £5,800 for getting her expenses wrong. She is innocent but, also, it seems to me, not.

MPs listened to her apology in silence. No one said 'hear hear'. I did not see anyone pat her arm . She walked out, untouched.

29 APRIL 2014

Tory rebels go off the rails

Tory MPs objecting to HS2 could hardly wait to tie their fervent objections to the tracks.

W E COMMUTERS ARE used to all excuses and so it was no surprise to discover, upon entering the Commons for the HS2 debate, that we were being delayed by rebels on the line. There was Cheryl Gillan, Tory battleaxe, dressed in silver sequins, rotating round the chamber like a disco-ball in search of a party. Michael Fabricant, aka Micky Fab, the llama-loving former Tory vice-chairman, had his 'important occasion' wig on for the debate. Worryingly, Cheryl's hair is beginning to look exactly like Micky's: they are spending so much time together plotting that they are starting to look like each other.

It was the most important day of their lives. You think I exaggerate, which goes to show how much you know about the HS2 rebels. Forget trainspotters, HS2-spotters are the new super-obsessives. Yesterday they were outraged at Labour's decision, completely unsurprising by the way, to back the scheme.

The 'debate' began with an achingly low-speed speech by Patrick 'Steam Train' McLoughlin, the token bluff northerner in the Cabinet who is, irritatingly, almost impossible to dislike. Yesterday his policy was to hug his friends close but hug his enemies even tighter. He allowed endless questions – 'this is the last time', he said, about 100 times – including a series of spirited queries on where, exactly, Stoke-on-Trent is located. (Answer: West Midlands! Who says MPs know nothing?)

His Labour shadow is Mary Creagh, an impressive performer who will go farther and faster than HS2 ever will, especially for those who live in Stoke-on-Trent. Now she hugged Patrick close too.

Micky Fab popped up, camel-coloured hair almost taking off. 'Are you not a teensy-weensy bit concerned,' he demanded, 'that when there is this love-in, this cross-party approach, it invariably means you are getting something wrong.'

Ms Creagh, who was wearing her kick-shin brogues, I noticed, looked a bit ill. 'Well, I don't share anything teensy-weensy or of any other size with you,' she said. Everyone, even Micky, actually especially Micky, for he is king of the double-entendre, rocked with laughter. For a moment, Mary was speechless (quite rare in the Commons). Wisely, perhaps, she said no more.

Cheryl arose with a gravity that befits her status as HS2 Rebel Queen. She is the Boadicea of Rail Routes. She began by thanking everyone. There were 'vast armies' who had helped her. She name-checked fellow MPs. We were in Oscar territory here. I looked to see if she was going to cry.

'I started as a Nimby,' said Cheryl. But then, after examining the plans, she decided to be a Niaby (not in anyone's backyard). HS2 was too secretive. The budget was suspect. The building should have started in the north and come south. Plus, it's not even green. Cheryl is also Queen of the Chilterns ('the lungs of London') and so she knows about green.

At some point, Cheryl let out a long sigh, an expulsion of air that felt much more than any one person could produce. This was not a grump, it was the sirocco of sighs. 'However,' she said. It was only one word and yet, in that, we all knew, there was defeat. She admitted she had lost the war but was going down fighting.

'It is a David and Goliath fight and, for once, Goliath is going to win,' she said. Then she told us her price: she wants a tunnel to go under the entire Chilterns. And I bet she gets it.

22 MAY 2014

Ed wrestles with a bacon sandwich

*It was the day before the European elections when the
Labour leader found something to chew on.*

ANY FOOL KNOWS that, for politicians, food is a danger zone. So
it's hard to explain what happened with Ed Miliband yesterday
morning. In his defence, not that he really needs me for that, it was
6.30 a.m., which is simply too early. They say that, in politics, the early bird
gets the worm but, of course, you are not supposed to eat the worm. And you
are never ever supposed to be photographed while eating the worm. Obviously.

So there's Ed, at New Covent Garden Market in London, at 6.30 a.m.,
suit immaculate at a time when most people are in their jim-jams, discussing
(incredibly) what he calls the cost of living crisis. This was the first stop of a
ten-stop, one-day tour of the country. In his words: 'I will be going all round
England – north and south, east and west – laying out Labour's ten pledges
from our cost of living contract.' (Some people know how to have fun.)

Ed, on his way to buy flowers for Justine, his wife, spied a café stall where,
after a chat with Tony Foufas, the owner, undoubtedly about the cost of living, he bought a bacon sandwich and sat down to talk – while eating – with
two people about you know what. With photographers present.

No! I could almost hear the incidental music – think Jaws but with bigger
teeth – as he opened his mouth and started to chew. Clearly he had forgotten
this basic rule: 'Never eat on camera.' Chewing while your mouth is full of
policy never works. But if you must eat (and if I was facing a ten-stop tour,
then I can see that a granola yoghurt, or whatever they eat where he lives in
Primrose Hill, may not be enough) then be especially wary of bacon sandwiches. They may be essential props for politicians trying to relate to 'real'
people, but they are greasy, unmanageable and full of gristle.

He chewed. The cameras recorded his teeth's epic battle with the bacon.
A witness reported that 'butter seeped between his teeth'. The photographers

clicked away. Incredibly, Sky TV was filming. Filming! The early bird was eating the worm – on camera. Finally Ed realised that the sandwich was winning. Lord Wood of Anfield, his adviser, took custody of the sandwich.

Ed rushed off to buy some roses and, to add insult to injury, the café owner announced he wasn't even voting Labour. 'I find the Conservatives are more pro-business,' he said.

So, Ed, here's the lesson you must never forget. Never eat on camera. In fact, in future, never chew in public. If you must eat, do it in the car.

The Fifth Year

Scotland, Tory Turmoil and the 'Ed Stone Election

JUNE 2014 — MAY 2015

THE FINAL YEAR of the coalition government started with UKIP coming tops in the Euro elections. Then, after years of Westminster pretending it wasn't going to happen, Scotland voted on independence (and almost won). Parliament bumped along the bottom as everyone became obsessed with the pre-election which gave way to the real election fought out on the belief, brought to us by the pollsters, that come what may, it would be a hung parliament.

•　　•　　•

6 JUNE 2014

Barack backs UK – and Dave loves it

*The G8 was due to be held in Russia but it was decided, because
of the ongoing Crimea crisis, to hold it instead in Brussels
where Dave and Barack had other things on their minds.*

I AM ALWAYS ON high alert when politicians say that, in a democracy, it's the
people who make the decisions. I want to shout: 'We know that!' Or, even,
in the immortal word of Homer (Simpson): 'Doh.' But, mostly because,
when a politician says those words, you can almost hear a tinge of regret.

'There is a referendum process in place,' said Barack Obama, 'and it is
up to the people of Scotland.'

I assumed the brace position as, I assume, did most of Scotland.

Next to Barack, at their joint G7 date night that was craftily disguised as
a press conference, David Cameron was looking at him in a way that, in any
other forum, would entail alarm, if not a slap. Dave stared at Barack's jaw,
his face struggling to combine the look of an international statesman with
the unblinking adoration of a dog hoping for a bone-shaped biscuit.

Barack's jaw is pretty busy. He is not exactly short on words. The voice,
which can be so sonorous, is mostly flat at these events, its lawyerly phrases
crowding against each other. When it came to the Ukraine, I can't imagine
there was even one phrase that alarmed Vladimir Putin, who has been exiled
by the G7 all the way to France.

But back to Scotland and Barack's vote. 'The United Kingdom has been
an extraordinary partner to us,' said Barack. 'From the outside at least, it
looks like things have worked pretty well.'

BRACE. BRACE. 'And we obviously have a deep interest in making
sure that one of the closest allies we will ever have remains a strong, robust,
united and effective partner.'

Ah yes, robust. I think we know what that means. 'But ultimately,' noted
Barack, 'these are decisions that are to be made by the folks there.'

So Barack's not so much a 'no' as a 'nope' then. Dave's eyes were boring into the jaw now. In Scotland, I suspect not even one vote swayed. 'I'm sure the people of Great Britain will make the right decision,' he added reassuringly.

The mutual adoration is uxorious. There is, of course, the staring; the lack of blinking can't be good for them. Then there is the constant referencing each other by first name – Barack this and David that – and the ostentatiously chummy banter.

At one point, vis-à-vis a question on the World Cup, Dave said: 'England is the home of football as it's the home and inventor of many sports: tennis, rugby, golf, skiing, table tennis, cricket.'

Barack chimed in: 'Baseball! Basketball!' David ducked his head, thrilled to be bantering with Barack. 'You did invent the English language though,' said Barack. 'We appreciate it.'

How I wish Shakespeare was on hand to write a riposte to that. But soon our ride in the Dave and Barack love boat was over. They shook hands and did some arm slapping as they left the stage, walking in lock step, to use one of their joint favourite phrases.

1 JULY 2014

Dave battles heroically with the Spitzenkandidaten monster

The Prime Minister lost the battle over the election of Jean-Claude Juncker as president of the European Commission but he painted himself as victorious anyway.

HAIL DAVID CAMERON, conquering hero of Brussels. It takes a certain kind of man to carry off being victorious in failure and, after yesterday, I can tell you that Dave is that man. He came to the Commons, cheered by his people, revelling in how he had stood up to the Eurocrat election machine.

'YEAHHHH!' screamed his backbenchers, for Dave could do no wrong. He had tried to block the presidential ambitions of Jean-Claude Juncker, who was that most dreaded of things, a Luxembourgian. (Is it even a country? Isn't it more a potentate?) It was, as they say in France and no doubt Luxemwhatsit, a triomphe.

Ed Miliband, who has never been victorious in failure, didn't seem to understand the idea. 'I know it is inconvenient to remind you, but you lost by twenty-six votes to two,' he carped. 'It is utter humiliation!'

Ha! Ed talked of humiliation even as he faced derision, screams and, in an interesting new tactic, yawns from the Tories. These were great theatrical yawns, with much patting of air. For Ed, it must have been frightening as he faced rows of gaping Tory mouths, expensive implants gleaming, molars visible from the Moon. When Ed finally sat down, the Tories broke into cheers.

'We've heard yet another performance worthy of Neil Kinnock,' jeered Dave.

'YEAH!' shouted the Tories, for in their minds Neil Kinnock and Mr Juncker are practically one and the same. (Isn't Kinnock's son married to a Dane? I rest my case.)

Dave explained the mechanics of his victory and how he had, single-handedly, taken on a monster called the Spitzenkandidat. Dave spat out the name with Germanic gusto. I just knew it had to be something unreal. What would a Luxembourgian version of Frankenstein look like? A bolted-together robot in an Arnold Schwarzenegger film, swaggering around Europe electing Mr Junk-yard.

Dave said that Italy, Sweden, Germany and, oh, probably everyone, had been captured by the dreaded Spitzenkandidat process that forced them to vote for Mr Juncker. 'Leader after leader found themselves strapped to a conveyor belt which they couldn't get off!' he explained. I had a vision of Frau Merkel, trussed up with one of those luggage straps for large suitcases, strapped to a travelator in the hell that is Brussels, forced to go round and round by the Spitzenkandidaten, until, finally, she voted for the Luxembourgian.

Dave explained his heroic battle of refusing to have a Spitzenkandidat. It was not democratic. It was not in Magna Carta.

But who was this? 'I congratulate the Prime Minister!' cried John Redwood, to even more cheers. It wasn't long ago that Mr Redwood was thought to have a touch of Spitzenkandidat about him as well. Now he was on the other side.

Dave preened as he was compared to Margaret Thatcher, though I am sure, in his mind, he sees himself as more Churchillian. 'I always knew you had lead in your pencil,' gushed one backbencher. Dave loved this. 'As for lead in my pencil, I will let the relevant people know.'

It felt surreal, but then we are living in Spitzenkandidaten times.

4 JULY 2014

Chancellor reveals sum total of his knowledge

George Osborne finds himself unable to answer a childish question.

SAMUEL RADDINGS IS seven years old and he's from Manchester. 'George Osborne is used to tough questions,' he said, filming himself on his phone as he prepared for his first Sky News broadcast, 'but wait till he meets us!' Wait indeed. 'Hi guys!' said George breezily as he entered the studio to do the first hot seat interview in which readers of the children's paper *First News* interview grown-ups. The children stared at him.

'Well, my name is George and I'm the Chancellor, and that means I'm looking after the nation's money.'

Samuel was the smallest of the six children, his brown eyes the biggest and his question the best.

'Are you good at maths?' George did something with his eyelashes. It was more than a blink. Was he fluttering them? I think he was. Where are the lie-detector test people when you need them? 'Well, I did maths A level,' he said, having another flutter. 'So I have been tested at school.'

Samuel stared at him, unblinking.

'I tell you the interesting thing,' babbled the Chancellor. 'Of course there is a lot of maths in my job, making sure you can get the books to add up.' (Fact: At the end May, public sector net debt was £1.284 trillion. I am sure you can see how that adds up.) 'But,' said George, dipping his head slightly, 'it is also about making judgements about where the country should spend its money.'

Samuel kept staring. I didn't really blame him. The George hairdo remains a source of constant fascination at Westminster: not many countries can boast a chancellor who is channelling a Roman emperor. George now explained that it wasn't his money, it was Sam's parents' money.

'What's seven times eight?' asked Samuel. The Chancellor pointed his finger at Samuel. 'I'm not going to get into a whole string of those!' he cried, though one question is hardly a string, as anyone with a maths A level must know.

George now announced another fiscal rule. 'I've made it a rule in life not to answer a load of maths questions!' he announced. Hmmm. Is that going to work if you are Chancellor? I can just see him telling Danny Alexander: 'Don't ask me about the deficit! I don't do maths questions! You know that.'

Back in the studio, Samuel was smiling as the presenter asked if he knew the answer. 'Fifty-six,' said the seven-year-old. The Chancellor, aged forty-three, nodded. 'You're right,' he announced. Of course he knew that. Of course he did.

11 JULY 2014

Dave fends off the Twenty Horsemen of the Apocalypse

*The long wrangle between the Lib Dems and the
Tories over what was known as the Snoopers' Charter
ended with a cliffhanger of an announcement.*

THE NEW NON-SNOOPING Snoopers' Charter was announced yesterday with an urgency so rarely seen in Westminster that I felt a blue plaque might be in order. Even the press conference with Nick Clegg and David Cameron, standing at their identical twin boy lecterns, was announced at the last moment, in the dead of night, in the middle of the Holland v. Argentina World Cup match. I felt that, like planes in the Second World War, we were being 'scrambled' or, as I think of it, scramble-egged.

'Just how close are we to the cliff edge?' asked a journalist. Dave explained that it wasn't just one cliff edge but two. It was a double Beachy Head situation. Legislation must be created more or less instantly. If we did not, the consequences were beyond bad: terrorism, paedophilia, murder, crime, mayhem. Like Gotham City before Batman. To do nothing would be like inviting the Four Horsemen of the Apocalypse to tea and complaining when they trashed the joint.

It was certainly dramatic. The message was sent out via air, land and sea. All three main parties had agreed (which, in Westminster, is cause for alarm and always requires snooping).

The morning flurry was capped by a statement in the Commons where Dave sat by as Theresa May told us about the Four Horsemen who, by then, had multiplied into at least twenty. She told us this was an emergency that must be fast-tracked and, as ever, her fan club, the May-niacs, agreed.

'I believe we have a duty to pass this fast-track legislation quickly,' said Colonel Bob Stewart, sagely.

The MPs split into two groups: those who had no desire to snoop into the non-Snoopers' Charter and those who weren't convinced. Tory David

Davis, who likes to live on the edge, if not the cliff edge, pointed out that the European Court of Justice ruling on data access was on 8 April. 'So if there is an emergency, it was a predictable one on 8 April,' he said. 'There has since been plenty of time to look at the twelve clauses that relate to data retention, so why is there an emergency now and not then?'

We snoops knew that the answer was the Lib Dems, but Ms May could not bring herself to say it. 'There was always going to be a need for fast-track legislation,' she insisted as if time, as we know it, did not exist.

Steve McCabe, for Labour, got personal. 'When I look back to the start of this parliament, I cannot help thinking that the Home Secretary is changing from the Protection of Freedoms Queen into Mrs Snoop. Is not the real reason we have an emergency that it has taken three months for the coalition partners to agree a deal?'

This brought forward such a furious denial that we knew it was, essentially, true. Labour's Chris Bryant, who has become a hate figure for Dave, which only makes him more important, asked why the legislation could not have two days instead of one.

Ms May noted she was publishing the draft Bill immediately so that MPs could have 'extra time' to look at it before Monday. She presented this as if it were a major accomplishment: never mind that your normal Bill would take months of scrutiny. This was an SOS. We were on a very quick fast track. It only made sense for Ms May to become Ms May Not.

15 JULY 2014

Thin red line is put on the defensive

Theresa May becomes the longest-serving Home Secretary since Rab Butler, despite her difficulties in finding someone – anyone – to head up her child abuse inquiry.

T O WATCH THERESA May before the Home Affairs Select Committee yesterday was to see a woman in control of her facial functions, if not her department.

She was there to be asked about her appointment of Baroness Elizabeth Butler-Sloss, who had just resigned as head of the mega-inquiry over child abuse.

But committee chairman Keith Vaz – or, as I like to see him, the Great Vaz, for he is like the Wizard of Oz in so many ways – never misses a chance to compliment. 'Can I congratulate you most warmly on becoming the longest-serving Home Secretary since Rab Butler,' he oozed.

'I expect to go downhill from there, Mr Chairman,' she said (this is her idea of wild frivolity).

'Did you celebrate the event?' Mr Vaz asked.

Her icy stare resumed. 'I am not somebody who celebrates that sort of thing.' I wondered, briefly, what it would take for Theresa to raise a glass these days? Global nuclear disarmament? 'I tend to get on with the job.'

The Vaz pounced: 'Well, the last few weeks have been somewhat shambolic! Why is it all unravelling?'

Mrs May's face was pale and stern, her scarlet lips pressed together in a thin red line. They matched her fire-engine red fingernails and shoes. She was dressed for a duel.

She certainly got it. She announced, quite early on, that she was very sorry that Lady Butler-Sloss had resigned. 'I reject entirely the suggestion she wasn't the right person for this. I am disappointed. I consider her to be someone of absolute integrity.'

The Vaz wasn't having it. 'This is not about her integrity. We are all great fans of Elizabeth Butler-Sloss's integrity!' he cried dramatically (he could end up in panto, you know).

The Vaz noted that there were obvious issues to do with the baroness, not least that she was a member of the Lords and that her brother was attorney-general at the time when allegations were swirling. He noted that no one from the Home Office had gone on television to defend her. He said this with horror, for the idea that someone wouldn't go on TV if asked was, for him, quite unthinkable.

'The Home Office was very clear in the statements that we made,' Mrs May said, though in my experience the use of the words 'very clear' almost always means entirely murky. She insisted that she had no regrets.

'This is a matter of judgement,' The Vaz insisted. Surely she should not have appointed her in the first place? The thin red line was getting thinner, the lips pressing so hard that I feared they might disappear, for so many things associated with the Home Office do go missing these days. 'Chairman!' she said, so clipped that, in grass terms, we are talking golf green. Of course 'consideration' was given to the 'appropriateness' of whether she should lead such an inquiry.

The whole spectacle had filled the Great Vaz with an alarming amount of confidence until, like a hot air balloon, I feared that he might float away. At one point, when they were talking about the Home Office permanent secretary, Mr Vaz said to her: 'Of course you are just the Home Secretary…'

Just the Home Secretary. Of course. No wonder she never celebrates.

16 JULY 2014

A good day for felines and facial hair

*David Cameron shuffles the pack, giving the women
a boost, and Adam Boulton swallows a fly.*

THE SHUFFLE BEGAN earlier than expected, with Michael Gove arriving at Downing Street at 8 a.m. He made a funny face as he began his walk of shame/fame. He disappeared inside the giant shiny black door. We never saw him in the street again.

I sent a message to my mole in No. 10 which, just to confuse things, is a cat. Yes, for the day I asked Larry to help me with my inquiries.

'It's a feline reshuffle,' Larry texted (he's a cat so he can't talk, obviously).

But where, I asked, was Gove? Where had the Cabinet's only meer-kat gone? But Larry would text only about the felines. We watched as three women marched into No. 10 – Nicky Morgan, Liz Truss and Esther McVey. All emerged with big smiles. The feline reshuffle had begun.

Now came an ominous tweet from David Cameron saying that Mr Gove was to be Chief Whip. We were then told that Michael Gove was to be 'Minister for TV'. And yet, still, no sign of him, even on TV.

The basic way a reshuffle works for the press is that we stand around in Downing Street waiting for the big black shiny door to open. All eyes, and cameras, are on the door. There is a lot of time to admire the hanging baskets. All ears are filled with the news anchor commentaries.

I had forgotten how entertaining Adam Boulton could be. 'COME TO ME!' he shouted at his Sky editors. 'I HAVE NEWS!' This turned out to be that Lord Hill of Oareford (who he?) is going to Brussels and Baroness Stowell of Beeston (who she?) is going to be leader of the Lords.

Boulton also provided my best moment of the day when in mid-sentence he paused in a rather alarming way. 'Are you all right, Adam?' asked his news editor. 'It's OK. I've swallowed a fly,' came the response. So Adam swallowed a fly. I don't know why.

Here are the other big winners of the day:

Beards. Stephen Crabb, the new Welsh Secretary, is a dead ringer for Conchita, the bearded Austrian Eurovision winner. Apparently he is the first bearded Tory in a Cabinet since 1905.

Esther McVey. The diminutive employment minister emerged from No. 10 and did an amazing pose, leg out (had she borrowed Angelina Jolie's leg from the Oscars?). She then did another twirl: well, she is being allowed to attend Cabinet, but that isn't exactly an exclusive club after this reshuffle. Even Larry texted me that he is going to attend.

Badgers. They have moved the goalposts again, firing Owen Paterson, who tried to blame them for his cull disaster. And now he's been culled. Liz Truss will take note of that.

William Vague. I always thought of the Foreign Secretary as Mr Vague but the world seemed to disagree yesterday as he was moved to Leader of the House and replaced by Philip Hammond, who will be even more vague, I am sure. 'What we are asking in Hong Kong is why?' a Chinese TV anchor said to me. Well, I said, it's because he wanted to go. I'm not sure that happens in China.

Felines. I'm sure it was pure coincidence but the second wave of women began arriving just as the lunchtime news began. How satisfying must it have been for Priti Patel, Penny Mordaunt, Amber Rudd and Claire Perry to go through that door. When Claire came out, she made a 'wheelie' motion with her hands. So that would mean she's doing transport. I can hardly wait to see her do that at the dispatch box. It's going to be fun.

4 SEPTEMBER 2014

The men who stare at goats also stare at Mr Speaker

*John Bercow's enemies, outraged that he had put forward
an Australian as the new clerk for the Commons, continued
in their endless campaign to try to remove him.*

YOU HAVE HEARD, no doubt, about the US Army's dalliance with the paranormal where it experimented with the idea that if men stared at goats long enough, they could kill them. It is my theory that Tory backbenchers have hit on their own version of *The Men Who Stare at Goats*. Readers, I bring you: The Men Who Stare at Bercow.

They were doing it yesterday. I saw them.

They stared at the Speaker throughout PMQs, a fairly serious affair in which everyone agreed on everything but Scotland. MPs were then supposed to move on to the Wild Animals in Circuses Bill (which should include goats, for they are often wild) but the Men Who Stare at Bercow had other ideas.

'Point of Order, Mr Speaker!' cried Simon Burns. The MP for Chelmsford has a silken manner but he did once have to apologise for calling the Speaker a sanctimonious dwarf and he hasn't been happy since.

If Mr Speaker's heart sank, he did not show it. He knows that the Men Who Stare at Bercow want to kill him and that, in the kerfuffle over the appointment of an Australian as the new clerk of the Commons, they think they have found their poisoned apple. On Monday he had to announce a 'modest pause' in the recruitment process. Bercow has now become even more punctiliously pernickety faux-polite (he likes words that start with p) than usual. Thus Mr Burns was assaulted with niceness.

But what was this? The flamboyant hairdo that is Michael Fabricant, whose big eyes have been staring very hard at Bercow, was also raising a point of (dis)order about an arcane clerk-related matter.

'Unfortunately,' said Bercow, allowing a modest pause, for he is fond of them these days, 'but fairly predictably, you are wrong.' Bercow, after a minor kerfuffle with the Hairdo, announced: 'I think the House will want to proceed with its business.'

The House, however, couldn't have cared less about proceeding with its business. Up popped Christopher Pincher, a dandified Tory. He said there had been a story in the press that Mr Speaker thought that most MPs hadn't a clue what the clerk did and thought he was 'just a man in a wig'.

It was the word 'wig' that did it. I saw Mr Speaker jerk when it was said. 'Order! Order!' he barked, telling Mr Pincher to 'resume his seat' (the words 'sit down' being far too direct). Mr Pincher did this, his eyes pinned to the Speaker for obvious reasons.

'I do invite you and other members as a whole to rise to the level of events,' said Bercow, just a little pompously, to sounds of outrage, though it was hard to discern whether it was pro or anti-Bercow outrage.

'I think perhaps we can leave it there,' said the Speaker.

Can we? It felt, on this day, that he had lost the House and that is a terrible thing for a Speaker. Sir Edward Leigh, the straight-talking Tory for Gainsborough who is a grandee-in-training, said: 'In my experience, if a democratic assembly is to function properly, it is absolutely vital to uphold the authority of the Speaker.'

This was met with a loud 'HEAR, HEAR'. Mr Speaker pounced on this comment as a sign of support (though I am not sure it was) and said, rather pathetically: 'Let us proceed in an orderly way.'

The Men Who Stare at Bercow glanced at each other. They think that looks can kill and maybe, if you aren't a goat, they can.

11 SEPTEMBER 2014

Team Westminster leave the bubble

*Shocked by the close polls in Scotland, Westminster
cancels PMQs and goes north on a mission of love.*

IT WAS THE day that Westminster love-bombed Scotland. Dave and Nick and Ed all went 'live and in person', as they say in entertainment – and, surely, that is what we have here – to spread the love. How much do they want to win? I'll tell you how much: Dave has praised Gordon Brown. Desperate times.

I felt a huge surge of sympathy for the Scots. They have had to put up with a lot from English politicians in the past month – fury, threats, sulks – but surely this was the worst of all. The Better Together team arrived separately for their separate events. It seems that some things, like photographs, are not better together. Just because they love Scotland doesn't mean they have to breathe the same air.

Dave headed straight for the financial district and to the headquarters of Scottish Widows, perhaps not the most uplifting of locations. He sat on a stool (how do they come up with these ideas?) and, basically, begged his audience of bankers. 'I would be heartbroken if this family of nations was to tear apart,' Dave said, eyes moistening. Tears! And, worse, English tears. As I said, desperate times.

But it was about to get odder. What is one thing that an English person might think that the Scots would like? (No, not whisky, for that would, of course, involve organising a piss-up in a distillery.) It's swearing. Or, because this is an English person doing it, quasi-swearing. Dave was explaining that the referendum is not like a general election, where you can make a protest vote. 'If you are fed up with the effing Tories, you give them a kick,' he said. As I said, desperate times.

Ed Miliband avoided Edinburgh. He didn't want to run into Dave. Instead, he headed up the M80 (he loves Scotland, he loves the M80) to the Forge

Community Centre in Cumbernauld. Ed also came bearing gifts: his very own Labour-patented, verb-free peroration. 'Solidarity. Social Justice. Together, not alone. From the head. From the heart. From the soul.' At least he didn't say from the effing soul. (Actually, I really can't imagine Ed Miliband swearing or, even, quasi-swearing.)

Then there was Nick Clegg who was sent to Selkirk in the Borders. This had the benefit of being quite far away from both Dave and Ed, but there was one snag: there were Scottish people there. It wasn't long before some of the Yes Scots made their feelings known. 'We have done extraordinary things together,' Nick trumpeted. 'Team GB competed together, we defeated fascism together, we created the NHS.' No swearing, I noted, to his credit.

But amid the love, there was also hatred. Alex Salmond (for it is he) said he thought that Team Westminster was going to throw the 'kitchen sink' at Scotland, which sounded painful. But what, he was asked, about the love-bombing? 'There is an understandable degree of cynicism', carped Mr Salmon, 'about people at the last gasp jetting up to a country to tell us how to run our own affairs.'

Oh, Alex. Where is the love? Or, even, the effing love?

12 SEPTEMBER 2014

Hoots Mons! It's a conspiracy plot

I watch as Alex Salmond, leader of the Yes campaign, takes on the world and, more specifically, the BBC.

ALEX SALMOND HELD an 'international' press conference yesterday in Edinburgh where he was introduced by no less than four people. (Is that enough? Why not five?) Finally he sauntered out, a bit like a game-show host, suited and booted, his snaggle smile flashing on and off like a beacon. He leaned against the blue Yes lectern, arms out like flying buttresses. Behind him was a huge poster of a baby's hand being held by an adult. I felt sorry for the baby.

Mr Salmond adored answering questions from what he called 'our friends in the international media'. He explained how he loves the EU, human rights, peace, the UN and pelagic fish (don't ask). He told us how the Basque country had received him with 'full proper respect'. I wondered what that could mean. Did they give him a special chair? A trumpet fanfare? Or maybe his own personalised pen?

Mr Salmond said the Yes camp had approached the campaign with humility. I quite enjoyed that because if you have to say it, well, you know. But I didn't dare laugh because this was a strange press conference in that it was packed with Yes supporters who heckled questions they didn't like.

Indeed, the BBC political editor Nick Robinson wrecked the whole 'international friends' mood thing by asking if RBS's decision to move its registered office to England had any consequences. 'BBC bias!' came a cry from the Yes people.

Mr Salmond, international statesman, raised his hand to quell the rabble. He explained that this move meant nothing, RBS was merely moving a 'brass plaque' from one place to another. Did he shrug? I think he did.

But then – did the sky darken? Did thunder flash? He held up a printout from the BBC news website. The RBS story was leaked to the BBC from a Treasury source! This was very serious, a market-sensitive bombshell, a Mons Meg of an attack. Mons Meg, he explained, for the benefit of his friends in the international media, is a medieval bombard at Edinburgh Castle.

'This is a matter of extraordinary gravity,' he announced, calling for a Cabinet Office inquiry. And when the inquiry is set up he hoped that the 'impartial' BBC would investigate. At the word 'impartial', the Yes men and women laughed and clapped. (If Scotland votes Yes, will all press conferences be like this? Will they get to fire Mons Meg at people they don't like?)

'Back to our friends in the international media!' cried Mr Salmond.

'Answer the question, First Minister,' insisted Nick Robinson. 'Are there any consequences to the RBS move?'

'I'm going back to our friends in the international…'

'Answer the question…'

For a moment, I saw (and felt) a flash of anger or, perhaps, frustration scud across Mr Salmond's fleshy moon-surface face. 'Nick!' he exclaimed but then he caught himself, his voice lightening, saying that now it was the BBC that was heckling (though, actually, Nick was just being a journalist, for Mr Salmond is as hard to pin down as a unicorn is to see).

Mr Salmond ranted on about the Treasury leak and expected the 'full co-operation' of the BBC in the 'inevitable' inquiry. (Why do I suspect George Osborne will have zero interest in finding this leaker?)

The Yes people clapped wildly and Mr Salmond returned to his friends.

'Al Jazeera,' said a man who then noted: 'A lot of people regard you as trying to present yourself as more peaceful than the English.'

I tried not to laugh for I didn't want to be Mons Megged. But we'd just seen Mr Salmond at his most combative. He'd turned a story about RBS moving its registered office into a full-on attack on the Treasury and the BBC. Peaceful? The man is a political street fighter.

17 SEPTEMBER 2014

Going walkabout here is scary – and dangerous

The Labour leader is mobbed and not in a good way
as he tries to talk to voters in Edinburgh.

ED MILIBAND IS a wanted man in Scotland. They seek him here, they seek him there. Yesterday, the Yes campaign was seeking the Labour leader everywhere because it was rumoured that he was going to do a walkabout. Labour, though, weren't giving any details.

'Edinburgh,' said one aide, sotto voce. 'Afternoon.'

We had the morning to get through first. This belonged to Gordon Brown, who blew the roof off at Clydebank Town Hall. 'I LOVE THIS COUNTRY!'

he bellowed. Gordo is furious at the idea that it is not patriotic to vote No. He is incandescent at Alex Salmond's 'lies' over funding for the NHS. He is, in general, apoplectic. It was a tub-thumper of a speech to a Labour crowd. I emerged, ears ringing, exhausted, with a desire to lie down in a darkened room.

But that was not to be because I had to find Ed in Edinburgh. The whisper was that Ed would be at the rail station. Then we heard it was the Parliament building. We scrambled, like fighter planes, only to be redirected again to the St James shopping centre.

The Yes protesters got there first, a scraggly bunch, a thin line of nine. They held up a flag and signs and barked slogans such as 'Shame on the BBC' or 'You don't need poverty'. My personal favourite was this one: 'Alistair Darling is finished – in Scotland'. About 100 people milled around, waiting for Ed. Back in a corner, away from the Yes protest ('Ban the energy companies!'), the media began to interview each other – always a bad sign. But then, suddenly, someone told someone else that Ed was already in the shopping centre.

Stampede! Yes supporters, suddenly far more numerous, No supporters, TV cameras, hacks and even a few shoppers pounded into the centre. I couldn't see Ed, just a doughnut of cameras and microphones, Yessers jostling against No-ers, trying to get their signs in front. It wasn't nice.

'F***ing liar!' shouted a Yesser at the heaving giant amoebic form that, I assumed, contained Ed Miliband. It was crazy, anarchic and dangerous. The crowd pounded by. There was a lot of abuse at Ed (even 'Murderer'). A man from the Socialist Workers Party had a sign saying: 'Don't let the Nazis divide us.' Actually, I thought, the Scots are doing a pretty good job of that themselves.

We pounded by Poundland and on to John Lewis. Ed's amoeba lurched towards Supercuts. 'Supercuts!' shouted a Yesser, 'That's what Westminster are doing to us!'

Through the maelstrom, I caught a glimpse of Ed's dark suit, trying to chat to two hairdressers. A voice bellowed: 'This is what the political class looks like when it's dying!' Ed was moving faster now, out of the centre and across a walkway over four lanes of traffic. The crowd surged behind him, the walkway trembling. And then – poof! – he was gone. The last I saw of him was the top of his head, rounding a corner. Never has talking to voters been quite so scary as in Scotland.

18 SEPTEMBER 2014

Yes frontman revels in rock star adulation

Hugs and kisses, and lots of cheese, for the perpetually triumphant Mr Salmond.

WE WERE STANDING more or less in a field, outstanding as they say, just beyond the rather rundown town of Kilmarnock in the west of Scotland, waiting for Alex Salmond.

'He's delayed,' says one Yes man who looks about twelve. 'Everybody wants a selfie with him! Everywhere he goes! It's like Beatlemania!'

Love, love me do, as the Yes campaign tells Scotland: you know I love you. Maybe it's just good planning, but wherever Mr Salmond goes, except at press conferences with pesky journalists, he seems to be greeted with open arms. Yesterday, on his final Yes tour, there were hugs and kisses, backslaps and arm squeezes, for the first minister is a tactile man.

This is either the best day of his life or, if the Yessers win, the second best. He's loving it, and, like any pop star, is keeping us waiting. We have gathered at Braehead Foods, a purveyor of fine Scottish grub. One hour goes by. Then two. We are corralled into the warehouse, surrounded by towers of roasted red peppers and crushed Oreo cookies. His protection team are here, plus his cadre of adoring aides, not to mention supporters draped in the Saltire, blaring 'Scotland the Brave' into the car park. 'This is almost certainly the most exciting thing I will ever do,' says one aide, big-eyed.

And then, suddenly, he is among us! We are allowed to watch him talking to the owner of Braehead, standing among the tomato purée and bamboo shoots. He is looking trim – I have just discovered that he has his own personal chef to make sure that he stays that way – and is wearing a hi-vis jacket. Why? I have no idea, but every politician covets a hi-vis photo op.

He heads over to the soy sauce shelf for interviews. The No campaign, he says, is totally negative. This, of course, is by definition true. It was one of Mr Salmond's genius tactics to phrase the question so that he was Mr Yes, the positive one, the one giving the thumbs up. 'People want to vote for something,' he says, 'not against something.'

The word 'Scotland' is ever-present. He rubbishes David Cameron and says the only bully boys in this campaign have been on the No side. He harrumphs with disgust that anyone would think that the country of Adam Smith would not know how to run an economy.

'It's a festival of politics!' he burbles. It's a grassroots movement, a joyful carnival, a wonderful vision, a conversation with the future. We are swept into the cold room, where Mr Salmond grabs two hunks of cheese (I am sure they are not allowed on his diet), one made on Arran, the other Mull. He announces that the Yes side is the underdog, because Westminster is against them. 'But in this festival of democracy,' he says, 'underdogs have a habit of winning!'

Alex, I ask, as he puts the cheese back, what does it feel like to be a pop star?

He grins from ear to ear. 'He's been a pop star for ages!' gushes one of his aides. He laughs and heads out, already late for his rally (Hello, Perth!) and his date with the future.

20 SEPTEMBER 2014

Less Mickey Mouse now, more a wee, timorous beastie

*It was a day of drama north and south of the
border as a grey day dawns in Scotland.*

W E SHOULD HAVE known what was to come when we saw
Alex Salmond as he was driven through the damp streets of
Edinburgh early yesterday. The Mickey Mouse face, so often
wreathed in smiles, was now sombre, reflective, broken. After all the selfies,
the love-bombing, the sheer exuberance of the Yes campaign, it had ended
like this. The picture, reminiscent of the famous Thatcher shot as she left
No. 10, was politics at its most brutal.

Voters had rejected independence, 55 per cent to 45 per cent, but it seemed
the weather was one of the 'yes' voters and so the day did not dawn here so
much as creep up, mist clinging to the night, refusing to give up.

Salmond, though, had had to do just that before sunrise. 'Scotland has,
by a majority, decided not, at this stage, to become an independent country,'
he told his deflated Yessers who had gathered at a 'space' called Dynamic
Earth. The words 'at this stage' were interesting. Mr Salmond was accepting
defeat but not, apparently, total defeat. And yet he knew, for he himself has
said it so often, that there would not be another referendum anytime soon.

We really should have guessed at 10 a.m., as we stood outside Bute House,
the official residence of the first minister (think Downing Street but much
nicer aspect), waiting for his press conference. We learnt, again by rumour,
for telepathy is big here, that it had been postponed, possibly until noon. I
couldn't help but notice the lack of joy on the streets. If Yes had won, Scotland would have been a party. But No had won, so it was back to work, time
for a wee tidy-up and then, maybe, half a lager.

Mr Salmond, we were told, wasn't ready for his close-up yet. So instead
we watched events in England, where the Better Together team, always linked
only by string and paper clips, dissolved. David Cameron had been eager to

claim victory, just after 7 a.m., as he walked out of Downing Street, where his special sustainable wood lectern, which had earlier made the journey to Aberdeen for his final plea to voters, had been placed. The look on his face was one of studied earnestness, but we experienced Dave-watchers could see that every pore exuded relief. Though 'delighted' with the result (not to mention keeping his job), he immediately began to play games with his devolution vow, saying this also meant that England must also have a deal.

The hated Westminster elite were back to playing politics. Nigel Farage added his voice to the call for English votes for English MPs. It seemed way too early in the morning to hear Farage, so calculating, so staged, so English. I felt like crawling back under the duvet. Mr Salmond, high on his campaign, emblazoned with passion for independence, must have been furious as the devolution deal got murkier. Ed Miliband gave a (very) small speech but where, I wondered, was Gordo? I already was missing his marvellous ranting total-rage events, which just might have swung it in the end.

I was just about to give up on the Salmond press conference when word arrived: it would be 4 p.m. but the journalists would be hand-picked. I would not be one of the chosen. Whatever happened to Mr Salmond's 'festival of democracy'? It seemed just a trifle Sovietesque but, then, as it was explained to me, Alex Salmond was a control freak. Besides, I had a mole. The big black door opened for those who were not banned.

Rumours of resignation were still being denied. The setting was magisterial: chandeliers, gilt, mirrors. Mr Salmond seemed calm, smiling, not cocky or ebullient but, strangely, at peace. I got the feeling, as he announced that he would resign but still be involved in the fight for independence, which he said would be achieved 'in his lifetime', that actually he was quitting to spend more time with politics.

24 SEPTEMBER 2014

Ed goes to the park and finds Gareth

The Labour leader roamed around the stage, telling us about everyone he had ever met and it was only afterwards that we realised he had forgotten to mention the deficit.

ED MILIBAND'S BIG speech in Manchester contained a ten-year plan to save Britain and transform our lives. But, to be honest, it's Gareth that I remember. And the fact that if I ever meet Ed Miliband in a park, I must run the other way.

Basically Ed has been roaming the country for the past year, meeting people and demanding to know their names. It's the Starbucks syndrome, where they insist on putting your name on a cup and calling it out. But Ed takes your name and puts it in a speech. So yesterday he told us about a woman named Josephine in Scotland and a chef named Xiomara.

Then we heard of Colin, aged eighty and in hospital, who died two weeks later. And Rose, a doctor from Devon. But for some reason it's Gareth, who works for a software company, has a five-year-old daughter and can't afford to buy a home, who became fixed in my mind. As Ed ploughed through his ten-year plan for tractor production (sorry, transforming Britain), I wondered how Gareth must feel being the star of Ed's speech.

Well, OK, co-star. For Ed doesn't just meet Gareths. He also goes for walks in parks.

'You know, the other day I was in the park,' he told us. 'There were two young women who were in the park and they seemed excited to see me.' I felt that this was, already, too much information. Ed said that one came over to him, which seemed highly unlikely, and said to him: 'So it's true, you do meet famous people in this park.' This seemed even more unlikely. Then, Ed told us, the other one said: 'Yeah, it is.' Then the first one said: 'No offence, we were hoping for Benedict Cumberbatch.'

This does seem the worst dialogue of any play ever written. But I could see the girls' point. I, too, would rather meet Benedict Cumberbatch. As I tried to imagine what Sherlock would make of this whole thing, Ed said that one of the girls then told him that her generation was falling into a black hole. Millions of people had lost faith in the future, including, Ed told us, Gareth.

Gareth! I looked around the packed hall. Ed had already made someone else he had met (Elizabeth) stand up. So I guessed that Gareth wasn't there.

Behind Ed were rows of happy people sitting under four huge signs that said 'Labour's plan for Britain's future'. The music was upbeat to the point of nauseating: there was 'Happy' by Pharrell Williams and 'Hakuna Matata' from *The Lion King*, which means 'no worries'.

But, of course, Gareth and Josephine and Xiomara do have worries. Ed has a new idea to tackle them. 'An idea that is just one simple word. Together, together, together,' he chanted. 'Friends,' he now cried again. 'Together we can.'

Can we?

'Together, a different idea for Britain,' announced Ed.

I felt underwhelmed by the 'Together' thing which, with or without Gareth, still felt like a slogan devised with fridge magnet words.

29 SEPTEMBER 2014

Give Grant Shapps a cigar, he's had his finest hour

The Tories are furious over the defection of Mark Reckless to UKIP.

AT LUNCH IN Birmingham yesterday, I watched the woman across from me – still clinging to her perm, as so many Conservative women are – reading a news story that screamed 'Tories in crisis'.

A large besuited man beetled up. 'Helloooo,' he said, lowering his head to stage whisper in her ear: 'There are media going round taking photos of people reading that.'

The woman, startled, cried 'Oh!' and quickly turned the page.

However, the hierarchy of the Tory Party itself was not in page-turning mood yesterday. They were mad and they didn't care who knew it. They were ripping up the page and eating it for good measure.

'We have been betrayed!' shouted a sharp-suited Grant Shapps, the party chairman, his fervour making him sound a bit like a cuckold. For a moment I couldn't figure out to which scandal he was referring, but it soon became clear this was not a sex scandal (I always think the Tories like those) but the far greater sin of Mark Reckless's defection to UKIP.

Mr Reckless, as Grant called him, the use of honorific making it clear that no one in the Tory Party would ever call him by his Christian name again, had let down every Conservative everywhere.

'Today your trust has been abused,' said Grant. 'You have been cheated.'

Grant told the audience that he shared their sense of 'betrayal and anger'. I looked around me. No one looked even remotely angry, waving the little plastic Union Jacks they had been given. Behind Grant sat rows of people wearing Union Jack T-shirts. The young fogey next to me had a Union Jack hankie. Sartorially, this Tory conference was a new low but, actually, spirits seemed rather high.

Not, though, it seems, in the Shapps household. 'We have been let down by somebody who has repeatedly lied to his constituents and to you,' he stormed. 'He lied and lied and lied again!'

There was something about the rhythm of the words that made me think Grant was, at this moment, channelling Winston Churchill. Indeed, I suspect that Grant was thinking quite a lot about Churchill when he wrote his speech: how, he asked himself, would Winnie have reacted to the Great Betrayal that had taken place twenty-four hours earlier at the UKIP conference in Doncaster?

'Let this be our rallying cry,' Grant now intoned, looking purposefully at what I soon realised was his autocue.

Grant lowered his head, bulldog-like. Perhaps he was trying to glower. I began to worry that he might be straining his neck. If only he could have a cigar clamped between his teeth.

'My friends,' he said, though that seemed a little presumptuous to me.

'We are going to campaign hard in Rochester and Strood. Because the people there deserve an MP who will keep his word.'

Grant Shapps tried to glare, eyebrows down, looking as resolute as it is possible for him (which, I am afraid, is not very). 'So let us resolve today. We will not waver. We will not be blown off course. We finish the job we have started.' Grant was fighting them on the beaches (well, the banks of the Medway at least). He was fighting them in the fields and in the streets of Rochester and Strood. He was never going to surrender. This was, make no mistake about it, his finest hour.

7 OCTOBER 2014

Vince's sense of humour? Atrocious

What does Ed Miliband not have in common
with Gladstone? Now we know.

YOU KNOW YOU are in trouble when Vince Cable is the one who is supposed to lift your spirits. It's like putting the Grim Reaper in charge of birthday party planning. Since Vince went into government, he has been as grey as an overcast rainy day in, well, to pick a place at random, Glasgow.

But a man's got to do what a man's got to do. Vince had to start with a joke. So, in true Vince style, he decided to make it about the Bulgarian Atrocities. Only a Lib Dem would see the comedy potential in mass death from 1876. But that's what makes them especially fun to watch.

Vince arrived looking, as ever, like the Nutty Professor without a satnav. He immediately spoke of Gladstone, but this is normal for Lib Dems. Indeed, if you don't mention Gladstone in the first few minutes you run the risk of being fined.

Gladstone's feats of oratory were legendary, Vince noted, and his speech on the Bulgarian Atrocities was especially so. At the word 'Atrocities', the man next to me perked up. 'Oh yes,' he murmured, as if it held fond memories.

'He is said to have spoken for five and a half hours, without notes, from memory,' said Vince, reading his autocue. 'As far as we know, he didn't have to issue a statement the following day apologising for forgetting to mention Bulgaria or the Atrocities!'

Laugh? They positively cackled, clapping wildly, thrilled to be making fun of Ed Miliband, who had forgotten to mention the deficit in his conference speech, thrilled to be listening to Vince (the 'guru of growth', according to his introduction) and not to be reading the polls that predict their near obliteration. To me, the Lib Dems this year deserve respect just for being here, an experiment in mass delusion that I hope is being studied by scientists around the world.

Vince reminded us that David Cameron had also memorised a speech, the one that won him the Tory leadership in 2005, in which he talked about how much he cared about the underclass and saving the planet. 'You might recall the hoodies and the huskies,' he noted. The man next to me did a mini-harrumph, a hiccup of outrage (though it may have been just a small burp).

'Which raises an interesting question,' noted Vince. 'Is it worse for politicians to forget what to say or to remember what to say but forget to do anything about it?'

More laughs! More claps! This from the party – indeed from the Secretary of State himself – who vowed to scrap tuition fees and then tripled them. Vince didn't mention that as he poured praise on his party (and himself). In all areas, he said, the Lib Dems had a 'massive responsibility: to be the voice of sanity, seriousness and sense'.

Sanity? The Lib Dems? I think not. Just before his speech, I overheard two Lib Dems gushing to each other: 'Oh haven't you met a viscount? Viscounts are LOVELY!' Another conversation began: 'Have you ever been to North Korea?' It's a chat-up line you would only ever hear here.

Vince likes to be seen to be against the Tory grain and so he extolled the virtues of immigration. 'The Tories are horribly torn between open economic liberalism and their inward-looking, UKIP-facing grassroots, who probably see Clacton-on-Sea as the new Constantinople – holding out against the alien hordes!'

The man next to me adored that. 'A bit of Byzantine history,' he chuckled, thrilled to be there and to be seen to be sane.

8 OCTOBER 2014

Nigel joins big guns with (at least) three pints on walkabout

*Farage arrived, tanks at the ready, to fight the
Heywood and Middleton by-election.*

IT WAS 12.01, one minute after opening time at the Gardeners Arms in Heywood, and so where else would Nigel Farage be but at the bar, ordering a pint of Wainwright's pale ale? He and other Ukippers were having a quick drink (well two, actually, but who's counting) on their way to what was described, unbelievably, as a tank museum campaign stop.

'No, I will not be standing on a tank!' insisted Nigel, his every sip accompanied by the flash and click of cameras. 'I don't do stunts anymore.'

Right. No stunts. So off we went up the A6045 to Collop Gate Farm where a line of tanks, yes, actual tanks, bought on the internet, had been set up as a unique sort of meet-and-greet for Nigel.

'I don't do stunts!' he shouted as he strode, double-breasted blue suit open, city slicker shoes splashing through the rain, towards a Chieftain Mk10 now decorated with a huge UKIP banner. Nigel chatted to one of the tank enthusiasts (as I think they are called). 'This is a great little hobby!'

In seconds, indeed, faster than you can say 'stunt', Nigel was up the ladder, standing first next to the Chieftain and then on the tank itself, looking slightly apprehensive as his leather-soled shoes slipped ever so slightly. 'My stunts never go wrong!' cried the man whose plane crashed in 2010 after the UKIP banner got caught in the propeller.

He was, for a moment, in boy's toy heaven, standing on a Chieftain, two pints inside him, flanked by the barrel of a gun that, in another place, had sent shells twelve miles into battle. 'We are parking our tanks on Labour's lawn!' shouted Nigel to the bedraggled posse of press in the farmyard.

You may be the first politician who has fought a by-election in an actual tank, I noted.

'I'm not a politician!' he insisted.

So what are you then?

The man who owned the tanks knew: 'He's a spokesman for this country.'

But Nigel didn't hear that, for he was, as usual, talking himself. 'I'm an ordinary chap', he insisted, 'who wants change.'

UKIP may indeed, as the polls suggest, lose the Heywood and Middleton by-election tomorrow, but Nigel Farage is having as much fun as it is legal to have on a campaign trail. The actual candidate, John Bickley, seems nothing more than a prop, though he didn't seem to mind, noting that he had been in the entertainment industry: 'I'm used to dealing with the talent.'

Our next stop was Kirkway shopping parade in Middleton. We arrived, wet and bedraggled, ready to meet some voters (as opposed to tanks). There was only one problem. We couldn't find Nigel.

'He's in the pub,' said one of his many bald minders. We scurried over to a place called Thornberries and, indeed, there was Nigel, pint in hand, surrounded by UKIP supporters carrying banners, grinning wildly.

Spookily, every voter that Nigel met (John occasionally getting a look-in) was voting for him. 'We want our country back,' said a woman named Sharon, escaping the rain in a café called, optimistically, Hopes. The rain began in earnest now. A reporter asked Nigel if he could see why UKIP is lagging behind in support from women. After all, it had been a day of drinking pints and tanks.

'In fact, there were more women Russian tank drivers than men at the battle of Kursk in 1943!' insisted Nigel. Right, well, you can't argue with that. Tanks, as they say, for the memories.

24 OCTOBER 2014

Woof woof as MPs fight to be top dog

The Westminster canine show was even more barking than usual.

I T WAS RAINING, or possibly reigning, cats and dogs at Westminster yesterday. First stop was the one event that gives MPs an excuse to be barking: I speak, of course, of the Westminster Dog of the Year show, held next to the House of Lords, in Victoria Tower Gardens.

I immediately spotted Nadine Dorries, MP and jungle star, gripping a white bundle. 'This is Darcy,' she explained to a media scrum. The five-month-old Westie, which sadly looked nothing like Colin Firth, jumped down. 'And is this Darcy's first professional engagement?' the man from the BBC asked politely.

I next met Inca, a fire dog, wearing feet-protecting booties. Her human, so to speak, was Penny Mordaunt, the fire minister, who I happen to know owns copious numbers of felines. 'Yes, I have cats,' she said defensively as Inca begged for a croissant. 'Alas, there is no search-and-rescue moggy division.'

But there was no time to interview Inca, or indeed Penny, for I was on my own mission. It was rumoured that Michael Gove was taking time out from his onerous duties as Chief Whip to appear with his Bichon Frise.

Instead, though, I ran into a former Chief Whip, Andrew Mitchell, attached to a rather beautiful Welsh Springer Spaniel named Scarlet. He told me that her policies were to be tough on cats and on the causes of cats, adding: 'Number two, she will abolish world poverty.'

How to respond? I was saved by Sarah Vine, newspaper columnist and wife of Mr Gove, who bustled up clutching something that looked like a small cloud with eyes.

'This is the ridiculous dog!' she announced. 'It's Snowy. We call him Fat Sheep. Can you see why?'

What to say? Did she say sheep or chic? It's so hard to tell at these events. 'He is very naughty and greedy and fat. It's a boy. Everyone thinks it's a girl. He is, in fact, a ferocious male.'

Snowy, a cheese-loving puppy-farm rescue, looked about as ferocious as, well, the Chief Whip. But wait, I said, didn't the Chancellor own a Bichon Frise too? 'George loved Snowy,' Sarah explained, 'and so he went and got Lola, who is proper-breed Bichon and they are married.'

'Married?' I asked, almost afraid to go there.

'Snowy is married to Lola,' Sarah said briskly. 'I have the pictures. There was a ceremony with flowers.'

Yowsers! I went inside, to the chamber, to see if I could find the Chief Whip, but instead I discovered that MPs were discussing, possibly in honour of heavy rain, the subject of cats and whether parliament should get one to kill the mice. 'There are very clear practical and technical difficulties,' an MP who sits on the commons commission insisted. Technical difficulties? With a cat? It seems that there were fears that more than one cat was needed: 'Herding cats is quite difficult.'

But where was the Chief Whip? I soon discovered he was outside, on the medal podium, with Snowy, who had come second to a lovely Alsatian owned by Labour's Robert Flello. 'Once again the winner is German,' the Chief Whip said. To which I can only add: meow.

11 NOVEMBER 2014

The question that be not now put? And they call this a democracy...

The non-debate debate over what was supposed to be
the European arrest warrant ended in madness.

I N THE END, it all came down to something that sounded like an absurdity worthy of Gilbert and Sullivan. 'I wish to put the question that the question be not now put,' said Yvette Cooper, the shadow Home Secretary, flying solo at the dispatch box. Across from her, Theresa

May's eyes flashed. There was a realisation, a bit late, that this was now serious.

'That is on page 404 of Erskine May,' burbled Mr Speaker, exceptionally ebullient, bouncing around in his giant chair, apparently thrilled that MPs were having their version of a 100-car motorway pile-up. The rubberneckers flooded in, the Civil Service box full, the gossip so intense that I could see it.

The device of The Question That Be Not Now Put is a way of making the House of Commons stop. Just stop. Cease. Have a nap. Come back another day. The decision by Ms Cooper to force a vote on such a thing – so arcane that, in the Russian Doll of Arcanery, it is one of the teeniest of dolls – came after hours of weird legislative behaviour caused by the oddity that the debate about the European arrest warrant was not, in fact, a debate about it at all. Instead, it was about a clutch of regulations but not the one thing that everyone wanted to talk about, rebel over, shout out loud about.

Why did the government choose to omit the key three words from the motion? No one knew. The Case of the Missing Words discombobulated all. 'I'm completely confused,' admitted Sir Edward Leigh. 'I read in all my papers that we are debating the European arrest warrant today. Apparently we are not now. What are we voting on?' Mr Speaker trilled: 'You are voting on the regulations!'

On the front bench, Mrs May, so icy that penguins cannot help but flock to her, barely moved her pale powdery face. In the farthest corner, Jacob Rees-Mogg's monocle trembled. He arose, legs as long as Lincoln, double-breasted suit covering the heart of an eighteenth-century gentleman on a parliamentary mission. 'This is not right!' he insisted. 'This does seem to be procedural prestidigitation.'

Prestidigitation agitation indeed. Sir William Cash called it 'chicanery'. Keith Vaz said it was a shambles. The vote that was now just an 'indicative vote' was an artifice, sly, contemptible. As the chaos grew, whips began to rotate like Magimixes at a cake contest. Michael Gove, the Chief Whip, who was described yesterday as having a brain the size of a planet – which made me wonder who lived there besides him – was in intense discussions with everyone.

The Mogg arose again, magisterial in his top hat. 'We have whips scuttling round this house! This is a procedural absurdity. It is legislative legerdemain!'

Kenneth Clarke wanted MPs to keep calm and carry on. 'Can I suggest, before we decide this is the biggest threat to parliamentary democracy since the Gunpowder Plot, we allow the Home Secretary to explain?'

But Mrs May, thawing herself just enough to stand, didn't seem too keen to explain the missing three words, which is a shame because everyone really wanted to know what the hell was going on. The government won the first vote by only nine votes. Mrs May's face was so pale that she was almost translucent, like an iceberg. She won the Question That Not Now Be Put vote by more. But this was no real victory. For surely, in any sane democracy, the Question That Not Now Be Put should not have to be put at all.

13 NOVEMBER 2014

There's no place like gnome for the Reckless defector

I head to Rochester to see UKIP's newest candidate in action.

MARK RECKLESS STOPPED in a small garden of a small house that was populated by six very small gnomes. 'Do you want a photograph of me with the gnomes?' he asked, somewhat recklessly, emitting a laugh that sounded a bit rusty for lack of use.

I cannot think of any other politician who might think that was a good idea. But then, Reckless is not A. N. Other. He is The Defector. The One the Tories Hate. The man they vowed to smash in the Rochester and Strood by-election. I have always seen him as a bit uptight and dour. Indeed, it is one of my theories that he has no sense of humour.

'You've got me bang to rights there,' he says, cheerily.

Wait? Did I hear something close to an actual chuckle? Reckless says he feels free now, and he does seem liberated, beetling down the aspirationally named Hero Walk in Rochester, meeting voters and their gnomes, talking about Europe. I daren't point out that the gnomes, original name Gartenzwerge, were one-time immigrants themselves.

But make no mistake. This is not politics as usual. Mark Reckless – dogged, ideological, earnest, emphatically uncharismatic – is in the fight of his political life.

'Mark is not *un*popular,' explains a UKIP aide carefully. 'He's just not known.'

Not known? With a name like Reckless? That seems unlikely.

The polls are in his favour, but every real person (i.e. not a politician or a journalist) I talked to thought it would be close. Actually, it's not that easy to find a real person in Rochester High Street, such is the influx from SW1 to this historic, if a little tatty, town. Dickens lived nearby, a fact that is hard to miss, with shops such as Tiny Tim's gift shop.

I stop in at a place called Sweet Expectations. 'The Tories have almost caught up!' burbles the owner, pointing to her window where customers are encouraged to choose an appropriately coloured bon-bon to put in the old-fashioned jars. Sure enough, the blues are almost up to the pinky UKIP ones (I wonder, briefly, if they are fruitcake flavoured).

Tragically, I must report that the Lib Dem jar contained only seven very lonely lemon sours.

In the street, I see Rob Wilson, the Tory minister for civil society. So, I ask, how's it going? 'Reckless is very unpopular,' he says. Not exactly civil, I thought, but then this is war.

Still, I have to say it: there remains something refreshing about UKIP. Yesterday's celebrity was Douglas Carswell, but Nigel Farage is a frequent visitor.

Ah, I ask Mark, who famously got so drunk that he couldn't vote on the Budget, have you been to the pub with him then?

Mark explained that he hasn't touched a drop for some years now. 'I'm encouraging Nigel to come with me to tea shops instead.'

That's a campaign he may not win.

14 NOVEMBER 2014

Intrepid Ed back on planet Earth to tackle dark forces

I cannot keep count of the number of times that Ed Miliband has relaunched himself, but this one, coming as the European Space Agency's robotic Philae landed on a comet, was out of this world.

WE GATHERED, AS you do for these historic scientific occasions, to watch the political probe called Phila-Ed attempt a successful re-entry on to Planet Earth. Scientists have been worried for some time about Phila-Ed: he has been off course, at times by millions of miles, and last week fears grew that he had become overwhelmed by negative forces, the victim of a vortex of bad news and worse polls.

This was not a relaunch, just to be clear, but a re-entry. The chosen location was 'friendly', i.e. University College London. Phila-Ed, well-known for his geek tendencies, gravitates towards brainiacs. Soft jazz played in the background, a strange choice, reminiscent of lost days in lounge bars with low lights and banquette seating where people drink Manhattans when they should be working. Still, ours is not to wonder why.

A hush fell over the crowd. Necks craned. Phila-Ed was among us! The man next to me jumped to his feet. A woman dressed in salmon (not, sadly, Salmond) punched the air with her fist. Applause rolled over us. I observed Phila-Ed's long disjointed legs bend as they absorbed the impact.

Phila-Ed stared in my direction. Why? A whole room full of Phila-Ed fans and he was looking at me.

'There is a saying', he said, voice programmed to hearty levels, 'which goes: "What doesn't kill you makes you stronger." In the last few days, I know what it means.' The crowd leaned in. 'You need resilience in this job,' he said. Actually, I thought, what you really need is an Alpha Particle X-ray Spectrometer, but maybe that is the same thing.

'You need thick skin,' he insisted. Why, I wondered, doesn't he mention his comet nuclear analyser? 'But, above all, you need belief in what you are doing.' Ah, yes, belief. Always handy if you don't have a spectrometer or even a comet to land on.

It was a good speech, not out of this world but certainly passionate as he set out his horror of a 'zero zero' economy (zero-hour contracts for the workers, zero tax for the bosses). Britain was deeply unequal, unfair, unjust. 'That's why I want to be prime minister,' said Phila-Ed. 'To change it.'

This was the speech that he should have given at Manchester. He was, I realised, actually reading it: he wasn't staring at me at all, but at the transparent autocue that stood, like a weird lamp, in front of me.

He does seem to believe that powerful dark forces are out to get him. Was he, a dark force in the media asked him, the victim of a media storm? 'I'm not in the whingeing business,' insisted Phila-Ed.

Perhaps his most revealing moment came when he was asked to name his biggest mistake over the past four years. Surely he would mention the missing spectrometer now, I thought. But Phila-Ed didn't pause for even a nanosecond. 'The lesson that I learnt most is about going out more and engaging more, spending less time in Westminster and more time in the country.'

So there we had it. It seems that his new mission is to give us more Ed, not less. He's going to boldly go to infinity and beyond or even, in a pinch, Woking. Brace yourselves.

26 NOVEMBER 2014

Gritty Dom brings us pearls of his wisdom

Michael Gove's former special adviser explains how Westminster works (or doesn't).

DOMINIC CUMMINGS USED to be Michael Gove's special adviser at the Department for Education but he has reinvented himself as a perma-critic of the government. He is the self-appointed grit in the oyster, the rash on the body politic, the man who speaks truth – more or less endlessly – to power.

I don't know why he doesn't make it his official job title, actually. Yesterday, when he appeared to discuss (i.e. trash) the Civil Service before the Public Administration Committee, he was asked what he did.

'Unemployed!' he cried. How much better if he were to just shout: 'Grit!'

So here's the World of Whitehall According to Dom: disaster strewn, dystopic, dangerous to know. 'When Michael and I arrived at the Department of Education in 2010, it was a complete and utter basket case. Everything that could go wrong did go wrong. Contracts blew up left, right and centre. Procurements blew up left, right and centre.'

He was talking so fast I thought that maybe, like a piece of grit, he doesn't have to breathe. The words were racing, Lewis Hamilton style, screeching round the room. 'You would get legal advice that this procurement would get blown out if you go ahead, it's blown out if you don't, judicial reviewed if you do. Whatever you do, you'll get judicial reviewed! Makes no difference. Screwed!'

Still no breath. I examined his large egg-head. The mouth just never stopped. 'There is also a culture where no one cares. It's normal. Oh you lost £50 million? Oh well, that's life. These things happen. Are you going to fire the guy in charge. OF COURSE NOT!'

There is no incentive to speak the truth, get to the bottom of things, criticise the system.

'FISH ROTS FROM THE HEAD!' explained Dominic, a marvellously succinct grit-based observation of how government works. But in Westminster the head just gets promoted, rotten or not. The Prime Minister isn't really interested, the Civil Service isn't interested if he isn't and, well, you get the picture.

Dominic wants Whitehall to work more like the airline industry. Failure there is very rare because the pilot would go down with the plane. I tried to imagine how Whitehall would work if people died as a consequence of failure. It wasn't a good thought, the street strewn with bodies.

'What about leadership? Leadership as a skill?' asked the chairman, Bernard Jenkin.

Dominic emitted a dirty laugh. 'If they got rid of most of the senior leadership now, what leadership would you be losing? You've got the blind leading the blind!'

I began to admire his relentless negativity. 'We had disaster after disaster and, at 3.30 p.m., you'd see the guy in charge slinking home in the lift. Why? Because he doesn't care. It makes no difference to him. The answer to that is not fear. The whole incentive structure is wrong.'

But why is that man so disengaged?

'It's totally widespread! It's normal. Failure is TOTALLY NORMAL!'

Wow. A brave MP asked what could make the system change.

'Historically, things change in a crisis,' noted Dom, adding brightly that after Pearl Harbor the entire American system of security changed.

Pearl Harbor? Surely we can get away without a declaration of war. Still, if you're the grit in the oyster, you should know about pearls.

21 JANUARY 2015

750 glorious years and it's all about mangoes

With a bit of time travel magic, I bring Simon de Montfort from 1265 to 2015 in action.

P ARLIAMENT CELEBRATED A big birthday yesterday – 750 glorious years – as only it could: by talking about fruit, fish and pillow power. Sadly there were no sketch-writers present when Simon de Montfort's merry band of prelates, magnates and knights gathered in 1265 and so we will never know what really happened. But yesterday, as I watched proceedings, I wondered what de Montfort would say if he were to join me, his body parts magically reunited and head reattached after his bloody end at the Battle of Evesham.

The first thing you need to know about de Montfort is that he clanks – but then, he was wearing the very latest in chainmail. And, of course, he isn't even English. 'Zut alors!' he cried.

I peered down to see the object of his fascination. It was the unmistakably orb-like figure of Keith Vaz, aka The Great Vaz, who represents Leicester East. De Montfort was the sixth Earl of Leicester and so may almost have been a constituent.

'Will the Foreign Secretary join me in welcoming the decision taken thirty minutes ago by the EU to raise the ban on the import of Alphonso mangoes from India?' the Great Vaz exclaimed.

Philip Hammond, tall and thin, a good candidate for chainmail, was effusive: 'I am absolutely clear that there should be full transparency on all issues concerning mangoes.'

'Mangoes?' repeated de Montfort, eyes quizzical, forehead no doubt furrowed under all that metal.

But I had no time to explain for now a real, live baron, as in John Baron, the MP for Basildon and Billericay, was on his feet asking a question about soft power. I wish that I could say that the baron was answered by a squire but, instead, it was a Swire, as in Hugo, who is a foreign minister. 'I am sure you would agree that this country probably does soft power better than any other country,' he insisted, as if we were leading the world in pillows.

'Soft power?' asked de Montfort before suddenly pointing (more clanking). I followed his gaze down to the not-inconsiderable form of Sir Peter Tapsell, the ageless Father of the House. 'Tapsell!' cried our founder. I was not surprised as I had always assumed that Sir Peter has met everyone, starting with Moses.

Our attention was taken now by Labour's Alison Seabeck, who was, appropriately, asking questions about angling. 'On democracy day,' she said (happy birthday to us!), 'I am concerned that the fisheries minister has made a statement on his personal Facebook page specific to changes in bass fishing, saying that he has made a breakthrough.'

De Montfort put his head (still attached) in his hands. Facebook! Fishing! Democracy used to be so simple in 1265 when all you had to do was imprison the king.

Ms Seabeck didn't think Facebook was the right place to make a formal statement. 'Fishers directly affected are finding out about it from cross-posting from sea anglers!' she despaired.

Mr Speaker called another knight, Sir Edward Leigh, who noted what a special day it was. Mr Speaker addressed this with his usual flowery con-flagration of words: 'All sorts of plans have been developed to mark and commemorate that anniversary, about which members will hear, and with which they will be involved. I will – of course – have something to say on that matter.'

Of course. I looked over at de Montfort but it was too late: he was already fleeing, back to the relative sanity of 1265.

28 JANUARY 2015

Sir Jeremy tells us all about his marvellous dashboard

The head of the Civil Service explains, in his own special language, how Whitehall works.

I HAVE TO SAY that to watch Sir Jeremy Heywood in action is a beautiful thing. He may look like a cross between Mr Benn and Tintin, with a really very impressive front cowlick, but the language is just so very, very special.

The head of the Civil Service slips and slides through sentences, an electric eel in the deepest of oceans, effortlessly gliding, eliding, making sure he never actually says anything of meaning. This is a tongue that is not so much Esperanto as Desperando. Yesterday I learnt about horizon scanning and stove-piping and something called 'deep functionality'.

My favourite sentence, though, was when Sir Jeremy said: 'That is on my dashboard.'

I tried to imagine what Sir Jeremy's dashboard would look like. I suspect there are no furry dice hanging over it. I can tell you that there are many, many things on his dashboard. Big Data is on it. Deep functionality in leadership is on it. There is also something called the 'talent matrix' that civil servants are scored on. Sentence after sentence amazed me: for those of us who love words, listening to Sir Jeremy was the linguistic equivalent of exploring the Great Barrier Reef.

Take this one. 'We need to keep an eye on mainstream skills like knowing how to succeed in Brussels.' (Brussels is very much on his dashboard, though not necessarily in a sprout-like way.)

I was there, at this hearing of the Public Administration Committee, to hear what Sir Jeremy had to say (or not) about the delay of the Chilcot Inquiry report. Sadly, as we soon learnt, Chilcot was not on Sir Jeremy's dashboard. 'I don't think I have been responsible for delays to the Chilcot process,' he said. Do you see how it's not quite a denial, more of a squiggle around any sort of responsibility? He told us, repeatedly, he could not speak for Sir John Chilcot. 'That is really a question for Sir John,' he said.

There were a few questions that were not for Sir John but for Sir Jeremy. (When you reach a certain level in Westminster, everyone is a Sir. It's a law.) There was an actual row about Sir Jeremy's interpretation of the code for special advisers that allows political activity. MPs were furious. Sir John just stared at them, eyes blinking behind wire specs, as if they were an exhibit in a museum. Eels don't fight, they squiggle.

But, mostly, we were talking about things on Sir Jeremy's dashboard.

Greg Mulholland is a Lib Dem, an endangered species himself. He said that civil servants talked about something called horizon-scanning and stove-piping. Why were they speaking such ludicrous jargon?

'Do you have strategies for horizon-scanning and stove-piping?' Greg demanded.

Sir Jeremy looked ever so slightly pained. Of course he could not just say 'yes'. Instead he explained, words swimming around him, about how people worked in different departments but didn't seem to realise there were common themes. They shouldn't stove-pipe. They needed to horizon-scan. 'I don't think there is any great obstacle in the language,' he said.

'Do you tell your very large team they are not to do any stove-piping?' demanded Greg.

'I have a very small team,' Sir Jeremy said.

But, then, it's hard to fit too many people into a stove pipe.

5 FEBRUARY 2015

Time waits for one man and his £9 million dithering

Sir John Chilcot explains why he can't explain what's happened to his inquiry into the Iraq War.

THE CODENAME FOR the attack on Iraq was 'shock and awe'. Yesterday, Sir John Chilcot, the man who time forgot, and who has forgot time, gave us his version when he launched Operation Shockingly Awful.

Sir John arrived, looking a bit doddery, more grandpa than mandarin, his face pleasantly crumpled in a Shar Pei way. It has been four years since I have seen Sir John in action (or 'inaction' as the case may be), taking testimony. The whole inquiry has cost us £9 million and counting. Finally, as dither turned to delay, and the long grass reached up to the sky, MPs have decided to ask what is going on.

It was the perfect Sir John setting. The foreign affairs committee, overseen by the urbane Sir Richard Ottaway, is about as scary as a kitten. One member, Nadhim Zahawi, whose family comes from Iraq, asked if there was a possible date for publication.

The face crumpled just a little bit more. 'One doctrine that I sought to establish is that while there is no running commentary of our progress, from time to time, when it's appropriate, I write to the Prime Minister to explain where we've got to,' he said. 'I have very much the feelings of the families affected in mind when I do that.'

There is so much wrong with that answer. Where to start? Running commentary? Inchworms move faster. Write to the Prime Minister? Why not just tell us or, better, the families? 'Surely you have an idea,' asked Nadhim, 'roughly, approximately?'

Sir John did not. He didn't want to raise hopes that may be dashed. Operation Shockingly Awful is not about setting deadlines. Instead, it is about Maxwellisation, the process in which Sir John writes to everyone criticised in the report and allows them to respond. Sir John calls these people 'Maxwellees'. So had he given the Maxwellees a deadline?

'We have a very clear doctrine about that, which is that people deserve a reasonable amount of time but a reasonable amount is by no means an indefinite amount.'

MPs looked at him through hooded eyes. Sir John couldn't tell us how long reasonable might be. He just knew it wouldn't be before the election.

I was beginning to see the vast scale of Operation Shockingly Awful. Sir John is ruthless in his reasonableness. He does not think the Iraq Inquiry has been delayed. It has taken years because, well, these things do. He, like Louis Armstrong, has all the time in the world. The report will have rigour and documents (150,000 have been examined). Plus, and Sir John said this with particular pride, it had a vast number of footnotes.

Sir Ming Campbell asked how many had received Maxwellisation letters. The face had another mini-crumple. 'I have thought hard about how far I could properly go about helping the committee on this particular point,' Sir John said. 'I don't think I can give even an indication.'

Sir John, when asked again, refused again: 'I am afraid that I risk you feeling that I am being obdurate.'

So, Sir Ming asked, did Sir John ever rue the day he took this on? Sir John, whose laugh is soundless, said: 'I try very hard not to rue the day.' But surely, Sir Ming, that question is for us. Do we rue the day? I think we do.

6 FEBRUARY 2015

It's a long way down for Lib Dems facing the abyss

Nick Clegg and Danny Alexander launch their
austerity plan in a sky-high champagne bar.

TO SHANGRI-LA, THEN, to hear all about the Liberal Democrats' fiscal plans. I mean the five-star hotel, not the Utopia, although as we zipped up to the fifty-second floor of the Shard, it was a little hard to tell the difference. This is the kind of place where you do not take just one lift to get there. You go to floor thirty-five and switch. For a brief moment, I allow myself to feel wealthy enough to afford this ride.

We emerge into a glass-walled James Bond-type lounge called the Gong Bar. Apparently, there is also an infinity pool up here, somewhere, but it is not in the Gong Bar. Instead, we find Nick Clegg and Danny Alexander standing behind lecterns that have little mottos that say: 'Stronger economy, fairer society.'

It takes a certain kind of genius to launch a fiscal plan about austerity in a champagne bar in the clouds. The view would be spectacular, if a bit scary – with the Thames reduced to a wide ribbon, the Gherkin almost pickle-sized – except that the mist and the rain meant that it was all a bit, well, white out there.

'For us, austerity was always a means to the end, and the end is in sight,' said Nick.

We peered out the window-walls. Murk. The end was not in sight, but then very little was.

Nick and Danny stood in front of a glass wall. Behind them was free-fall. It looked perilous, but the Liberal Democrats are used to that. Nick, for instance, is facing decapitation in Sheffield with the most recent poll showing him trailing Labour by ten points. Danny is fighting for his political life in Inverness against the SNP. In the circumstances, abseiling down the Shard is probably almost calming.

The fiscal plan was all about the centre ground (so, so far below, I thought, for I am not great with heights). The Lib Dems are cutting less than the Tories and borrowing less than Labour.

Nick compared the Tory economic plan to a Tea Party manifesto.

'Only the Liberal Democrats can offer light at the end of the tunnel,' said Nick. Again, we peered behind him. Total mist.

The first question was brutal: 'Aren't you both personally on the edge of the abyss?'

Nick hit back: 'I think the poll today was – surprise, surprise – from the Labour Party's paymasters in Unite. I think it is complete and utter nonsense!'

Danny burbled: 'You are very welcome to come and visit Inverness and see a wee bit for yourself!'

Nick seemed to reserve his special dislike for his coalition partner. 'The Conservatives are literally coming up with totally kooky made-up figures – oh, have a tax cut here, have a tax cut there, we don't know how to pay for it. It is nonsense. They know it is nonsense. It is implausible and undeliverable.'

Then came the Ed Balls question. As you may know (and if you don't, you are spending too much time in the infinity pool), Ed Balls, when asked this week to name a business supporter, could only come up with 'Bill Somebody'.

So who could Nick name?

'We have more than Bill,' said Nick. Who? 'Richard Reed. The founder of Innocent drinks. He's a big support, as are many others.' Who? 'I'm not going to give you a litany of names!' spluttered Nick. 'I will send it to you on a postcard!'

A postcard from Shangri-La. That will be special.

9 FEBRUARY 2015

How do you solve a problem like Tristram and the nuns?

*Labour's education spokesman learns why he
should never have taken on the Sisterhood.*

I AM NOT GOING to make a, er, habit of writing about Tristram Hunt and nuns, although I still can hardly believe that he has managed to pick a fight with the Sisterhood.

The nun question did not come up so much as ambush the shadow Education Secretary on *The Andrew Marr Show* yesterday. Tristram, whose name I simply cannot write enough, has been putting himself about lately and I wasn't surprised to see him there, looking raffish and talking earnestly about the Sure Start early education programme.

'This is about making sure those disadvantaged children enter reception "school-ready",' burbled Tristram, who should know better than to say such things. (Surely 'school-ready' should be banned? Meals may be 'oven-ready' but kids cannot be compared to lasagne.)

Anyone but a politician could see the nun question was lurking. Last week Tristram had managed to enrage all nun-lovers (not to mention *Sound of Music* fans) when he'd inferred that nuns weren't as good in the classroom as trained teachers. Ever since, he has been the victim of something I would call 'Wimple Rage'. Really, he should have apologised immediately: 'Forgive me, Sisters,' he would have said, 'for I have sinned.'

Sadly Tristram did not take my advice. Indeed, I think that he thought he'd got away with it when Andrew Marr, upon switching topics, chose Mammon over God. Was Labour, he asked, really so anti-business? 'I'm enormously enthusiastic about businessmen and women making money,' gushed Tristram. 'We are a furiously, passionately, aggressively pro-business party.'

Right, said Andrew, so what about nuns then? A gulp travelled down the side of Tristram's neck. He beetled his eyebrows and put on a super serious pious face. Yes, I thought, pray. It's your only hope.

So, asked Andrew, could nuns be good teachers? 'I'm hugely in favour of people working in education,' feinted Tristram. 'That's not an answer,' thwacked Andrew.

Tristram explained, his face brimming with good intentions, that he wanted the best-qualified teachers in the classroom.

'Including nuns?' asked Andrew.

'Well, we are not...' waffled Tristram.

'Yes or no?' A look of fatigue passed over Tristram's schoolboyish features. 'Look, I said on Friday if I had offended nuns in any way, that certainly was not my intention. My point was this...'

Andrew, now impersonating a battering ram, asked again.

'We need a highly effective qualified teacher cohort,' whimpered Tristram.

As the questions continued, something inside Tristram died. 'I am sure', he said finally, 'there are brilliant teachers who are nuns who are doing a fantastic job.'

So there you have it. Nuns are not just good teachers. They are brilliant. They are fantastic. Indeed, they are nun-tastic. I don't think Tristram will mess with them again.

12 FEBRUARY 2015

Democracy in the pink (or is it magenta?)

There is only one question on everyone's lips as we
rush to Stevenage to see the bubblegum bus.

I T IS NOT the first time that I have waited for a bus, but this, of course, was not just any bus. It was, or so I was led to believe, a Barbie bus. Well, maybe a bit bigger. This is because it was pink or, possibly, magenta.

'There it is!' we cried as the bus turned into the approach road to the Stevenage Arts and Leisure Centre. The barrier rose and the Women to

Women bus crept forward, as pink as you can be and still be legal, a giant blob of bubblegum on wheels. Cameras rolled. Cameras clicked. The media mini-scrum surged.

'I'm here in front of the pink bus,' reported a TV reporter, 'or is it magenta?'

The pink side door slid open. Labour's deputy leader, Harriet Harman, emerged and we all noted that she was not wearing pink. Other Labour MPs followed, also wearing an array of non-pink-ness. I waited until the last had emerged but, disappointingly, Barbie was not among them.

A posse of photographers, all male, circled the bus, shooting it from all angles. It reminded me of those automobile shows when photographers clicked away as a woman dressed, if not in pink then in not in very much, writhed on the bonnet of a new car. Now, in Harriet World, there was no need for a scantily clad woman. The vehicle was fascinating in itself because it was, amazingly, defiantly, eye-poppingly, pink.

There was only one question on all TV reporters' lips.

'Why pink?' they asked Harriet, before adding: 'Or is it magenta?'

Harriet did not answer directly (she is a politician). Earlier she told us it was, in fact, the 'correct colour'. Now she added: 'It's an eye-catching colour. This bus is not just a colour. It's about something. It's about our democracy.'

Is it? I thought it was about being pink. The entire (and overwhelmingly male) Westminster world is excited by its colour, deemed to be patronising and sexist, a gender stereotype on wheels, an insult to all. I must admit that I like pink (and magenta), but I may be wrong.

Harriet, shamefully veering off-pink, tried to talk about childcare and equal pay and how to reach the 9.1 million women who didn't vote in the last election. But what was this? A protester had come up behind Harriet, holding a giant pink sign. Later I would discover his name was Bobby Smith, a New Fathers for Justice campaigner who is angry that a court has ruled that he cannot see his two girls.

'You didn't want to see men in pink,' said Mr Smith. 'Well here I am. This is the last straw. It's definitely not equality.' He added: 'When is the blue bus coming?'

Mr Smith opened his jacket and, chest pumped up, exposed a white T-shirt that said: 'This is what a victim of feminism looks like'. Mr Smith quickly became a commonplace part of the scene, roaming round, posing before the bus, a man on a mission to make this all about him.

The women gathered for one last pink-tastic photo. Mr Smith sidled into the picture, sign aloft. A woman tried to move him along. He refused. 'Hands off me!' he said. 'Hands off me!' He stood firm. A moment later, a photographer boomed out at him: 'Hey, get out of the picture, mate!' Mr Pink obeyed immediately, leaving the women to their photo in front of the pink (or possibly magenta) political icon of the day.

25 FEBRUARY 2015

Give Baroness Jones, the Genghis of Green, her own TV show right now

Green leader Natalie Bennett, fresh from her brain fade moment on radio, is forced to fight to speak at her own press conference.

THE GREEN PARTY campaign launch was an unforgettable joy. The event, in a small, boiling sludge-coloured room in central London, was chaired by someone who introduced herself as Jenny Jones, a Green baroness.

She was a bird of a person, wren-like, with cascades of grey ringlets and a manner that I might, kindly, describe as Stalinist. 'You can ask as many questions as you like about our manifesto,' she snapped, 'but we are not going to be answering them today. It is not our manifesto launch. It is our campaign launch.'

Jenny peered out, eyes darting. A man raised his hand. 'Man in the middle!' she commanded before having an immediate rethink. 'Is there a woman who wants to ask a question now?' But there was not a woman. A man (Kevin from *The Sun*) would have to do.

Green leader Natalie Bennett, fresh from her morning of radio Armageddon, told us all about how the Green Surge was changing British politics. I must admit that I rather like Natalie, with her nasal voice and clumping unpolished ways. We also heard from Caroline Lucas, the MP who everyone loves but who induces narcolepsy in me. Tacked on the end of the top table, we knew not why, was a man named Darren, a candidate from Bristol.

When Kevin was finished, Jenny's eyes raked the room. 'Is there a woman?' Thank God there was! A female from Austrian television, of all things, asked about nuclear power.

Jenny moved briskly on: 'OK! A man?' Joey Jones from Sky News was exactly that. He asked Natalie about her interview on LBC that morning. 'It was fairly excruciating,' he noted (extremely kindly). 'I can't imagine what it was like in the studio. Would you agree you are letting your party down?'

Jenny, jumping up, snapped: 'She's not going to answer that!'

Natalie, sitting down, protested quietly. 'Yes, I will.'

'No! No! No!' ordered Jenny.

Natalie nodded, numbly. 'I will…'

'No! No! No! No!' Jenny was furious, barking, the Mummy Dearest of politics, the Genghis of Green, ordering around her leader as if she were a very, very small dog on a very short leash. We all watched as Natalie, bravely, resolutely arose. 'I thank Jenny for her kind attempt to protect me,' she said as Jenny glared. 'But yes, it was absolutely excruciating in the studio. All I can say is occasionally one just has a mind blank. That happens.'

Jenny, colossally dissatisfied with us all now, turned to the room and barked: 'A woman?'

We struggled on, boy-girl, until Jenny announced: 'One more question. Anyone with a question for Darren? He is very talented!'

A man named Adam asked the cost of their Green policies.

'I wish I hadn't picked you, Adam,' snapped Jenny.

As the event ended – but not before Darren had said something talented – I felt Jenny's irritation radiate out at us, fizzling frazzling rays from a very frown-faced sun. We the press had let her down. We were all the wrong sex and we had no questions for Darren. We were, simply, not good enough for the Green Surge.

But, as far as I am concerned, Natalie Bennett must never, ever, leave politics and Baroness Jones of Moulsecoomb should be given her own TV show, immediately.

17 MARCH 2015

Sturgeon turns into the soft option

*To watch the new SNP leader in action was to see
a woman whose time had finally come.*

I T SEEMS TO me that Nicola Sturgeon is rather keen on London these days. Indeed, the SNP leader hates the elitist enclave that is Westminster so much that she talks of little else. Yesterday she jetted down to England (those frequent flyer miles must be adding up) to give a speech about, yes, Westminster.

'With possibly forty or more SNP MPs in a hung parliament after the election in May, Nicola may well find that she holds the key to No. 10,' said the man introducing her at the LSE.

Everyone laughed and Nicola rewarded us with one of her almost-smiles, a facial expression in which her eyes crinkle up and her lips open just enough so we can see the tiny pointed teeth.

'Thank you for that warm and – interesting – introduction!' she said, teeth flashing.

You had to admire the chutzpah. Basically, her speech to the LSE students (who loved her, by the way) was her fantasy of how she would go about giving a Budget at Westminster. There would, apparently, be a lot of consensus and co-operation. She doesn't like surprises. She doesn't like rabbits.

But what she really doesn't like are the Tories. 'Remember, as long as there are more SNP and Labour MPs than there are Tory MPs, we can lock the Tories out of government. There is no question about that.'

There was that little pointy near-smile again. She, like everyone these days apparently, doesn't like coalitions (they are soooo last parliament). But no one is ruling out informal working arrangements.

I have always seen Nicola Sturgeon as a boiled sweet, so hard that bits of her chip off if she runs into something. But these days she is on a mission to soften. Industrial amounts of Downy fabric softener have been used and the result is rather impressive. Gone is the helmet hairdo, so effective that the army has asked for permission to deploy it in war zones. In TV make-up, there is a spray-on foundation that they call 'airbrush'. Nicola Sturgeon yesterday had that airbrushed glow.

There was only one hostile question. 'You spend the referendum banging on about Scotland's oil,' said one student. 'Now the price of oil has plummeted, don't you thank your lucky stars that you lost?'

Nicola's almost-smile faltered. 'Is that a technical term, banging on?' she asked.

The man shot back: 'It is technical enough for the SNP.'

Nicola almost flirted in response. 'I sense that I have not persuaded you,' she said, saying that she hoped she would. 'I never give up on these things.'

I instantly knew this was true. She never gives up. We are never going to get rid of her (barring independence). All of these London events are orchestrated to give us that message. She wants her progressive politics, with its gender-balanced Cabinet and consensual Budgets, and she wants it after May.

But, noted one questioner, people in this audience cannot vote SNP.

'Can you put a candidate in Wimbledon please?' cried a student.

So, who would she advise that the English should vote for?

The Greens, said Nicola, or perhaps a progressive Labour type. 'It's not for me to tell people in England how to vote,' she said, deploying her almost-smile. Though, of course, she just had.

19 MARCH 2015

The Madness of Sun-King George

*The last coalition Budget is all about walking
tall and choosing the future.*

THE COMMONS WAS heaving. The galleries were full. The Osborne family was there, peering down on what is left of the man who is always on a diet. The peers' gallery was particularly impressive for there, in a row, sat lords formerly known as Nigel Lawson, Peter Mandelson, Jeffrey Archer and Tory Party chairman Andrew Feldman. It is frightening how they all look more like *Spitting Image* puppets than themselves.

It was a classic George Osborne speech, full of the kind of slightly mad things that he loves to say.

He began with this. 'Britain is walking tall again!'

I looked at his thin form bent over the dispatch box. Can you hunch tall? If so, he was doing it. Surely 'walking tall' is the kind of thing they say in a Clint Eastwood movie, a line best delivered by someone wearing holsters. Actually, the whole thing doesn't bear thinking about. Britons aren't tall. We are medium-sized. Plus, we are a couch potato, Gogglebox nation. If anything, we sit tall.

Now he announced another imperative. 'We choose the future,' he announced. Do we? I'd always thought that the future was just out there, an inevitable factor of life, the universe and all that. George looked immensely pleased. I wondered, not for the first time, how long it takes him to come up with this stuff. And then, as if in rebuff to this thought, he repeated it: 'We choose the future!'

But then, like a sugar-aholic in a sweet shop, he started choosing everything. A few of them made sense. 'We choose economic security,' he said. 'We choose jobs.' He didn't stop there. Soon we were choosing 'the whole nation' and 'aspiration'. Then, my personal favourite came. 'We choose families,' he said although, patently, it is families that choose us.

So now, there we were, walking tall, choosing the future and our families, listening to George read out a catalogue of numbers, each chosen to show that his chancellorship has been a stunning success. Everyone always thinks Budgets are about rabbits out of the hat. This year there was a lack of rabbits ('We do not choose rabbits!'). Instead, George gave us an intricate connect-the-numbers exercise that was aimed to make austerity look less austere. 'The sun is starting to shine,' he announced, 'and we are fixing the roof!'

This brought Labour groans. Well, it is Britain. The sun isn't exactly reliable.

George continued to explain how wonderful we were. 'Within fifteen years, we have the potential to overtake Germany,' he announced. ('We choose Germany!')

He was on a roll. We were giving money for driverless cars, church roofs, energy catapults, white vans. Then there was racing, orchestras and something called the internet of things. Confused? Well that's what happens when you walk tall.

27 MARCH 2015

Paxman grills Dave and Ed

The real election campaign began with the strange non-debate debate that was Dave and Ed being grilled by Paxo. I was just glad that, unlike so much else in this campaign, it wasn't in a kitchen.

FOR DAVID CAMERON the Battle for No. 10 became, within a nano-second, the Battle to Make Jeremy Happy.

'Could you live on a zero-hours contract?' scowled Jeremy.

Dave, formerly known as swashbuckling Flashman, not to say the Prime Minister, looked spooked. 'That's not the question!' he insisted.

In the spin room at Sky, everyone laughed. That's not the answer either.

Dave sat forward. Then he sat back. He hated the way Jeremy bopped around various topics, always scowling, finding Dave wanting in almost every way. 'You couldn't live on a zero-hours contract,' he frowned. 'This is one of the things that people find really problematic about you.'

Dave tried not to quail. Jeremy told Dave off for fibbing about immigration, not putting up VAT and, actually, just about everything. 'I don't want to be rude,' said Jeremy, hilariously. 'Do you know and you're not telling us, or do you not know?'

Dave looked earnest. He had no idea if he knew or not. The questions just got ruder. 'Let me ask you…' said Jeremy, dangling Dave on a hook. 'What do you think has been your biggest foreign policy disaster?'

Dave started babbling about how great it was that he cut the European Union budget. That's not the question, Dave! And that certainly wasn't the answer.

I so wanted this interview to continue. I haven't seen Dave act quite so un-prime-ministerial in ages. But now the most irritating 'debate' format in the world decreed that it was time to go to a question-and-answer session with 'real people', as they say in politics. It was, not to put too fine a word on it, tedious. Dave seemed a totally different person and we learnt absolutely nothing new.

Then, even more irritatingly, Ed Miliband began not with the 'debate' with Jeremy but with another Q & A session, where he rambled round the stage for eighteen minutes, unnervingly close to a giant picture of himself (he kept bumping into his own nose, which was bizarre).

He got better questions, specifically about the rift the leadership contest created with his brother. 'It's hard!' said Ed, arms out. Most people were peering at him as if he was an alien, which some, of course, think he is.

I could hardly wait for Mr Rude to be back on stage. Then, suddenly, he was before us (I speak of Paxo) and even ruder than we could have hoped for. 'Your figures were farcical!' he cried at Ed.

Ed, more or less, agreed. 'We got it wrong.' I was surprised by how relaxed Ed looked. He was sitting back. He was engaging with Jeremy, who was enjoying badgering him about immigration.

'Let me make the point,' said Ed, interrupting Jeremy. (Is that even allowed? Isn't it against the law?).

'You are making up a question to yourself!' insisted Jeremy. (This is one of Ed's irritating habits.) But a few minutes later Ed said back to Jeremy: 'Now you are asking yourself questions.'

The audience laughed. Ed had said it tentatively, with a smile. But he was standing up for himself. I think the actual turning point came when Ed confronted Jeremy: 'Don't be so obnoxious. You're important Jeremy, but you're not that important!'

Isn't he? I think we all know who won this debate and it wasn't Dave or Ed.

I APRIL 2015

Welcome to France? Don't tell Nigel

I head to Dover – and beyond – to catch the latest UKIP poster launch.

AS I DROVE down the twisty narrow road to the Coastguard pub at St Margaret's Bay near Dover to meet Nigel Farage, I heard my phone go 'ping'.

'Welcome to France!' said the text.

Welcome indeed. Or, perhaps in Nigel's case, not.

St Margaret's Bay is as close as you can get to France (Welcome!) without being there. We were under the White Cliffs, looking out over the glitter-strewn waters of the Channel. There were seagulls, surfers, but not, at least yesterday, swimmers. Up above us were some lovely homes, including two once owned by Noël Coward, one of which he rented to Ian Fleming.

Yesterday, though, the star was Nigel. He arrived, as stars must, by law, in a car with blacked out windows. The Kippers were waiting dutifully in the pub car park: thirteen of them all lined up in front of a giant display truck, the poster hidden for now.

Nigel was dressed in his version of man-of-the-people mode. Mustard corduroys, battered Barbour, checked shirt, tie with hares on it. The poster was unveiled: a picture of the White Cliffs with three escalators going up them. It was the ugliest poster ever, even worse than an earlier UKIP version with only one escalator. I hoped that Dame Vera Lynn would never have to see it.

'We want a different relationship with Europe,' said Nigel, peering out over the sea at Calais and its unwelcome hordes. 'You can't see it, normally you can...'

The villain of the piece was David Cameron. Once in a while, Nigel would mention the Lib Dems or Labour but, mostly, it was all about the Prime Minister and his unfulfilled promise to cut immigration to the tens of thousands. 'When Cameron made that promise he was being wilfully dishonest,' said Nigel, savouring the last two words, which lingered in the salty air like two men spoiling for a fight. 'He knew the truth. You cannot have an immigration policy, you cannot set any targets, all the while you are members of the European Union.'

Nigel now announced: 'And by the way, we are not being negative about this subject!' No, I could see that. (My phone pinged again: another 'Welcome!' Don't tell Nigel, I thought.) Nigel explained that his goal was to get back to 'normality'.

What, I wondered, was Nigel's idea of 'normality'? It was, he said, the kind of numbers we had seen in the 1950s (surely his favourite era) up until 2000.

What was his target? 'A return to normality...' said Nigel.

A figure? 'A net level of about 30,000 a year...' He liked this figure so much that he repeated it, a lot.

Soon he was back in star mode, walking along the seafront for the photographs, spotting a surfer ('He must be off his chump!') and telling us he likes vaping ('Jolly good!'). Then it was off to the pub – but for a coffee. After all, he is in pre-debate training mode.

It was time for Nigel to leave this little corner of French-England. I looked up at the houses. What would Noël Coward make of this scene, with Mr Normality in his mustard cords and ugly poster, surrounded by us media seagulls. Normal? Who is he kidding?

21 APRIL 2015

Nail-biting stuff at the SNP cliff face

*Labour launched their manifesto on the old Coronation Street set
in Manchester, the Lib Dems chose London and the Tories held
a utilitarian, pared-down event in marginal Swindon. But the
only manifesto launch really worth going to was the SNP's.*

THE CHEER BEGAN before Nicola Sturgeon had even finished saying the word.

'The SNP will always support independ…' The sound arose as if on the wings of a huge bird, a phoenix of a battle cry, and some of the 700 or so people at the SNP manifesto launch stood and clapped.

It was a moment just for them, the SNP faithful, the losers who refuse to act like losers. The cheer was for Nicola, for themselves, for the dream.

Nicola took a moment, her timing perfect: 'But this election is not about independence.' Now they laughed, for they got the joke. Of course it wasn't! Or was it?

The question hung in the air until Nicola supplied the answer: 'It is about making Scotland stronger!' Ah yes, that's what it is about. Cue more wild cheers.

They love her. There is no other word. Adoration poured forth from the moment Nicola, for she is a first-name only politician now, arrived. We were seated at the bottom of cliffs at the International Climbing Arena, built inside an old quarry, just outside Edinburgh.

As you drive up to this place, there are little signs that say: Nail-biting! Heart-pumping! Life-changing! They are about climbing but what are the SNP now if not the best free-climbing politicians in the UK?

I looked up at the soaring cliff faces. Many parties in this election are between a rock and a hard place. This, I thought, was what it felt like to be between a rock and an easy place. The SNP are only fighting, like the Lib Dems, to be the balance-of-power party but, wow, did it feel better than that.

Nicola Sturgeon has been a politician for years and yet, yesterday, she seemed entirely fresh. As she ambled almost towards the front to make her speech, her hapless deputy, Stewart Hosie, was talking into the microphone almost ignored by all.

'This is a manifesto to make Scotland stronger,' she cried to more euphoria. But, actually, it wasn't just that. It was also a manifesto to make England different, and often she was speaking directly to them, the Other.

The SNP would be 'constructive'. It would be 'responsible'. And yet, all around me, the energy felt much more visceral. This wasn't about revenge.

It was, however, about power. Not that Nicola would ever say such a thing as she stood in front of us, tickling up Labour policies, giving them an SNP twist (a minimum wage of £8.70, rather than £8, by 2020). But, as she progressed, killing off the bedroom tax (screams) and curing poverty (ditto), I noticed something was missing.

Alex Salmond! Where was Mr Charisma? He seemed to be entirely absent – and not only in body. I leafed through the glossy manifesto (actually, as it was munificent, then it should be a muni-festo). He was a missing person, airbrushed out, for now. I guess Nicola didn't want the past hanging round, getting in the way of her close-up, being bumptious.

The raptures of the muni-festo speech (truly, other parties might try to get a little bit of whatever these people are taking) were followed by a mini-press conference that began with Nicola pleading with members to let the media ask questions without being booed. The first question, about whether she was a hypocrite, received only a tiny hiss. So, it seems, Nicola rules. Or, in this place, perhaps, Nicola rocks.

23 APRIL 2015

Dynamic duo in joint appearance, but it's a bit secret

I have never felt more like a stalker on the day that I was banned from watching Boris and Dave fingerpaint. This was not about campaigning, it was about control.

I SPENT THE DAY desperately seeking Boris and Dave. The rumour was the dynamic duo were going to appear together on the campaign trail for the first time. But Boris's people wouldn't tell me where they were going to be. Dave's people wouldn't either. The Boris and Dave show was, ridiculously, being kept a secret.

I put on my Secret Squirrel decoder ring and headed out. I heard a whisper on the wind that the event would be in Kingston and Surbiton in south-west London. This made complete sense. Surbiton was the home of *The Good Life*, the sitcom that the Tories have adopted as their campaign theme. It is also the marginal seat of Lib Dem Ed Davey, the distinctly unsparky Energy Secretary. It had to be.

At Surbiton's wonderfully retro train station, I scanned the horizon. Nothing. Where were they? Boris's people were mute. The Tories the same. I was operating in a sea of murk. Still, everyone was always saying that Dave needs to meet more (or indeed any) Real People. There were plenty here.

'Have you seen the Prime Minister?' I asked one. No one had. The decoder ring was letting me down. I was joined by a colleague and we rushed to Kingston station and – eureka! – saw a group of Tories (the clue was in the big blue rosettes).

Were they meeting Dave and Boris? No, they said, they were going to a park to meet Grant Shapps, the Tory co-chairman embroiled in a mini-media storm over whether he tweaked his Wikipedia entry. I couldn't believe it. Surely it was a decoy. Still, we followed them.

'Have you seen the Prime Minister?' I asked a Real Person in the park. No one had. Grant Shapps wasn't there either. A Tory aide said it was 'too hot' for him to appear. Instead, the group of twenty Tories, who looked tiny in this park, rattling round like marbles in a pin-ball machine, were addressed by the wet blanket that is Theresa Villiers, the Northern Ireland Secretary. Never was a group more in need of Boris.

Where WERE they? The Tory candidate, James Berry, was here, with us, in the park. Surely it made no sense for Dave and Boris to come here and not meet the actual candidate? 'We heard the Prime Minister and Boris are here,' I said. 'Do you know where?'

The candidate looked confused and just a little trapped. I felt bad. It wasn't his fault that Conservative HQ had decided to turn this into a farce. Now, finally, we heard another whisper of a rumour – shhhh! – that Boris and Dave were visiting a children's nursery in Surbiton.

Screeechhhh! That was the sound of our tyres as we headed through the not-so-mean streets of Surbiton. At the Advantage Day Nursery we found the giant blue Tory bus and a few chosen journalists (and the candidate, who also knows a bit about screeching tyres). The Tory press team produced a portable barrier in the car park so we could stand behind it.

'The Tory campaign,' said James Mates of ITN into his camera, 'has been criticised as on the dull side…'

Dull? I can't imagine why they say that. This is exactly what happened next. Dave and Boris appeared and, without speaking, went into the nursery. Dave's people said I couldn't tag along with the press pack because space was limited, although twenty-three people now followed them in. Why was I being banned from watching Boris and Dave fingerpaint? The decoder ring didn't know.

The Tories moved the portable barrier to another bit of the car park so we had to move. Then Dave and Boris emerged. Boris waved. Dave slapped Boris on the back. Dave waved. They drove off. So that was it, the big event, two waves and a slap. Welcome to the world of campaign control freakery. Dull? Surely not.

29 APRIL 2015

No laughing matter as Passionate Dave lets rip

The campaign, fought on the idea that the Tories and
Labour were neck-and-neck, seemed to be conducted mainly
by candidates standing in their kitchens until, finally,
Dave decided he had to show us how much he cared.

I BRING YOU NEWS from the front line of Passionate Dave. Yesterday our new pumped-up Prime Minister went to Enfield to talk to workers. I say talk but really it was more like barking.

'If you want to let rip, LET RIP!' Dave ordered. 'Elections should be lively!'

Lively? Try bonkersroony. This was the verbal equivalent of Formula 1, screeching round sentences, screaming down the straights with the occasional pit stop to take a breath. After an hour with Passionate Dave, I felt exactly as I used to after hosting a birthday party for two-year-olds. My first desire was to sit down and be very, very quiet. But I couldn't sit down because there were no chairs.

Rule one for Passionate Dave is no sitting. Chairs are so last week. So we gathered, forming our own mosh pit on the shop floor of a company called Kelvin Hughes which makes 'situational intelligence' systems or, basically, radar, in far-flung north London. Dave strode towards us (Passionate Dave always strides, never walks). He'd thrown away his jacket. And his tie. He'd rolled up his sleeves, something he does in a methodical fashion, so they looked almost perfect. Can you iron rolled-up shirt-sleeves? I suspect you can.

Dave stood on a little metal stand – a post-industrial soapbox, if you will – in the middle. He began to shout, immediately using words like 'buccaneering'. He machine-gunned us with exclamation marks. 'There is one simple issue!' he shouted. 'People tell you it's about the hospitals! Yes, it is! It's about the schools! Yes it is! Above all, it's about the economy! The economy is everything!' Then, suddenly, Dave barked: 'Questions! Points! Let's have some "real people" first!'

One of the unreal people, i.e. the press, noted this was the third day we have seen Passionate Dave and wasn't he jealous that he had not been granted an audience with Russell Brand as Ed Miliband had.

'First of all,' shouted Dave, 'we are in Year Five of Passionate Prime Minister!'

I laughed. For months on end, we have been governed by Tick-Box Dave, so risk-adverse he no longer held press conferences much less met 'real people'. But now, nine days before the election, all that had changed. And he did look different: the face glowing, pinky-red, the veins in his neck standing out.

'As for Russell Brand, I think I profoundly disagree … He says, "don't vote". That's his whole view. Don't vote! You know, it only encourages them or something.'

The real people laughed at this. 'It's funny!' cried Dave. 'Right, it's funny! But you know POLITICS and LIFE and ELECTIONS and JOBS and the ECONOMY are not a joke! Russell Brand is a joke!'

The PM was live, unplugged and unstoppable. 'Ed Miliband can hang out with Russell Brand. This is not funny! This is about the election. It's about the future. It's about jobs. It's about the recovery!' And still he shouted. 'I haven't got TIME to hang out with Russell Brand! This is more important. These are REAL PEOPLE!'

So, basically, yes, he was a little jealous. Now he was asked why he didn't get out and meet more real people? Suddenly Dave focused on Ed Miliband's lectern, which the Labour leader is never seen without these days. 'I don't have to go everywhere with the lectern,' he shouted. 'I think we need to free this lectern. I'm worried. I think it's been taken hostage!'

The real people laughed, though a little uncertainly. There is a fine line between passionate and bonkers. Dave may not yet have the balance exactly right.

4 MAY 2015

Holy Moses! Ed is rock solid

The Labour leader unveils the 'Ed Stone, as it was immediately called, to an unbelieving nation.

THERE IS ONLY one word for Ed Miliband's giant stone tablet carved with his six election pledges and that is, surely, monumental. OK, you may have another word in mind but it takes a certain kind of genius to come up with such a notion. As I watched Ed standing by his 8 ft 6 in limestone pledge card in a car park in Hastings, I just knew that Moses would be jealous. 'These six pledges are carved in stone,' said Ed, in a suit and not a toga, wind whipping around and his head not quite reaching pledge No. 4 ('controls on immigration').

What would Moses say? Actually, I know. 'Why only six?' he'd say to Ed. 'What if I'd stopped at six? I'd have missed out adultery, stealing, lying and jealousy!' Then Moses would have tilted his head back, beard blowing in the wind. 'And the title?' he would muse. '"A better plan, a better future"? What does it mean? Mine was catchier.'

Yes, I quite like the idea of The Six Commandments. I think Labour missed a trick there. But, other than these sub-editing quibbles, I think Moses would have been impressed. Not for Ed some little dinky tablet that you could hold in your hand. Hell no, as Ed (not Moses) would say.

Back to the car park. 'They are carved in stone,' said Ed, surrounded by supporters with little red flags, 'because they won't be abandoned after the general election.' Abandoned? How would you get rid of an 8 ft 6 in limestone pledge card? It wouldn't exactly fit in the green bin. Where could you leave such a thing? Stonehenge? I think the Druids would object, and I wouldn't blame them.

How did this happen? How did it come to pass that such a thing could be thought of, much less organised, chiselled and actually erected in a car park? I tried to imagine the planning meeting as Labour aides sat down with Ed.

'We need something symbolic', said one aide named Adam, 'to regain people's trust.' 'I know!' cried Noah. 'Let's do something rock-solid! A stone
tablet! Like Moses, but bigger.'

So there you have it. Like Moses, but bigger. 'I want the British people to
remember these pledges,' insisted Ed. I noticed that his signature, carved in
stone, was at waist height. The fifth pledge was: 'A country where the next
generation can do better than this'. I began to feel sorry for the stone mason.
It's not exactly poetry.

Ed wants us to remember these pledges but, frankly, how can we forget them? Why can't he just put them on a Post-it note like everyone else?
Apparently the plan, should things go Labour's way on Thursday, is for this
object, surely to be titled the 'Ed Stone, to be installed in the Downing Street
garden, possibly the naffest garden accessory ever.

Now the Downing Street garden is a thing of joy. It has a beehive and a
wormery and a lovely old magnolia tree. The grass here really is greener on
the other side. It is tended by the Royal Parks and is a little piece of heaven
that is (mostly) untouched by politics. Indeed, I think the idea is that, like the
Civil Service, it carries on regardless. The last political act was Sarah Brown's
herb garden. Ed's monument would stick out, towering like Marx at Highgate.

Still, breaking news, as I write, the Labour Party has said that the 'Ed
Stone is now 'in storage'. Even Moses might rejoice at that.

6 MAY 2015

Nick Clegg finally sets this campaign on fire

The Lib Dem leader ends his campaign by cooking a bhuna, as you do.

NICK CLEGG IN charge of a frying pan is a fire hazard. It was
alarming to watch the Deputy Prime Minister, dressed in a pinny,
in a tiny kitchen at the Indian restaurant Dabbawalla in Cardiff,

trying to get to grips with the basics of a bhuna. I know they say that flames 'leap up' but with Nick they do not leap so much as trampoline to the moon.

'I'm not a very good cook,' he said beforehand. This may be the case – his wife, Miriam González Durántez, did look a tad anxious behind him – but he is, certainly, a great conflagrationist.

Welcome to the Nick Clegg Culinary Tour. He had started out at 6 a.m. at Land's End and made breakfast in Newquay. Actually, I say 'made', but I am reliably informed that, basically, he hovered over a pan with sausages and eggs and then placed two rashers of bacon on a plate. The next stop for Nick and the great big yellow Lib Dem bus was Dabbawalla, where sixty-eight people had gathered for lunch, a (very) small bit of which was to be made by Nick.

As I watched him, flames dancing, one word entered my mind. Why? But then I realised it was obvious. It was a kitchen! He was a politician! Where else would he be but here, almost singeing his eyebrows as the photographers clicked away?

Nick had, of course, been late. But then 'Clegg Time' is always at least a half hour behind BST. The Lib Dem bus, named Plucky because that is what this party is always called, blew into Cardiff about 1.30 p.m., bringing the rain. We were in the final forty-eight hours of GE2015 and everyone looked bushed. The journalists had the weariness of marathon runners in the final straight. The aides, in their 'Leader's Tour 2015' T-shirts, looked exhausted.

Only Nick, the Peter Pan of politicians, looked perky (or even plucky) in his high-top sneakers and a blue V-neck jumper. He, and Miriam, received a rhapsodic reception before he gave a pep talk about how only the Lib Dems could provide stability, unity, decency. Actually, I thought, forget all that. Only the Lib Dems provide lunch.

I think this must have been peak day for Nick's coalition pitch about how only the Lib Dems could provide a heart for the Tories and the brains for Labour. Every time I got within hearing distance, he was talking about hearts and brains. 'The last thing we need is another election before Christmas!' announced Nick.

Then it was time to set fire to the kitchen. The first panful of lamb bhuna

filled the place with the smell of burnt garlic. We watched as he put his creation into a small dish, and placed it to one side. Surely, we thought, it must
be eaten. It seemed only right to taste it (as journalists, we like scoops of all
kinds).

'What do you think? Too salty?' we demanded of the (real) chef who was
too polite to say (he gave it, even more politely, seven out of ten). Meanwhile,
behind us, Nick was creating yet another fire hazard that resulted in another
small bowl of bhuna, which we also took to taste. This one was much better,
not too salty, or garlicky. But, as Nick took off his pinny (surely politicians
should wear them at all times), I felt it was true: only the Lib Dems have
heart, brains and, yes, bhuna.

8 MAY 2015

Lib Dems were hammered before the real party started

The fantasy election ended at 10.03 p.m. on election night
when the exit poll landed to everyone's disbelief.

I T'S HARD TO shut up a roomful of opinion-formers, but the shock exit
poll accomplished it: for a moment there was a distinct lack of opinion
in the ITV Opinion Room.

But only for a moment. 'Ten!' cried a group of opinion-makers, staring
at the TV screen and the number of projected Lib Dem seats. 'They won't
go into coalition,' said one immediately. Everyone nodded: 'They will lick
their wounds.' More nodding. I do love watching a cloud opinion forming.

This room, one floor above the actual election studio at ITV headquarters in London, existed to put the party into politics. For now, though, the
commentariat was fizzing quite nicely: no need to pop the prosecco – yet.

Everyone clutched a phone and almost everyone had a laptop. There was
a Facebook pod, a Twitter screen to show us the Twitter worm. There was a

woman holding something called a Twitter mirror (don't ask). There were radio presenters, political spinners (even very brave Lib Dem ones) and, possibly most impressive of all, Brian May's hair.

However, this was not the only party in town. As I left, someone on the TV (and, honestly, it did feel like the people on TV were in the room with us) said something about the Lib Dems: 'It looks as if they have been hammered.'

Hammered is a good party word, of course. So to Shepherd's then, for the party of the night, the Westminster restaurant where, somehow, 600 people (actually, lobbyists, but I don't wish to split hairs) had to fit in. The noise, even early on, was thunderous. The first person I saw, unnervingly, was Nigel Farage. He was made out of cardboard, which I didn't mind at all. Actually he wasn't alone: there was Dave, Ed and (even) Nick. They were the only ones in the room not talking.

Or drinking. Hammered could very much be a theme here. The cocktails looked lethal and all featured champagne. There were blue Conservative ones (with blue curaçao) and Labour (with vodka and crème de fraise). The Lib Dems had orange juice and UKIP had crème de violette (which seemed a bit Frenchified to me).

But the most terrifying looking of all were the Green ones with crème de menthe. 'I'm worried people aren't pacing,' one man said. Hmmm, I thought. You try pacing yourself on crème de violette. Not easy, really, even if you are Farage and made of cardboard.

But surely the final word of the night must go to Rory Bremner, star turn at the buzzing Institute of Directors do on Pall Mall. 'I hope you enjoyed the election,' he cried at the end of his turn, channelling the plummy voice of David Cameron. 'I hope to see you at the next one – in December.' Cheers!

9 MAY 2015

Dave finds Love Finally

It was the day that Nick, Ed and Nigel resigned and
Dave, at long last, said goodbye to coalition life.

WHAT A MORNING! We rushed from one political funeral to another, careers crashing round us. In just under an hour, there were three resignations. Nick Clegg, Ed Miliband and Nigel Farage all decided they had to go – although, in Nigel's case, it sounded like he was merely off on a long holiday.

We arrived at Downing Street, still pre-lunch, all jangly from the morning's tears and trauma, dash and drama. You know the frantic hurry at the start of the film *Four Weddings and a Funeral*? Well, I can tell you that's nothing compared to this post-election version of Three Funerals and a Wedding. But, as this was Dave's day, and he'd been waiting to be our elected Prime Minister for five long years, surely the better Richard Curtis film title would be: Love Finally.

For once, Downing Street didn't feel cold and clammy grey. It wasn't sunny (as the sun is yellow, it may be a Lib Dem, which would explain that), but it was bright and cheerful. Above us, two Union Jacks flew. I remembered how, during the last tense days of the referendum, the Saltire rippled here. Not yesterday, it must be said. A top-floor lace curtain twitched. The official Downing Street lectern was lugged into the street. There were hundreds of photographers, an air of growing expectation giving it all a party feel.

The buzz of a helicopter overhead told us the Camerons had left the palace and, within minutes, the black Jag drove through what I like to think of as the Andrew Mitchell Pleb Gates, its headlights strobing blue lasers. David Cameron opened the door for Samantha, who was wearing a dress that shouted 'holiday', with palm trees outlined against calypso colours. As they walked into No. 10, it reminded me of five years ago, when it was Dave and Nick who went through the door together. Now, after 'the sweetest victory' – as Dave had called it the night before – it was just him and, finally, he was free to do what he liked.

The speech was gracious. Pumped-up Dave, with his shouting and his shirtsleeves, was nowhere to be seen; nor did we see the man who, fresh from winning the Scottish referendum, immediately began haggling over English rights. He started, instead, by thanking Nick Clegg for working so hard for the coalition. I wondered what Nick would think: only an hour or so earlier, he had given an impassioned farewell speech about how fear and grievance had triumphed.

Dave noted that Ed Miliband had rung him that morning to wish him luck. 'It was a typically generous gesture from someone who is clearly in public service for all the right reasons.' It was the nicest thing he had ever said about Ed, who has been ruthlessly caricatured, and who, of course, had also resigned less than an hour earlier, at a sombre occasion lightened by an occasional flash of humour, such as when Ed noted that the eruption of Mili-fandom was the most unlikely cult of the twenty-first century.

Dave seemed to be in Father of the Nation mode. He was careful to name-check all four nations and referred to 'these islands' and 'our proud history'. He told us we could all lead the Good Life and that we were on the brink of something special. 'Together, we can make Great Britain greater still.'

Then he and Samantha stood, cameras flashing. 'Kiss!' shouted the pho-tographers. Dave declined. Perhaps it really will be Love Finally, after all this time.

The Show Must Go On…

THE TORY GOVERNMENT, surprised to be in power, stumbled into action and immediately ran into an obstacle known as the SNP on subjects such as fox hunting and constitutional change for English MPs. The official opposition seemed mostly interested in its own navel and embarked on a leadership contest in which no one appeared to be a winner. The Lib Dems were also in disarray. Indeed, the Scot Nats were the only ones who seemed to know what they were doing and they, we all could see, were most definitely not all in this together.

· · ·

13 MAY 2015

Blue-collar Cabinet gets to work – for the cameras

The first meeting of the Tory government was almost painful to observe.

IT LOOKED LIKE the dinner party from hell. You know how people like to do their fantasy dinner party where they invite the most fascinating people from history? The first Tory Cabinet meeting in eighteen years was like a spoof version. This was not history so much in the making as in the faking, with the camera showing Cabinet ministers chatting to each other with such animation that you just knew it could not be true.

Thus we saw the Foreign Secretary Philip Hammond talking to Michael Fallon, possibly about the finer points of back-stabbing, for the Defence Secretary is an expert on the subject. The camera panned back. There was that guy with the beard. I guess he must still be the Welsh Secretary. We saw a painful shot of newbie Amber Rudd, the Energy Secretary, listening with every fibre of her being to Jeremy Hunt (you really know it can't be that fascinating).

There was Nicky Morgan, eyes orb-like as always. Theresa May drew the short straw (Chris Grayling). There was a shot of someone who is, apparently, the Scottish Secretary (i.e. the only Tory in the Scottish village). Where, I wondered, was Larry the cat?

David Cameron bustled in and Iain Duncan Smith (identifiable from behind by his white-fringed bald head, like the perfect Caribbean beach, minus the palm trees) started to thump the table. Everyone else thumped too: MPs love to thump tables and I have always feared that dinner at their homes involves jumping cutlery and sloshing glasses.

Yesterday, the cut-glass water glasses and white coffee mugs, which looked like the ones you get free with petrol vouchers, did a little disco. Everyone had name cards. Maybe this is something they do at home as well. Dave gave a pep talk about how they must give everyone in Britain the good life. 'Some pundits might call it blue-collar Conservatism,' said Dave, his shirt blindingly white, 'or being on the side of hardworking taxpayers. I would call it being the real party of working people.'

Ah yes. Never mind that the blue-collar Cabinet had caused a limo crisis outside Downing Street. Or that I have never heard anyone refer to the Tories as the 'real party of the working people'. But, of course, I have never been to a dinner where people greet each other by thumping. 'Those are the down to earth, bread and butter issues that we were elected to deliver on,' said Dave, who is, as you may remember, an expert on artisan bread-making.

Dave brandished his manifesto. Ever since he won a majority, Dave has carried the manifesto everywhere. I understand he has had one laminated, just in case he wants to check something in the shower. 'This will be a different government,' he announced, 'it's not a coalition government so we can have accountability, no trading away of things that are in here, the ability to deliver this.'

Everyone, including the back of IDS's head, furrowed their brows and looked serious. Lecture over, Dave looked up: 'I think we can say goodbye to the cameras...' IDS waved at the furry boom microphone, which went out of shot. 'And start our work!' The screen went blank, just when the interesting bit started.

19 MAY 2015

Day One: Let the Battle of the Buttocks commence!

As Churchill almost said: 'Let's fight them on the benches.'
Thus the Battle of Buttockburn began as the SNP and
Labour fought over where they were going to sit.

MPS MET FOR the first time yesterday to elect a Speaker but, frankly, that was a sideshow to the real action, which was all about Dennis Skinner, aged eighty-three, and Mhairi Black, aged twenty.

There was the Beast of Bolsover, wearing the ever-faithful sports jacket, looking like the personification of a growl. He was in his usual place, the aisle seat of the first opposition bench, which he believes that he owns. But now the SNP, incredibly overexcited to be the third-largest party in the Westminster they claim to hate, have that bench, and so they want his seat.

It was a stand-off or, more accurately, a sit-off. Think O. K. Corral but with chairs. The SNP sat first but then the Beast spotted a gap and out-buttocked them. When the smoke cleared, and Black Rod entered the chamber, walking by the front bench in all his finery, it was the Beast, not Braveheart, who was in situ. The SNP can make all the noise they like but if they are going to declare war over that seat then I can tell them who is going to win, and (whisper it) he's English.

I knew it was my duty to report on the Battle for Skinner's Seat, but there were many distractions. There was, for instance, the furthest back Labour bench, where I spotted Keir Starmer, former director of public prosecutions, next to Tulip Siddiq, whose aunt is Prime Minister of Bangladesh, and Stephen Kinnock, whose wife is Prime Minister of Denmark. That's a close-to-power trio if I ever saw one.

Then there were the missing. Ed Miliband? Absent (probably still in Ibiza). Nick Clegg? Awol. Indeed, I scanned the benches for any of the eight Lib Dems until, finally, I spotted Norman Lamb crammed in with the Welsh. In the end it fell to Alistair Carmichael, a man who would be jovial in the middle of a locust plague, to speak on behalf of 'the elite cadre' of Lib Dems.

But the best show of all was watching the face of Mhairi Black, who is SNP and 'baby of the house'. She may be the youngest MP in centuries, but she may also be the most unimpressed. To watch her face as Black Rod flounced by, lace collar pristine, stockings perfect, was a joy. She wore an expression of prolonged incredulity, as if she had just seen something magical and strange – and truly ghastly.

For reasons unknown, Mhairi was sitting in the Labour benches. It was enemy territory and it can't have been an overly comfortable place to watch the re-election of the Speaker, John Bercow, an arcane ceremony given added piquancy by the fact that, on the day before the Commons broke up, the Tories had tried to kill him (politically).

But Bercow, like Skinner, is a survivor, and so there he was, buttocks on bench. He was given an almost torrid introduction by Jacob Rees-Mogg, sadly without his top hat and monocle. Mhairi's forehead creased in consternation, as if she was discovering an entirely new species. As is traditional, two MPs then went over to 'drag' Bercow to the Speaker's chair. It was all very am-dram: Bercow, bent over, staggering by, pretended to be reluctant. This made Mhairi look even more perplexed while Skinner just glared. But then he always does.

15 JUNE 2015

The debate is not about Scotland, it's about Nottingham

The Scotland Bill turned out to be mostly about somewhere else entirely.

THE DEBATE OVER the Scotland Bill often didn't seem to be about Scotland at all. And, confusingly, it didn't even seem to be the Scots who were doing most of the debating.

Indeed, we had barely heard the first Scottish vowel when Labour's Frank Field was on his feet. 'This is a debate that England needs to have herself now,' he announced.

Ah yes, England. I had thought that the clue to the Scotland Bill was in the name, but everywhere you looked yesterday, in every corner of this not-so-foreign field, they were thinking of England.

Or, perhaps, even Nottingham. Labour's Graham Allen sees himself as THE constitutional expert in England and, indeed, in his mind may have even been there 800 years ago at Runnymede. Certainly he saw the debate yesterday as the beginning of a new Magna Carta, a Magna Scotia if you will, although perhaps an even better term would be a Magna Allen.

The Scotland Bill was, as he told us, about Derby, about Wales but, mostly, probably, about Nottingham. 'One of the key things is to say, from the benches which represent England, in my own case the city of Nottingham, that nothing in this Bill should be something which cannot apply the liberation of the progress to a city like the one I represent,' he announced, tall and imposing, rocking forward, like an earthquake-proofed building during a tremor. I felt sorry, as I often do when Mr Allen opines, for that is the word, for that great city. (I can hardly wait for the film: Cry Freedom, Nottingham!)

However it wasn't just about Nottingham. Magna Scotia was also about Dudley. For now Ian Austin, the Labour MP for Dudley, jumped up to object to the SNP, which, inconveniently for Mr Austin, now speaks for fifty-six of the nation's fifty-nine seats. 'The people sitting there,' he said, 'clearly want to create a one-party state in Scotland whose supporters...'

I heard a rumble. The SNP does not object in the same namby-pamby way that other, shall we say English, MPs do. It creates a collective noise, the human form of a thunderstorm approaching.

Mr Austin raised his voice, for the weather is always bad in Scotland. '… whose supporters engage in the most disreputable bullying tactics to silence any dissent in that country!'

An SNP voice sliced through the chamber: 'Silly boy!'

Almost all of 'Team 56' as the SNP calls itself, was in the chamber, tartanising half of the opposition benches. (If 'tartanising' is not a word now, it will be soon.) As a group, it feels explosive but it doesn't, often, explode. Yesterday, I gave the group credit for self-control, as it listened to yet another non-Scot arise to explain what the most important thing about this Bill was.

It was John Redwood, now fully rehabilitated after his Vulcan period. 'The more we hear the Scottish voice,' said Mr Redwood (chance would be a fine thing, I thought), 'the more I have to be not an advocate of the Union but an advocate of England.' So now we are not just crying freedom, but crying Redwood. 'Someone needs to speak for England!' he cried. I think we know who that is.

17 JUNE 2015

The Eurorebels scream blue purdah

Tory backbenchers find yet another subject to be outraged about concerning the EU referendum.

I DO WONDER SOMETIMES if the Eurorebels are just addicted to rebelling. They have won their battle to have a referendum. On the eve of yesterday's debate, they also won a grudging concession not to have that referendum next May, on election day.

The SNP's Alex Salmond, who is not a Eurosceptic but has never let a rebel bandwagon go by without flirting with the idea of jumping on it, crowed yesterday over the government's amendment to change the referendum date. 'It was tabled, I understand, at 9.35 p.m. last evening in a disorganised, spatchcock, humiliating climb-down!'

There is nothing MPs love more than a humiliating climb-down. David Lidington, the minister for Europe, sat on the front bench for seven hours, his face set in stone: it is possible he is in training to become part of Mount Rushmore.

So the rebels had won. For a brief moment, they faced the ghastly possibility that there was nothing left to rebel over. Thankfully there was the issue of 'purdah', the period before an election when the government doesn't do much. The government doesn't want to go into purdah for the referendum because they say (I paraphrase) that they won't even be able to tie their shoelaces then. The rebels are convinced that the refusal is a cunning plan to skew the result.

The rebels pounced on purdah with the kind of hyperbole we have come to expect from them. The idea to abandon purdah wasn't just bad, it was an affront to democracy, to our way of life, to the Magna Carta. Purdah, purdah, purdah. Never has the word been said so many times. It felt inappropriate for a word that is about drawing a veil over something.

Actually, Mr Lidington tried to do just that, saying that he wanted to go into purdah over whether to go into purdah. He said the government would 'consult' and produce (I paraphrase) a fudge in the autumn, during the report stage of the Bill. The rebels fought back as only they know how: they sought to bore the government into submission.

Arise Sir Bill Cash! In fact the man who is never at a loss for words when it comes to Europe had some difficulty arising yesterday and, at words of concern from the Deputy Speaker, he sat down. 'I am sorry to have to make my speech in this way,' he explained, 'but I have been in hospital for the last four days.' Now that is commitment.

Sir Bill explained that the purdah rebellion was nothing to do with Maastricht. 'There was a rebellion then because we did not have a referendum. On this occasion, we merely wish to ensure that the voters are given a fair choice.'

It sounded oh-so-reasonable. Mr Lidington's face stayed immobile. The rebels pushed it to a vote and the government was saved by Labour. But be under no illusions: this is only the first battle in the Purdah War. The rebels won't draw a veil over it.

24 JUNE 2015

Lord chancellor isn't one to complain. However…

*Michael Gove was already making his
(punctuation) mark on his new job.*

I AM TYPING VERY carefully today, given that no less a figure than the lord chancellor has made a decree banning the use of the word 'impact' as a verb and starting a sentence with 'however'. If I were lord chancellor, I would concentrate on far more important things, such as the correct use of apostrophes.

We haven't heard much of Michael Gove lately and now we know why. He's been sitting in court, watching how antiquated and Dickensian it all is and fulminating whenever anyone starts a sentence with 'however'. He's discovered what the rest of us knew already: that the wheels of justice turn very slowly and often not at all. The result of all that toil was a speech called, according to the press release, 'What does a One Nation justice policy look like?' I winced when I saw those capital letters for Mr Gove has also decreed that words should be lower case unless absolutely necessary.

'Were Mr Tulkinghorn to step from the pages of *Bleak House* or Mr Jaggers to be transported from the chapters of *Great Expectations* into a crown court today, they would find little had changed since Dickens satirised the tortuously slow progress of justice in Victorian times,' said Mr Gove.

I suspect, however, that Mr Gove has already been in contact with Messers Jagger and Tulkinghorn. Certainly, his idea that some top lawyers – 'people in our best chambers who are not doing enough, given how well they have done out of the legal system' – should do more work for free is straight out of Dickens.

But then Dickens and Gove have much in common, both being prone to feverish activity, constant tinkering, inventing, writing, lecturing, opining. Yesterday, in the chamber, Mr Gove did remind me of some sort of Victorian factory, steam pouring out of his ears. He seems to be reviewing everything that he can: legal aid, freedom of information, the court system, humanist marriage, the Human Rights Act, not to mention the use of 'however' at the beginning of a sentence.

There are five Ministers (I am capping this, m'lord chancellor, to avoid confusion with vicar-types) sitting on the bench. They look an extraordinary group. There is the housewife heart-throb Dominic Raab, in charge of human rights, and Caroline Dinenage, whose brief is family justice, who does not walk so much as sashay, something that may prove distracting for some. There is Mike Penning and Shailesh Vara, both ministerial veterans. Finally there is the tall stooped figure of Andrew Selous, whom Mr Speaker always refers to as 'Selooo'.

There was a Dickensian exchange between Mr Selous and the smooth operator who is Sir Edward Garnier. Sir Edward noted that he had visited sixty-five prisons as an MP (in the course of his parliamentary duties, I assume, and not for the incorrect use of 'impact') and that most work done by prisoners was almost useless. 'In one prison, I saw people making hairnets. No doubt there is a market for hairnets…'

Michael Fabricant, whose strange Heidi-yellow locks continue to fascinate, shouted: 'There is!'

Mr Selous responded by almost bowing to Sir Edward: 'I have great respect for your seminal work, "Prisons with a Purpose"…'

Mr Gove looked absolutely thrilled with this. However, as he wouldn't write, actually, it's only the start.

14 JULY 2015

The Hustings Four desperately try to be human

I tune in to the Liz and Yvette, Jeremy and Andy show and find it less than riveting.

THE *Victoria Derbyshire* show's Labour hustings began with the holy grail of politics. 'Part of the brief is to sound as much like a human being as possible!' announced Victoria. Andy, Liz and Yvette all laughed in a cunningly human way. Jeremy is too far to the left to do fake laughter and so he pursed his lips. (I haven't included surnames as this is daytime television and no one has them.)

The seating plan was a nightmare. The only person facing the audience of 100 of the pickiest voters in Britain was Victoria (well, it is her show). The four candidates were sitting in the front row, so whenever they answered a question they had to swivel their heads round. It was an osteopath's dream come true, making everyone pretend they are owls.

I feared for the Hustings Four, as I think of them, these brave Labour MPs who have condemned themselves to appearing in every possible hustings format devised in the world. It's a scientific experiment usually reserved for rats. And now, Victoria, with her human requirement, had set the bar at the very highest level. They could, I knew, only fail, but – being politicians – they did not know that.

So Andy burbled about his three children, being from Liverpool and the fact that when his wife appeared on *Blind Date* she had chosen a Tory. Also, he had been out canvassing and an ex-girlfriend had opened the door. This was way too much information. Being human does not equate to being on a dating site.

Liz is forty-four and from Watford. (It did sound a bit like a dating site, actually.) She wanted to be a dancer but then realised she should be a politician, as you do.

Yvette, who is passionate about diversity, by the way, has driven a tractor.

She wanted to be a Doctor Who assistant but now realises that was lacking in aspiration and she should have wanted to be the Doctor.

Jeremy said his hobbies were equality, justice and human rights (dating site disaster).

'Have they passed the human test?' demanded Victoria as the audience glared. I heard two claps and a groan. 'That's a good start,' said Andy perkily.

It was not. The audience thoroughly disapproved of the Four. It was like therapy but with microphones. The Four were too left, too right, too centrist, too Tory, not passionate enough, not apologetic enough, not human enough. 'We are seeing no leadership!' announced an audience member.

Andy swivelled his head and redoubled his dating efforts. 'We need to believe in things again,' he said. Andy believes in giving the country back its heart and soul.

'What does that mean?' demanded Victoria, who was becoming a bit of a stickler on this human thing.

Yvette, head boinging like a pinball, is into high-tech. We've had the Industrial Revolution, now it is the Digital Revolution. I felt a yawn coming on. She wants to invest in coding (I'm only the messenger) and, more specifically, women coding.

Liz is into people. 'We have to start with our best asset, which is our people,' she said. Some of 'our people' in the room accused her of being a Tory. She pointed out that Labour lost the election and had to change. The people frowned.

And then there was Jeremy who was, one woman noted, not 'the right person'. Jeremy leaned forward. 'Is it the beard?' he asked. She shook her head. 'Are you sure?' asked Jeremy, who may seriously think he can win by a shave. So who won? Why, the osteopaths, of course.

15 JULY 2015

Barking animal lovers are here to stay

The foxes declare victory as the government runs for cover over hunting.

THE ANIMAL KINGDOM gathered yesterday across from the Palace of Westminster and went a bit wild. It was mostly foxes, urban of course, and in a leap of evolution that Darwin may struggle with, many were standing on two legs. I was behind one named Victoria, of K-9 Angels, who was wearing fox ears, had long blonde hair and a strategically ripped T-shirt, her arms covered in fake blood and scars.

If Nasa's New Horizons spacecraft were looking down, or indeed if the planet of Pluto had a pair of binoculars trained on us, it would have looked as if we were worshipping a man whose hair is its own solar system. I speak, of course, of Brian May, guitarist of Queen, who was now standing on the statue plinth of a king (George V) in Old Palace Yard. 'This is an important day for our wild animals,' shouted Brian, 'and an important day for our democracy!'

The wild animals went, er, wild. I had not realised that foxes could whoop and whistle. A smoke canister or two were let off, red smoke drifting over us. I looked up at Brian and, suddenly, realised that next to Brian's outer hair ring was a man in a grey suit. Was it a Westminster version of the wolf in *Little Red Riding Hood*? I peered closer. Well, it certainly looked like Angus Robertson, the Westminster leader of the SNP. Grandma, I thought, what big teeth you suddenly have.

'What's happened,' cried Brian, 'is the government has backed down!'

I am told that the collective noun for foxes is a 'skulk'. I can confirm that the skulk now went a bit feral. Brian said his first reaction was one of disappointment because he wanted to watch the debate and win the vote. He thanked the SNP, for it was their decision to take part in the vote that had prompted the government retreat. Brian thought they could have won without the SNP because there were many Tory MPs on their side (not least a new vegan Tory, Andrea Jenkins, who beat Ed Balls). 'This is a team effort. This is Team Fox! This is a win!'

Now Grandma, or even Angus, took the microphone. 'Today is YOUR victory. It is because what you have been doing is to convince MPs like myself to take part in the debate and vote. My message to David Cameron is that you are a coward! The reason you pulled the vote is that you knew you would lose!' Caroline Lucas, of Green fame, arrived to shout: 'This is what the Big Society looks like. It looks like you. It's beautiful!'

The hunting horns were in full voice now. Two-legged foxes holding signs that said 'For foxes' sake' and 'Team fox' were having selfies taken with a creature who was about 6 ft tall dressed top to toe in (fake) fur. Was it a fox? Or was it a bear? I peered into its mouth and saw only a very large hipster beard.

'I am worried that you may be a bear,' I noted tentatively as the selfies went on. 'I think I am a mongrel,' admitted the bear/fox as he danced for joy.

The fox/humans had sat down in the road, briefly stopping traffic, as the skulk shouted: 'Blood on your hands! Blood on your hands!' Brian was shouting again: 'We will never give up!'

And you know what? I believe him.

16 JULY 2015

Dressing down for mayor comes loaded with schadenfreude

Achtung! Boris gets blasted as the Home Secretary announces her decision on water cannon.

THERESA MAY, AS dry as burnt toast, had come to the Commons to tell us her decision on water cannon. She explained that it was classified as a 'less lethal system', the same as Tasers and baton rounds. Behind her, slumped in a corner, sat the dishevelled garden gnome that is Boris Johnson.

Theresa explained in a voice as desiccated as coconut that in June 2014 the Mayor of London had approved the purchase of 'three Ziegler Wasserwerfer 9000 water cannon' from Germany.

Did I see Boris flinch? Theresa spoke the words 'Ziegler Wasserwerfer 9000' as if each was an illegal alien who had arrived in her mouth without papers. The Wasserwerfer had cost £218,000. The Wasserwerfer had sixty-seven 'outstanding issues'. The Wasser was werfer wobbly. She'd consulted every expert in die Welt and had decided Boris was ein Dummkopf. (I paraphrase, but I think you will find my translation is sound.)

She was speaking to the House but every word was aimed at Boris, her competition as a future Tory leader. You did not need to be Freud to feel that there was a certain amount of schadenfreude in the air; indeed, schadenfreude loaded into a Wasserwerfer and werfed directly at the mayor. But as Boris's normal dress code is 'riot', it was hard to tell what impact this had.

The shadow Home Secretary, Yvette Cooper, was a geyser of approval. 'The Chancellor has now grounded the mayor's airport ambitions and can I strongly welcome your comprehensive pouring of cold water on his cannon ambitions!' Other Labour MPs gushed their approval.

Boris pitched up to a standing position. 'May I remind you that the decision to buy the Wasserwerfer was taken in the light of the strong support of the commissioner of police of the metropolis, and of the strong support of the Prime Minister and indeed of the people of London? The decision was also taken in the interests of economy, since we were able to buy these machines and save £2.3 million.' (It's an interesting economic theory that when you spend £218,000 on something you can never use, you save £2.3 million. Still, I know what he means: I often 'save' money while shopping.)

Alex Salmond arose. 'Have I got this correct?' he crowed. 'The Mayor of London bought three antiquated, expensive, dangerous and now totally redundant German-made water cannon, aided and abetted by the Prime Minister?'

At this Boris shouted: 'Nothing to do with you!'

Later, the Sky presenter Kay Burley had some ideas for how the

Wasserwerfer could be used; for instance, to help Boris wash his hair. She also referred to Theresa May as his boss. 'I don't know why you say she's my boss,' grumbled Boris. 'She's simply the Home Secretary.'

Ah yes, simply the Home Secretary. I do hope Theresa was listening.

Acknowledgements

THIS BOOK WAS the idea of my publisher Jeremy Robson who has proved unfailingly supportive throughout. My thanks also go to my agent, Rebecca Winfield, for her practical help, guidance and advice. I must also give a bow to my fellow 'sneer' of sketch-writers and of course politicians of all hues, without whom this book really would not have been possible. All of these sketches appeared in their original form (they have all been edited and/or augmented) in *The Times* and I owe a great debt to my acute, enthusiastic and appreciative readers. My thanks go to everyone at *The Times*, including the news desk and the sub-editors who so regularly save me from myself and also, in particular, John Witherow and Emma Tucker, as well as Robert Hands, and all my fellow *Times* occupants of 'The Room' at Westminster. I must salute Morten Morland for doing another superb cover. Last, but not least, I am indebted to my family and my husband, Ian Berkoff, who has smiled through it all.

Index